IDEOLOGY AND MYTH IN AMERICAN POLITICS

IDEOLOGY AND MYTH IN AMERICAN POLITICS

A Critique of a National Political Mind

H. MARK ROELOFS
New York University

LITTLE, BROWN AND COMPANY
Boston Toronto

This book is for Joan,
Cora, and Danny,
without whose help
it would have been longer.

Library of Congress Catalog Card No. 75–36959

SECOND PRINTING

Published simultaneously in Canada
by Little, Brown & Company (Canada) Limited

Printed in the United States of America

PREFACE

This book is an attempt to comprehend critically the American political system. Its primary themes are described in the introduction that follows. Two prefatory comments may be made here.

First, wherever possible, references to illustrative material, evidence, and supporting authorities are to the plain and obvious. There is a temptation in any effort to reinterpret the American political experience, to steer away from materials grown hoary with overuse and sticky from too much patriotic handling. But a theory of American politics couched in novel references risks not only misplacement of general emphasis but also failure to deal solidly with the primary problems. Accordingly, references are mainly to the major historical events (the Revolution, the Civil War, the two World Wars, the New Deal, the Kennedy assassination, Vietnam, Watergate), the major documents (the Declaration of Independence, the Constitution, the Federalist papers, the Gettysburg Address, important Supreme Court decisions), the major figures (Washington, Lincoln, Franklin Roosevelt, Boston's Mayor James Curley, New York's Robert Moses), the major problems (economic development and management, race, poverty, crime, governmental corruption), and writers in the mainstream of American political culture (Thoreau, Calhoun, Turner, authors of prominent textbooks, the editors of The New York Times).

These are "schoolroom" materials. Placing primary reliance upon them will guard against the book becoming esoteric. It will also express a primary assumption underlying the book: that no real advance can be made in the interpretation of the American political experience by bringing in new evidence. (See the Appendix, "The Study of America.") We all know what the evidence is; the question is, what now, in the 1970s, are we to make of it?

The second prefatory matter is to acknowledge the great assistance received during the writing of this book from personal friends. Encouragement, always precious to any author, at the outset came especially from Ralph Hummel, Gerald DeMaio, and Stan Norris. They also read the final manuscript and were generous and helpful with their comments. So also were Patricia Albin, Nanette Beatrice, Jane Dahlberg, Theodore Lowi, John Mason, Theodore Norton, Kim Ezra Sheinbaum, Steven Waldhorn, and Kathryn Yatrakis. Ann Cattell not only read the manuscript, but also generously supplied critically important editorial assistance later. I am especially grateful to Professor Herman Brautigam of Colgate University, a mentor for me for twenty-five years. He not only edited the manuscript throughout but also challenged me to rethink and rewrite important sections of it. But neither he nor those mentioned above can be held in any way responsible for the result. That burden may be shared only by me and my owl.

CONTENTS

IDEOLOGY AND MYTH IN AMERICAN POLITICS

INTRODUCTION:
CONTRADICTIONS
AND CONSEQUENCES

American political life displays a seemingly endless succession of contradictions, even paradoxes. These are alternately baffling, outraging, agonizing, disillusioning, sometimes horrifying — but as often as anything else strainingly hopeful.

On the one hand, it is broadly evident that the American political system is corrupt, inefficient, and, with terrible regularity, brutal. The corruption is ubiquitous, both high and low, petty and serious, and the situation is of long standing. History testifies to that as much as do current revelations. History and recent events also show that the complexities of American government make it grotesquely clumsy at defining social needs and hurts, and appallingly wasteful in allocating resources to their solution. As for the brutality of American government, that is amply exposed in the treatment of minority groups, the conduct of our military forces in Vietnam, the conditions in our prisons, mental hospitals, and nursing homes, and the operation of our public welfare systems. Moreover, in all this corruption, inefficiency, and brutality, there is nothing to suggest that the instances in which they appear, whether taken collectively or individually, are somehow un-American, mere occasional, accidental aberrations. On the contrary, they give every appearance of rising directly from fundamental features of the American political spirit.

Nevertheless, there is another side to American politics. However much corruption exists, there is also the fact that American citizens are sincerely shocked by it. They never tire of seeking it out, exposing it, and striving to bring its perpetrators to justice. In addition, for all the monumental inefficiency of American government, it must be noted in fairness what it is inefficient at. The nation's massive, free, and comprehensive public education system exists. The Department of Health, Education, and Welfare, with its polyglot programs for every kind of human betterment, exists. And the concern of the laws and courts for the definition and preservation of the rights of all citizens exists. Finally, alongside the brutality of American government both overseas and at home, lies its record of outbursts of generosity and humanitarianism. And again it must be said in sum that all this moral outrage, social concern, and humanitarianism is as profoundly and characteristically American as its contradictions.

The essay that follows grapples with these contradictions,

with the paradoxes of American governmental behavior and aspiration, by locating in the American "political mind" three disparate frameworks of political consciousness. The first two of these are labeled "Bourgeois ideology" and "Protestant myth." Despite the fact that they are in important ways radically opposed to each other, they can be seen as locked in unhappy embrace. Together they are the dominant elements shaping American political life. The third factor in the American political mind is labeled "the rational/professional mentality." Like the others, it is a form of political consciousness. But both analytically and historically it is only loosely connected to the other two and relative to them plays a clearly subordinate, however otherwise significant, role.

For the purposes of the analysis that follows, all of these terms will be given specialized meanings. But this much can be said about them now.

As stipulated in what follows, *myth* denotes the nationally shared framework of political consciousness by which a people becomes aware of itself as a people, as having an identity in history, and by which it is also prepared to recognize some governing regime within its community as legitimate. Myth is a people's legend and its hope. *Ideology*, in contrast, is a narrower and more practical term. As stipulated in what follows, it is the framework of political consciousness, the set of ideas, by which a people, or at least its dominant, governing element, organizes itself for political action. Myth gives meaning to national existence and endeavor. Ideology gives patterns for political action.

Because myth is so oriented toward national identification and aspiration, and ideology toward patterns of operative behavior, it is probable that in almost all organized societies there are discrepancies between ideologies and myths. Both are fundamentally concerned with human memory, human action, and human aspiration. Both, in the jargon of scholars, are norm and value laden. But ideology is the thought pattern of persons whose work must be done day by day. Myth is the ancient memory and the generational hope of the whole people, its "civil religion."

The thesis of this book is that in America the discrepancy, the tension, between myth and ideology is extreme, so extreme as to be self-crippling.

The problem is congenital. Its roots antecede by far even the nation's founding. The labels Bourgeois and Protestant as applied to elements of the American political mind designate forms of political consciousness which had developed in Europe as early as the sixteenth century. They had been united into a single syndrome and given vigorous articulation as a political creed by English middle class Liberals by the 1680s. But even in those early years the tensions within Liberalism, between its Bourgeois and Protestant components, were evident.

What had united the two was their common affirmation of an individualism which was radical in its insistence upon the primacy of personal vocation and revolutionary in its opposition to prevailing social structures. But they were divided by their conflicting understandings of human power and destiny. On the Bourgeois side these were interpreted in terms of materialism and self-aggrandizement, on the Protestant side in terms of love and piety.

In Europe, the tensions within early Liberalism were moderated by the general complexity of the historical and cultural context, which contained much else besides Liberalism.

In America, Liberalism was alone, isolated, and knew only itself. The very emptiness of the environment excited its energies and teased its aspirations. Its Bourgeois side grasped and defined in its own terms the emerging nation's political institutions, virtually to the exclusion of all other considerations. The Protestant side was thus rendered, in operative political terms, impotent. But it did claim with growing success the right to define the nation's mythic self-understanding. In this guise, it trailed behind the nation's political practice as unstilled, harping conscience. As persistently, it thrust ahead proclaiming idealisms hopelessly beyond the capabilities of the operative political system. The result was — and is — an extremity of tension between ideology and myth, practice and hope, and action and conscience, that proves, often enough, more than human endurance can handle rationally.

The result is also that in this situation myth takes on, as if by conscious assignment, the social function of masking ideological practice. *That* is what we may do, but *this* is what we aspire to be, what we truly are. Myth becomes virtually a lie, falsifying the nature of actual political practice and concealing actual modes of operation and actual achievements.

But the masking is never complete. The avaricious transactionism and other features of America's actual, "Madisonian" political institutions are regularly uncovered. Then the contradictions between actuality and the aspirations of myth are exposed, and the myth's "Lincolnesque," humanistic egalitarianism rages against what it has found. But these bouts of reactive behavior, for all the horrendous dimensions they may on occasion achieve, accomplish little. The American political mind offers few alternatives and the tendency of its political processes is always, after exhaustion, to go back to the beginning.

This explication of contradiction and paradox, of the tensions and interactions between myth and ideology in American political life, points to a conclusion: that, in its own terms, the American political system is inadequate. It satisfies the claims of neither its myth nor its ideology. Protestant hopes remain unfulfilled; efforts to realize them often bring on disaster. Meanwhile the Bourgeois ethos is lashed for its privatistic materialism; it is even denied that tranquility in the possession of its gains, which is its primary political goal. The final consequence is mostly a political process in which illusion and disillusion chase each other across the spectrum of political consciousness.

The role of the rational/professional mentality in the totality of this political process is subordinate but indispensible. Judges and bureaucrats, the two types of political actor in which this mentality is especially prominent, both perform roles essential to American political life as a whole. Judges conserve the law, that is, the "cage" within which American political life goes on. Bureaucrats, to the best of their professional competence, try to get the nation's public work done. But the American political system gives neither judges nor bureaucrats sufficient long-term discipline and direction. Both, while experiencing some sense of accomplishment, are also distracted and frustrated by inabilities to carry through as professionals dedicated to the public interest. Moreover, if they try to force solutions to their problems, they are more likely to join and be corrupted by the system, than to transform it.

The overall outlook for American politics is bleak. There is no prospect for any revolution in it. The system simply does not possess the required self-understanding and conceptual apparatus to perceive the need, mobilize the resources, or lead the forces for that kind of creative self-transcendence. On the other hand, mere reform — a tinkering with party financing, the organization of Congress, or the powers of the presidency — would not significantly affect the basic problems. They are too deepseated for that. But there is also little prospect that the system will go totally to pieces. The record shows the American political system to possess quite extraordinary capacities to sustain itself virtually unchanged through every kind of disaster, civil war, depression, military defeat overseas, and even the sustained corruption of itself. We must expect more of the same, more failure, more chaos and disintegration, but also more recovery and endlessly reasserted hope. To all appearances, American government is destined to go on forever, just as it is.

There is a final feature of the book that should be noted at the outset, a methodological dimension which determines the kind of book it is intended to be. What this book offers is a "general theory" of American government. It amounts to an indictment of that government, but the argument is more analytic than empirical, more concerned with explaining why and how the logic of the system fails than with listing all the wrongs that have been committed by its operation. It is assumed that readers are well stocked with the historical facts and that they know, perhaps in some detail, how our federal, presidential system of government works.

The question this book addresses is, what are we to make of all these facts? Is there a single theory which can successfully make the relations between them intelligible? The Civil War was a breakdown of the political system. Why did it happen? What should its occurrence mean for us today? Why Vietnam? Why Watergate? What next?

This is to put the matter very imprecisely, and even in an introduction something more exact should be attempted.

A theory is characterized not only by the facts it claims to relate and explain but also by the kind of reality in which those facts are seen to be imbedded. Natural scientists, and those social scientists who imitate their procedures, work in a realm we tend to think of as "external," an "out there" arena in which objects are related in time and space and reproduce patterns of regular behavior. This kind of external reality may reasonably be called the realm of objects. Another kind of reality, the kind explored in this book, is a more internal sort.

It is the intersubjective world of shared human consciousness. It springs into existence the instant you and I and perhaps others agree to do something together — and vanishes as rapidly when our agreement breaks down. But as long as we agree and work together, our world of mutual consciousness exists.

Of that world, it can be asked, what is happening in it, what are we doing in it, how are we doing it? The answers to these questions are superficially obvious. What is happening within our shared intersubjective world is whatever we agreed to do (build a house, play a game, eat a meal, go to war) and we are doing it according to the rules and conventions we have for such activities. However, just as in the world of objects where appearances can deceive, so in the intersubjective world of shared endeavor, observers can be deceived, confused, or simply ignorant of what the participants in a particular community are "really" trying to do. Even the participants can be confused.

Within this methodological perspective, the themes of this book, together, declare a didactic general theory about what is happening inside the intersubjective realm of American political consciousness. It holds that while Americans in shared consciousness are actually submitting to the imperatives and operations of Madisonian politics, a very limited kind of game, they also persuade themselves that they are playing Lincolnesque politics, a much more ennobling pastime. Then the conclusion: This is a highly frustrating kind of politics but it is likely to continue for some time.

The first chapter examines the methodological questions in detail. It concentrates on identifying the kind of knowledge this book is trying to find out — the ideas in terms of which a people acts politically, their ideologies and myths — and how this knowledge can be gained — the so-called "critical method." The chapter is largely abstract. It has been included in an otherwise practical book for two reasons.

One is that in the present confused state of political science, prudence alone requires that each writer, as he begins, set out not so much his moral bias as an explanation of what kind of work he thinks he is attempting. Nowhere is this more true than in discussions of political ideas.

The second reason for prefacing a treatment of the problems of American government with an extended methological exposition is that the most serious of those problems only become visible if the perspective selected for viewing them is appropriate for that purpose. Events of recent years have convinced many observers that something must be seriously wrong with how Americans do politics. The argument of this book is that the sources of these difficulties lie more in the ways Americans think politically than in the ways they act politically. Consequently, a methodological perspective that emphasizes the primacy of mental forms and habits has been adopted. The prime question is always, what is the way this people thinks and *therefore* acts?

In this book, the argument is ultimately that Americans are trapped inside their historically given political mind, that they cannot escape from it, and that they are bound to go on repeating patterns of political behavior which are essentially unproductive if not worse. That argument will gain substantive weight as it works through historical evidence and institutional analysis. But its final force depends on more analytic and abstract considerations. What are political minds, and how entrapping *in concept* can they be? Is it conceivable that a whole nation can be caught inside its own head? The purpose of the extended discussion in Chapter 1 is to show that especially that last question can be answered in the affirmative.

Chapter 2 begins the substantive discussion by examining in a general way the Liberalism that dominates the American political mind. The treatment is both historical, looking at origins and patterns of development, and analytic, determining the propositional content of the Liberal creed as it was hardened in the American environment. This chapter sets out the fundamental equation of America's political culture, the Protestant-Bourgeois syndrome, in all its individualism and anguish.

Chapters 3 through 6 examine the articulation of the underlying American Liberal creed in the nation's practical political life. The stress throughout is on the creed's disparate emphases and resulting contradictions.

Chapters 3 and 4 follow the Bourgeois, ideological side of the equation first into the nation's founding constitutional documents and then into the political institutions erected upon them. The general characterization reached is that the American political system is a system of "baronial" politics fundamentally vulnerable to such problems as corruption. It is in no descriptively accurate sense a system of "responsible government," and it is creakily immobile before the kind of broad social problems that plague modern societies, to say nothing of the problem of reforming itself. It is, however, extraordinarily stable, as it was designed at its founding to be.

Chapter 5 reverses the focus and concentrates on the nation's political myths. It shows how the Bourgeois operative political system and its works are masked by the Protestant mythic beliefs that America (1) is an egalitarian community, (2) is organized into an electoral democracy pursuing goals of social justice, and (3) is led on into triumph and tragedy by presidential greatness and power. Each of these myths is shown to cover over with some success particular ranges of American political practice.

Chapter 6 stands by itself. It shows how the covering up function of myth can sometimes fail and how a perpetually dangerous but always sterile myth/ideology cycle of interaction can then unfold.

The final chapter treats the mentality of the rational/professional, and the work of those institutions in which that mentality is especially prominent. It also shows why the rational/professional mentality in the American environment has been unsuccessful in any possible challenge to the dominance of the Protestant-Bourgeois ethos.

The book's concluding section raises the question of the American political system's capacities and prospects for self-transcendence. The negative answer advanced to that question is seen to rest on the analysis that extends throughout the book. In sum it asserts that if the Americans were to alter their prospects they would have to root out and radically reconstitute major elements of their political *mind*. That may be too much to ask of any people. It is certainly too much to ask of Americans.

CRITICAL
KNOWLEDGE
IN POLITICS

IDEAS AND ACTIONS
POLITICAL MIND
IDEOLOGY AND MYTH

IDEAS AND ACTIONS

This book is about the American political mind. But what are "political minds"? Can they be said to exist? Do they have enough substantiality to be examined and analyzed as are other objects of experience? Or are "political minds" intellectual constructs by which scholars piece together in convenient ways traits of "national character?" Are they, therefore, merely metaphors, perhaps dangerously misleading ones?

The central themes of this book are assertions that within the American political mind systematic and permanent dichotomies exist between its ideological and mythic elements. For example, it will be asserted that, contrary to widely and fervently believed myth about the American presidency being a grand and powerful office, this position, in operative ideology, is a weak one. But how can such dichotomies come into existence and persist? Why cannot the myths be exposed and the operative "facts" left to speak for themselves?

The major conclusion of this book is that the contradictions and tensions between American political ideology and myth foster in the nation's political system self-crippling tendencies that often issue into disastrous consequences, but that next to nothing can be done about them. Why not?

The answers to all these questions depend on the answers given to the first, which asks what political minds are and whether they are real. In this book, political minds are held to be the functional abstracts produced by the historically developed understandings nations have of themselves as politically active. As such, political minds are real, in a wholly literal sense of the term, and can be subjected to objective study, if appropriate methods are used, as much as any other feature of human experience. But statements of this sort are both controversial and obscure unless carefully explained.

The same comment could be made about the methods to be used here for determining the content of political minds. In their formal aspects, these methods are virtually unknown in the field of American political studies, yet only their use can isolate and bring into clear focus the ideological and mythic elements underlying the nation's political institutions and behavior. In sum, these methods can be called "the critical method" in deference to their descent from Immanuel Kant's techniques in performing what he termed "transcendental analytics." On the other hand, these methods are not sharply different from kinds of analysis which almost all of us practice from time to time in ordinary life, albeit informally and unself-consciously. And it is surprisingly easy to explain how these methods are used once their yield, "critical knowledge," is understood.

But to do any of these things, we must go back to the simplest beginnings of the argument for which all of these matters are conclusions.

That argument begins with an understanding of personal, human action in which action is distinguished from motion, from mindless bodily movement, and from reflex. Action is purposive behavior undertaken in accordance with the intentions of an actor. Consider the assertion, "I have no idea what you are doing!" How naturally we assume in this kind of language that the meaning of an action lies not in its external manifestations but in the internal ideas which give it structure. In the absence of those ideas, an action is unintelligible, a jumble of observed manifestations. We only learn what an action really is by determining the intentions of the actor. Moreover, it is possible to call the actor's intentions, intangible as they may be, objectively real.[1]

Even in a process as subjective as human action, those who act do so with certain intentions rather than others. It is a question of objective fact. Did they have these intentions, or those? Obviously actions themselves in the external, physical world are also objective fact, and statements about them are subject to various kinds of verification. That most of those methods of verification are different from the methods we use to determine an actor's intentions does not alter the *objectivity* of the knowledge sought about what intentions were factually present. Whatever they may have been, they were present in the actor's comings and goings in a way that is wholly independent of any possible observer's knowing about them.

A man leaves a building. That is attested to by a number of observers of the physical facts: one saw him leave, another

---

1. See Stuart Hampshire, *Thought and Action*, Chatto and Windus, London, 1960, especially Ch. 2.

heard his footfalls and recognized his gait, a third smelled his cigar in the hall. But what did his leaving mean? We ask him and he replies, "I'm going to take a taxi home." Even such a simple statement of intent may be difficult to verify, but it is structurally as open to verification as any other statement of fact, because it, too, is a statement of fact.

The themes of this book are broad generalizations about the nature of American political life, about what Americans in politics have done and how. Much of the argument in which these generalizations are presented is analysis, more or less cogent, and much of it is evaluation, more or less agreeable. But the generalizations are about facts. This book is not about what America might have been or ought to be politically. It aims to depict what America really is politically. It attempts to trace the actual historical configuration of American political intentions.

If we think about intentional actions, even very simple ones, it cannot escape our attention that there is more to them than just the actualized idea. Invariably the idea for a particular action is connected to and may even be a direct response to other ideas in the actor's mind. This man we mentioned may habitually go home from work at the end of the day without consciously thinking about it. Or perhaps he is a conventional sort of fellow who leaves when his fellow workers leave. Or he may be an acutely self-conscious, philosophically inclined person who makes it a rule to go home promptly every day from work to be with his family, participation in which is for him not only agreeable but ethically satisfying. Abstracting from these illustrations, we can say that the intention (idea) behind an overt action can be the product, or the application of a habit, convention, and/or rule. These, in turn, comprise constructions in the mind by which an actor, aware of himself in a situation, formulates particular intentions of a certain sort with a high degree of regularity. "Good old Joe! You know him. End of the day, he'll go home, every time." Joe's mind, it seems, has built-in tendencies to think daily, "Go home!"

The focus in this book is on the fact that Americans, as citizens, act in certain characteristic ways. We can anticipate with assurance that the Americans will adhere to these patterns. That assurance is rooted in the ascription to the American political mind of certain enduring constructions, which determine that the citizens of this nation will in politics act in accordance with certain identifiable habits, conventions, and rules.

But this is to point to the very end of the present argument. So far all that has been seen is a distinction between the immediate intention behind a particular action and certain possible, more permanent constructions in the mind out of which the immediate intention may come. The enduring constructions of the mind do more than prompt particular intentions and overt behavior here and there. Before they do that, and in order to do that, they must first define for the actor what his situation is; they must delineate in more or less specific terms the context in which his action is to appear as meaningful behavior.

This man we have been discussing has an intention, on a particular afternoon, to take a taxi home. The intention is a response to a habit, convention, or clearly formulated rule that after work he should regularly go home promptly. But this regularity-prompting habit, convention, or rule is itself only meaningful and then operative in the man's behavior as it is set in the context of the associated meanings of all its terms, *work, after, go, taxi,* and above all *home*. The association of these terms, and their understanding as applicable to his situation at the end of the day, make it possible for the man to lay an imperative upon himself and respond in turn. In this sense we can call these constructions of the mind *frameworks of consciousness;* they are the means by which an actor organizes his understanding of his existence in the world for the purpose of acting in it. A framework of consciousness for action includes an imperative; but it also includes a great deal more, a whole matrix of understanding within which the resulting action is placed as meaningful.

Another observation should be noted here about these constructions in the mind, now termed frameworks of consciousness. The frameworks of consciousness a man possesses or can put together on any given occasion determine the actions he can take, the range, variety, and quality of the behavior he can engage in, and the kind of man he is. Suppose the man taking a taxi home is severely mentally retarded. His teachers, with utmost patience, rigor, and an extended period of training, have finally fixed in his mind a pattern of consciousness such that he can go home by taxi at the end of the day and not attempt any alternatives. Such a man may exhibit regularity in his behavior, but little versatility. An intelligent man equipped with a broad understanding of his daily situation and with a wide range of conceptions might be just as regular in his overt behavior as the first. But he would be infinitely more capable of generalizing the basic imperative about going home, of understanding its full import, and, of course, of adapting his behavior to the unexpected.

This may appear a simple point but its relevance to what follows cannot be exaggerated. It will be contended later in this book that Americans, politically, are equipped with an extremely simple-minded conception of the electoral process. Elections for them are largely personality contests which, though often psychologically exciting, are on a rudimentary level of political maturity. But the dominant American conception of the electoral process is imbedded in and intricately related to the American conception of political life generally. It is but one aspect of the American political intelligence.

All this suggests that, when studying a person or a people, a reasonable objective can be to inventory their minds — to examine, analyze, catalogue, and evaluate their frameworks of consciousness for action. But how do we go about such study? How do we apprehend for study frameworks of consciousness? The answer to these questions is that the process is obvious, often difficult in practice, but not impossible, especially if we are systematically aware of what we are doing.

To determine what a person, or a people, intends to do and why, one can make inferences from appearances, in accordance with the adage that actions speak louder than words. One can also be introspective and then empathize, "That is what I would do in those circumstances." But these methods are indirect. To gain direct access into the minds of actors the plain, obvious route must be taken: ask them what they are doing.

They may lie, of course.

Even if they do not, there are difficulties. The immediate intention in an action may be revealed easily through ordinary modes of communication. It may be only slightly more difficult to formulate the imperative that prompts the immediate intention. But to reach back to those whole frameworks of consciousness by which actors, whether single persons or whole peoples, understand situations, define themselves in them, and then set out to act individually or collectively, is a very difficult undertaking.

One problem is the range and complexity of underlying frameworks of consciousness. Another is the usual lack of self-awareness, especially of whole peoples, about the ways they understand their world and themselves. We will return to these problems in the next section of this chapter, but a third problem, basic to all the central themes of this book, should be noticed directly here at the outset.

When we seek to penetrate the subjectivity of actors, whether persons or a people, to determine through conversation and other techniques not just their intentions but also their underlying understandings, we may find our subjects honestly confused. This is different from simply not being aware of why they do certain things. They may honestly believe they are acting out of one world of understandings even though investigation will contradict them. That man going home from work in a taxi may believe, and state with every evidence of sincerity, that his objective is to honor, protect, and participate in his family. He may further nearly convince us that he is doing this in pursuit of a deliberate conception of himself as a philosophical moralist. But we may notice that he argues all this with a suspicious trace of sentimentality and forced idealism. Sustained conversation and reflection might finally persuade us that his guise as a philosophical moralist is almost a sham. In fact, for all his heated protestations to the contrary, he is guided almost entirely by unalloyed and highly conventionalized fear of what his neighbors might think. Moreover, were we to confront him with this alternative interpretation of his acts, he might become angry, giving further evidence that we are right.

This kind of behavior is a kind of irrationality. Yet it is a familiar situation that raises all kinds of questions about why people often cannot acknowledge the operative intentions behind their acts. There is no reason to go into these psychological issues here. We should simply note that situations of this sort exist commonly and that to deal with them as they appear in American political life we will have to develop clear conceptual tools. We must find ways to distinguish accurately and systematically between what people proclaim and perhaps sincerely believe they are doing and what they truly intend, in operative thought, to do.

It should be obvious by now that the subject matter of this book and its analytical methods are straightforward, relatively simple, and familiar. All of us, more or less frequently, ask not only questions like "What is he doing?" and "Why is he doing it?", but also more complex questions like "I wonder what the dickens he *thinks* he is doing?" But to ensure that we proceed systematically, we should put the understandings we have gained into formal terms. The best way to do that is to go back to Immanuel Kant and borrow and adapt some of the technical terminology he set out in the *Critique of Pure Reason* and other works.

Kant was concerned with the most general, philosophical problems of human experience. His central focus, especially in the *Critique of Pure Reason*, was on determining the absolutely certain, *a priori* contribution made by the rational mind to the experience of scientific observers. Our concern in this book is with political philosophy. Our central focus is on determining the particular ideas by which in certain societies political actors experience life in concert with their fellows. We can apply Kant's ideas to our narrower focus because the tradition of "critical philosophy" which Kant founded flows directly from him through many intermediate figures (such as Hegel, Marx, Weber, and Dewey) to the present. In that passage, the tradition broadened its interests in psychology, sociology, and history and deepened its concern with problems of social and political action and organization. And it did so without any significant loss of Kant's original intent.

The core of Kant's philosophical effort was to determine and analyze the ideas which made human experience possible.[2]

2. "Before objects are given to me, that is, *a priori*, I must presuppose in myself laws of the understanding which are expressed in conceptions *a priori*. To these conceptions, then, all the objects of experience must necessarily conform." *Critique of Pure Reason*, tr. J. M. D. Meiklejohn, Everyman's Library, J. M. Dent, London, 1934, p. 12.

That is clearly the kind of thing we are trying to do in this book; to determine and analyze the ideas by the possession and use of which the American people have political experience. And it was by analysis of the "transcendental" that Kant said we could uncover the ideas which make experience possible.[3] Again the term is formally descriptive of our own efforts. If we were to analyze the transcend*ent,* we would talk of things beyond human experience, God for example. If we confined our attention to the immediate, we would be bound to describe in endless particulars only "what happened." When we focus on the transcend*ental,* we are looking beneath the immediacy of what happened to find in the human agents acting there the conceptual mechanisms they use to construct, organize, and make intelligible their experience, their action.

In one area it may appear that this book moves some distance from Kant. He assumed in his observer a high degree of rationality. It did not occur to him that his observer would experience actuality in other than consistent and systematic ways. However, as was indicated by our example of the man who might give a confused explanation of his daily activities, in this book we have a central interest in at least one important kind of human irrationality. Nevertheless, Kant's general approach can serve us uniquely well even here. Too many times in discussions about myths and the confusions they may engender, the subject is handled as fantasy to be brushed aside easily by clear thought about realities. Myths, in that light, are cobwebs in the mind without reality or function in political life. Following Kant's general approach to the problem of human experience enables us to see, from the very outset of our investigations, that this may well not be the case. Kant says men have conceptions which enable them to have experience. We add that they may also have misconceptions about their experiences. These misconceptions can be as much built into their minds as the conceptions by which they actually have experience. Moreover, these misconceptions themselves generate a kind of experience of their own which is added onto and laid

3. "I apply the term *transcendental* to all knowledge which is not so much occupied with objects as with the mode of our cognition of these objects. . . ." *Ibid.,* p. 38.

over the actions actually performed. Following Kant's general approach allows us to see the complexities of this kind of situation as arising from the same source, the constructive and synthesizing activity in human experience of the mind of the observer and actor.

There is a final point. To gain what we are now looking for, knowledge of the transcendental elements of American political experience, is to have "critical knowledge." This is a tribute to the method by which it is obtained. A transcendental analytic is not done by speculating upwards into distant philosophical heavens. On the contrary, the whole point of the critical approach is to start with actual life as it is lived, as it is experienced and observed by real people. That is what is then subjected to sustained "critical" analysis.[4] In our case, we must start with the actual, raw material of American political practice, the documents, institutions, spokesmen, and processes by which Americans daily do politics. Then we must lift off the material manifestations and other particularities of this and that situation, and search down to find, isolate, expose, "purify" (in the Kantian sense) the underlying ideas by the possession and use of which Americans are enabled to have their political experience in all its possibilities and limits.

What we will then have is the American political mind. This mind is a substantive, cultural reality, as tough and enduring as any other. But to see this we must go back to our step-by-step analysis.

---

4. ". . . principles existing a *priori* in cognition . . . are the indispensable basis of the possibility of experience. . . . For example, if we take away by degrees from our conceptions of a body all that can be referred to more sensuous experience — colour, hardness or softness, weight, even impenetrability — the body will then vanish; but the space which it occupied still remains, and this it is utterly impossible to annihilate in thought." This is a very simple statement of Kant's critical method. Note how a much more technical example retains the same basic approach: "General logic is again either pure or applied. In the former, we abstract all the empirical conditions under which the understanding is exercised; for example, the influence of the senses, the play of the fantasy or imagination, the laws of the memory, the force of habit, of inclination, etc., consequently also, the sources of prejudice — in a word, we abstract all causes from which particular cognitions arise, because these causes regard the understanding under certain circumstances of its application, and, to the knowledge of them experience is required. Pure general logic has to do, therefore, merely with pure a *priori* principles. . . ." *Ibid.*, pp. 27 and 64.

POLITICAL MIND

The argument so far has introduced the actor, largely isolated and alone, who acts out of a world of understandings we have called frameworks of consciousness for action. We have also indicated ways by which the transcendental elements of his life could be revealed. This figure conforms in many ways with American conceptions of the citizen-actor, a self-motivating, self-understanding and self-identifying entrepreneur, whether in politics or business life. But reflection will show that these conceptions, if taken as characterizing any person's mental state for action in the world, are grotesquely insufficient.

Any person, mentally equipped for action, cannot be conceived of as isolated. The human animal — even the American, for all his obsessive individualism — is a social animal. That statement means vastly more than that individuals are physically dependent on their fellows for survival, that they are garrulous and enjoy company, and that even the meanest of human aspirations can only be achieved in social situations. Human sociality in the present context means even more than that only in society can humans gain ethical fulfillment. What is being pointed at here is that the individual can only come into existence as an author of actions as a social product.

Where do the frameworks of consciousness we use for action come from? It is true that in action situations, we all organize our understanding of what we are doing subjectively. We all think of ourselves as "I, acting." But we did not ourselves invent the frameworks of consciousness out of which we act.

Biographically, it is simply objective fact that we did not invent them. Beginning in infancy, continuing through childhood with great intensity, and extending throughout adulthood, we are taught how to understand the world in which we act. In that world each of us is an individual, acting and responding anew in each situation that arises. We are not social robots; we are individually situated and we often act by and for ourselves. But our equipment for action comes to us from without. The very language by which we not only talk to each other but also organize, grasp, and render intelligible to ourselves our situations, comes to us from social training. Most importantly our

sense of ourselves as subjects, as egos having intentions, projects, careers, and the like comes from without. It can be force-
fully argued that we only become aware of ourselves as selves
as we participate in social life. We distinguish ourselves as
selves only as we distinguish ourselves from other selves like
us.[5]

All this is established by reflection on the biographical and
social process by which each of us grows to maturity. Its full
import becomes apparent when we introduce into the discussion, beyond subjectivity, the term *intersubjectivity*.[6] The term
designates the level, or better, the world, in which "I" can meet
"you" as self to self, as subject to subject, and in which we
relate to each other in ways qualitatively different from the
ways material objects relate in the physical world.

Consider a formal invitation to an intersubjective relationship. You meet a friend on the street. He or she stops, looks at
you, and says, "Hi!" You have been recognized.

Recognition is the original political act and perhaps the
most primitive of deliberate social acts. To have it omitted, we
sometimes say with a more poignant literalness than we may
intend, is to be "cut dead." On the other hand, to receive that
greeting is to be socially revived, to become socially real, to be
translated in a trice from being a mere object for others into
being a subject for others. Even more interesting is the profound sense in which your friend's having recognized you is a
welcoming of you "in." Before, you were clearly "out." It is this
sense of being in rather than out that prompts phrasing about
intersubjective relationships constituting "worlds."

To extend the argument, let us suppose that after recog-
nizing you on the street your friend asks you to join some

5. "The self has a character which is different from that of the physio-
logical organism proper. The self is something which has a development;
it is not initially there, at birth, but arises in the process of social experience and activity, that is, develops in the given individual as a result of
his relations to that process as a whole and to other individuals within
that process." George Herbert Mead, *Mind, Self, and Society*, ed. C. W.
Morris, University of Chicago Press, Chicago, Ill., 1934, p. 135.

6. "The very assumption of the existence of the Other . . . introduces the
dimension of intersubjectivity. The world is experienced by the Self as
being inhabited by other Selves, as being a world for others and of others
. . ." Alfred Schutz, "The Dimensions of the Social World," in *Collected
Papers*, Vol. II, ed. Arvid Brodersen, Martinus Nijhoff, The Hague, 1964,
p. 20.

project, share a meal, join a seminar, go on a crusade, or whatever. Your friend may have to explain the project in some detail and then argue on its behalf at some length. Even then, you may refuse. But if you agree to join the project, notice all that follows in concept.

First, the project you have joined is precisely a framework of consciousness for action as defined in the preceding section of this chapter. Moreover, it will inevitably be a framework of consciousness of very considerable complexity, even if the invitation your friend proffered was to the simplest of meals. There is not a culture in history which has not worked out in considerable detail the relationships to be maintained between host and guest, and these details themselves are understandable only in the general social context in which they appear. Your friend may have pronounced only the imperative, "Come to my house at six for pot luck!" But these words spoke and assumed volumes.

The obvious new element in this framework of consciousness compared to those we noticed earlier is that this one is shared. From this fact flow crucial consequences. The most important is that the shared framework of consciousness, once agreed to, turns back upon its orginators and organizes, or constitutes, them as a group engaged in a certain project. In a literal, straightforward sense, it is their constitution. It not only defines their relationships within the group, but also regulates, even governs, their behavior in it. By subscribing to this constitution and on the basis of its terms, the participants in the project achieve membership in the resulting group and possess the rights and obligations that go with such membership. How important and distinctive the status of membership is can be seen in the fact that objects in the physical world, however much they may be related one to another by proximity, causal patterns, or correlation, can hardly be said to be related in common membership in the sense now being discussed. Finally the project, the shared framework of consciousness for action, and the intersubjective world its underlying agreement created can all vanish if that underlying agreement weakens. If minds no longer meet, commonality ceases. If at times it seems that America is disintegrating all around us, it may be that what is going to pieces is nothing physical but that tenuous social agreement by which we work and live together. We may be no longer solidly and trustingly of one mind.[7]

The quality of relationships in intersubjective worlds, as was just noticed, is substantially different from what exists between objects in the physical world. This is because what is being related in the two worlds is substantially different: in one case subjects, selves, actors, persons undertaking purposive action and, in the other, objects with no relevant consciousness of themselves or of each other. But that distinction alone is not enough to characterize the difference in the quality of the relationships. The essential distinction is only revealed by noting that relationships in the intersubjective world are internal and inherent, while those in the world of objects are external and imposed.

In the "out there" physical world, objects act upon each other, as billiard balls do, and this is the case whether the objects and relations involved are physical, chemical, or biological. Even in the instances of greatest interpenetration or outright synthesis, the elements involved, insofar as they are distinguishable by the observer, remain for him external to each other, particular, and separate. When we perceive relationships between objects, we do so in our own terms. The apple fell, it is said, on Newton's head, but it was he who imposed the theory of gravity on that phenomenon for his own theoretical convenience. It is people who impose relationships on things. The relationship between chalk and blackboards is real and obvious — but only for men and women and children who know and impose that relationship. Certainly the chalk and the blackboard know nothing of it, even when in use.

The situation is very different in an intersubjective world. To reverse the customary phrase about the physical world of objects being an "out there" world, we can say that an intersubjective world is an "in here" world. The source of its interior character and the feeling that it is always a bounded, not a boundless, world, lies in the internality of the relations that obtain in it. Every element in an intersubjective world is reflected back into itself by the other elements. If I am master,

7. ". . . social relations really exist only in and through the ideas which are current in society. . . ." Peter Winch, *The Idea of a Social Science,* Routledge and Kegan Paul, London, 1958, p. 133.

then you must be slave; in fact I am only master at all to the degree that you are slave, and vice versa. Similarly, father is only meaningful as related in mutuality to son, wife to husband, citizen to other citizen, and so forth. To talk of one of these inhabitants of the intersubjective world is to define the other. Often these reverse relationships are obvious. Sometimes they are veiled. It took a black man, enraged and possessing acute artistic sensitivity, to perceive that the underlying function of the black man in the intersubjective world of America has been almost from the beginning to make the white man white.[8] His particular point is well taken. But the general point is also important: the American political world or mind is a closed system relating each and all of us within one whole.

Intersubjective worlds do not come to us in bits and pieces. They are wholes. They are systems whose elements are related internally to each other through networks of reciprocal meanings. Moreover, these relationships are inherent in the role each element plays in the system as whole. If I am master, then master I necessarily am insofar as I am in the system at all. If I would not be master, I can escape only by abolishing not only my role as such but all that defines it as well.

The practical effect of intersubjective worlds being so tightly related internally is to make them closed worlds. To enter one of these worlds is to enter it totally, to a degree rarely appreciated in abstract terms. To act within it is to accept and act within its definitions and rules virtually to the same degree. Imagine yourself, as a stranger, approaching a major university or municipal library. The building, in all its bulk, has meaning for you, but that meaning is *its* meaning, not any meaning you might assign it. And once inside the building, you must accept and act not only in terms of a host of petty regulations about smoking and silence and so forth, in terms of the arrangement of reference facilities and stacks, in terms of the principles of the cataloguing and shelving of books, and in terms of the physical layout of the building, but also in terms of the very conception of what a library should be that was operative in the minds of the building's architect and his employers when they first conceived it and made the decision to build. You accept all this, and it closes around and enfolds your mind as

8. James Baldwin, *The Fire Next Time*, Dial Press, New York, 1963.

you sit and read your book. In fact, its envelopment of you is the essential conceptual precondition of your sitting and reading there at all.

A final point should be made about intersubjective worlds in general before turning to their directly political aspects. Intersubjective worlds or minds are real. For all their fancifulness, complexity, and fragility, for all their being ultimately rooted in individual subjective consciousnesses, they possess an objective existence through time. People really do get together, agree on projects, and sustain shared frameworks of consciousness for action. These are their social and political minds, and there can be little question, in the light of the analysis we have been through, that they can be studied objectively. To call such work empirical research is probably an abuse of the technical content which ought to be allowed that term in careful discussions. But study of actual intersubjective worlds or minds is nevertheless as much a study of "what is" as the weighing of rocks or the observation of mice.

We can now turn to the distinctively political aspects of intersubjective worlds, to the constructs of consciousness employed when men and women are of a mind to do politics together. Politics is preeminently a range of purposive social behavior, an arena in which men and women deliberately agree to act together in accordance with authoritatively determined programs. Political life begins when a people creates an intersubjective world in which each recognized person appears as a subject and as a member of the resulting community. Political action, as a type of social action, can take place in that world when the people together adopt and share mutually understood forms of consciousness for action which authoritatively define relationships and allocate roles.

The political mind which such a group may intersubjectively create must be willed aloft by each of the participants in a conscious subjective effort. Though individually they may be unable to articulate the particular character and details of their shared mind, it is for each of the participants, for all their subjectivity in holding it together, objective. This is doubly so. Obviously, the political world to which he belongs is objective for the individual as it is willed up and presented to him by the others in his group and as they, through recognition, accept him into it. But this political world is also objective for him as he presents it to himself, that is, as he becomes aware of what he must do and is doing to sustain himself as an accepted member of the group.

Thus, if the particular political mind willed aloft by a group is an absolute despotism in which only one leader has power, then all the rest are, objectively, slaves, both in the sense that they are in slavery to the one leader and in the way in which each of them understands his own condition. Even more remarkable is the objectivity of the equality each member of a group can gain if what they will aloft is an egalitarian political community. In such a community, a Quaker meeting perhaps, almost as if by magic each can have conferred upon him, both by the rest and by his own understanding, a virtually perfect equality of status whose objectivity can be sustained even as it flies in the face of all those empirical facts which distinguish human beings by age, sex, physical appearance, and so forth. If the community is truly egalitarian, then *in it* its members are really equal, regardless of all other differences.

This general understanding of the nature of political reality as objective patterns of intersubjectivity, as communal minds or worlds, can be applied to an analysis of what are, in concept, the two most important features of political life: political institutions and power relationships.

On the basis of the analysis presented so far, political institutions are one class of formations of consciousness for action adopted by a people. Political institutions may be more intricately arranged than other formations of social consciousness in common use, and they are usually much more explicitly defined. But qualitatively they are of the same order of intersubjective agreement for common action that extends from the most casual shared meal to the most ancient and complex religious rite.

This may be clear enough when theoretically stated, but we must be aware of the ways in which ordinary language can be misleading. Ordinary language has it that "The United States Senate *meets*," which is to imply *is*, "in Washington." Leave it to language like that and the impression will be strong that the United States Senate is an "out there" thing which one could journey to our nation's capital to look at and study as one would rocks. But in fact all a student can see there is a building and an assortment of people who more or less frequently assemble in it. These are the appearance of the Senate, the outward show of the political reality behind that term as it is employed in the American intersubjective world of politics. But they are not that reality itself. It is to be found only by another route.

The would-be direct observer of the reality of the United States Senate must make himself a subject and then relate, as subject to subject, to the persons intersubjectively constituting that reality. To do this directly and overtly, he would approach a member of that body and talk to him or her. He would say, effectively, "Excuse me!" that is, "Notice me as subject, please!" and then go on with the question, "Is this a meeting of the United States Senate?" The reply might well be, "Yes!" and contact with senatorial reality would have been made. On the other hand, we can suppose a different reply, one more revealing of the complexities involved. The answer might be, "No, we are still assembling. But we'll be in session soon and I'll let you know when we start." That kind of answer separates the immediate imperative that the Senate meet at a particular time from the more general and on-going constructions in their minds by the use of which the members of that body are able to meet and do business on a regular, continuing basis. These mental constructions are the true, relatively permanent, inner reality of the United States Senate.

The complexities of the senatorial concept, as an example of an operative formation of intersubjective consciousness for action, should be stressed. The concept of the Senate, like any element in an intersubjective world, cannot be understood except as internally related to a host of other institutions, the House of Representatives, the presidency, the courts, and the totality of the American political system. The American political system is emphatically an intersubjective whole, a single "mind," an intricately contrived system of internally related elements each of which is only finally comprehensible in terms of all the rest.

These points apply even more vividly to the concept which most distinguishes political life generally, the concept of power. The presence of explicit power relationships is what most distinguishes political institutions from other social institutions, but it is not the essence of them. The essence of a political institution is that it is an expression of social agreement to act in accordance with certain established patterns. The presence of power relationships in such an institution in no way diminishes this essential character. Far from being some force exerted willy-nilly by one on others, power in its political sense is itself inherently an intersubjective relationship resting ultimately on reciprocal agreement.

This may not be immediately obvious. Force is an object-to-object affair, in which one object is imposed upon the other. The effects are visible or otherwise fully accountable in the physical world perceived by the senses. Power in its political sense, on the other hand, is not only a more complicated matter; it is also blatantly paradoxical. It exists and is effective within an intersubjective world only on the basis of that mutual consent which creates the intersubjective world in which it appears. This means, specifically, that persons over whom power is held must consent to the fact of their subservience as much as those who hold the power. Moreover the power held, its nature, and its extent must be defined in advance. It cannot be employed beyond the limits of its definition except at the risk of the breakdown of the power relationship itself and of the whole intersubjective world in which it appears. We normally think of power as involving coercion; we imagine persons compelled to do things they otherwise would not do. On an immediate, superficial level, this popular impression of power is obviously true. If it were not, there would be no need for political power, and the whole world would be governed in a spirit of cheerful, unprovoked cooperation. But placing power relationships in their sustaining intersubjective worlds exposes a deeper level at which the coercive element in power must be seen as "coercion by consent."[9]

Paradoxical as this expression may be, it is descriptive of political life of all sorts. Consider a game played by teams. Each side must elect a coach or other leader to call and run the team plays. Obedience to his commands may have to be instantaneous if the team is to be efficient, and individual players, very much against their instincts, may be required to submerge their talents and personal aspirations into the team effort. Nevertheless this blunting of themselves, and acknowledgement of the team captain's powers, were both prefigured in the

9. H. D. Lasswell and A. Kaplan, *Power and Society,* Yale University Press, New Haven, 1950, p. 99.

original responses of each player to the basic invitation to join the intersubjective world within which the game can be played, "Let's play ball!"

The paradox of political power is even more sharply revealed in the classic example (all too American) used in discussions of this sort, a police officer arresting a suspect. Drawing his gun, the police officer orders the suspect, in the name of the law, to surrender and come quietly. Viewing the situation as an intersubjective one shows that, no matter how imperious the officer's command or how threatening his gun, his words are effectively an invitation to the suspect to remain in (or perhaps rejoin) a world of shared consciousness for common action. In that world of shared consciousness police officers, by the authority general agreement and social law assign to their office, have the power to arrest those they think have violated the law, and ordinary citizens when so arrested should surrender quietly. The police officer is asking the suspect to join a game the rules and terms of which — *officer, suspect, law, arrest, surrender* — have all been clearly and reciprocally defined in advance. If the suspect joins the game, the police officer's power to coerce the suspect into behavior he would not otherwise have undertaken has been proven effective. Notice that the police officer's drawing of his gun played no special or distinctive role, since we are supposing the arrest to have been made peacefully. Like the officer's uniform, it symbolized his authority. Like the officer's words, "In the name of the law . . . ," it underlined the peaceful nature of the game the suspect was being asked to join by drawing attention to the game's alternative. The presence of the gun says simply, "Surrender *or else. . . !*"

". . . *or else* no game!" If the suspect resists and tries to escape, in an instant the subject-to-subject, dialogic relationship the officer had proffered vanishes. Both men still regard themselves as subjects, but they now regard each other as objects, qualitatively no different from any others in the physical world. The officer's power has in this same instant also vanished and he is compelled to subdue the suspect, if he can, by force. Stripped of all symbolic meaning, his gun has become for him only a more or less effective manipulative tool. For the suspect, the gun is now a force of nature the effects of which he must somehow avoid. What happens thereafter is for physicists, biologists, and psychologists to predict and describe. Politics and political mind are irrelevant.

IDEOLOGY AND MYTH

The analysis so far developed has shown concrete political mind to consist primarily of intersubjectively shared consciousness for cooperative action. Secondarily, power relationships, the distinctive element in political life, appear within such a system of shared consciousness. Their presence makes the more general agreement a people may have to work and live together more secure and more comprehensive. Nevertheless, for all their practical indispensibility and their capacity to distinguish political situations from social situations generally, power relationships are not the essence of political life. That essence lies in the deliberate effort to live life cooperatively.

Even so, much of what has been said is artificial. How many people, in the ordinary course of everyday life in American politics, consciously agree to live cooperatively under the terms given by the extant norms we usually abide by? We do things together, of course, but mostly without conscious thought. Moreover, even while we may agree that abstract analysis must show our agreement to participate in shared frameworks of consciousness, there is still about our actual daily lives an uncomfortable sense that we are caught, that we have few viable choices about the patterns in which we play out our ordinary affairs with each other, and that we are trapped inside social, economic, and political systems we had no hand in devising. These have been handed to us out of history. Perhaps we can rebel on this point or seek reform on that, but generally we must do the best we can within the ways of life we have inherited.

Placing a world of social action in its historical context adds to it a third dimension of complexity. The patterns of reciprocal, internal relations connecting the elements of an intersubjective world now can be seen extending deep into the past, and the same can be said of the elements themselves. Each will have an individual history and perhaps interconnecting histories. Insofar as this history is known, it will impinge upon the totality of the intersubjective situation along with consciousness of whatever present roles are being played. Thus in the intersubjective world of a congressional committee meeting, a chairman's gavel plays a certain role: it symbolizes a present chairman's authority. It will fill that role especially well if committee members and observers know that this particular gavel has a long, special history. If this historic gavel is wielded by a revered, elderly gentleman with a long record of service on the committee and in Congress generally, the effectiveness of chairman and gavel, meaningfully related to each other, will be further enhanced. Finally, when the chairman is seen in the committee room in the company of the other committee members, and when all this is set in the context of the gradually accrued, historic role that congressional committees have come to play in the United States, then at last will the full complexity of the concept labeled "Mr. Chairman," by which the committee members grasp their leader in shared consciousness, begin to emerge.

This kind of complexity in totality and depth comes about only on a highly particularized level. There may be general similarities between the meanings given the term "Mr. Chairman" as applied to a chairman of a committee in the Congress of the United States, the chairman of a board of directors of a major business, the chairman of an academic department of a university, and the chairman of the Presidium of the Soviet Union. But at the level of actual daily life, the differences between the myriad details and the operative substance of these concepts in their separate intersubjective environments set them worlds apart.

Both the complexity of formations of consciousness for cooperative action and the particularity of their highly individualized relationship to particular cultural and historical contexts point to a final characteristic, their viscosity. No culture can endure without shared memory and historical repetition of form and symbol; conservatism is a natural instinct of social self-preservation. Formations of consciousness for cooperative action are achieved only with great difficulty, and the range and intricacy of detail which must be consciously agreed upon greatly exceeds what is required of other cultural formations. Once a group, especially a national society, has worked out shared understandings about how to do things, it is difficult to get them to change not so much their "habits" as their "minds." What is at issue here is not perfunctory, repetitive behavior but shared formations of consciousness for common action. Once a group has an idea of how they wish to carry out certain kinds of actions, they will generally stick to the chosen method because, in both a technical and a literal sense, they will have no *idea* of how else to proceed.

The viscosity of formations of consciousness for common action in particular societies can be demonstrated in a variety of ways. Especially in the United States, the accepted modes of consciousness for political action, both in terms of institutional patterns shaping overt behavior and in terms of underlying philosophical assumptions and imperatives, are the subject of deliberate, systematic, and sustained instruction in the schools and universities of the nation. Further, when deviations from these accepted modes occur, a great hue and cry is raised in defense of "law," "the Constitution," and the American sense of "justice," "fair play," and the national "way of life." This reaction effectively reinforces the schoolbook lessons. Even the disputes which arise when there is suspicion and controversy over ambiguities in the inherited teachings achieve the same end. In such disputes, as much as in the teachings themselves, resides the underlying assumption that in the shared world of political consciousness we all inhabit, there exists a massive body of conceptual formations for common action, an American way of political life. To attack that assumption, to suggest that some of these inherited modes of political action might be changed or replaced, is to speak sacrilege. All that is socially permitted when doubts about how to proceed spring up, is to peer ever more closely into the massive inherited conceptual complex and discover there what is to be done.

Sometimes in America today some of us, individually or in little groups, will claim not to be included in the all-encompassing national political mind. We will hold that because we personally are Marxists, or flower children, or members of spiritualist communes or of splinter, extreme right-wing groups, we do not think or act in the orthodox ways and neither have nor owe any allegiances to their underlying assumptions. We will claim that we are free people. But this claim is specious. It is honored only if we are quiescent and/or if the bulk of the society largely ignores us. But if those conditions are not met and if, instead, we try or are forced to enter into even the edges of the common political life, then one of two things will happen. We may to some degree start to play the game by the accepted rules, and whether we know or like it or not we will begin also to assimilate accepted definitions and goals. It is remarkable how far this process can go even when the dominant order is attempting to punish deviants in a court of law. On the other hand, those drawn into the game may nonetheless refuse steadfastly to follow the rules. In that case they will lose disastrously, as if they had entered a football game determined to play by basketball rules. Unless they succeed in destroying the dominant society and making it over in their own image, they will be charged with being "out of their minds" and treated accordingly.

None of this is to suggest that cleavages cannot exist within the dominant political mind of a society. It is rather to argue that there must be a foundation of agreement if the society is not to face disintegration. In America there are serious cleavages between racial and ethnic groups and there is often little assimilation between them. Yet for all their differences and hostilities, it has not been shown that any of these groups has refused to accept the norms, rules, definitions, and goals of the dominant social and political culture. When they play the political game, even for purposes of opposing each other, the nation's minority groups willingly join and play the American way. This is also the case with Democrats and Republicans, whether conservative or liberal, and with most other groups that voluntarily work within the established laws and mores of political action. Much like lawyers in court or players in a sports contest, if only to make their differences of opinion known and felt, they accept the context of "the game." Sometimes explicitly, mostly inarticulately, they know that without the context there would be no contest. More specifically even than this, they know that there are recognized limits and accepted modes for disagreement, and they are careful to observe these as they press their special points of view.

All this is relatively straightforward. Such is not the case, however, with the most serious cleavage problem that can arise within a concrete political mind, one associated with the problem of irrationality raised at the beginning of this chapter. There the distinction was made between what a people may think and sincerely believe they are doing, and what they are in fact doing in operative idea but are reluctant to admit even to themselves. Unlike the others just mentioned, this cleavage can cut to the very bottom of a political mind and lock a whole nation into fundamental war with itself. The remainder of this book is designed to show that the most serious of America's political agonies arise from divisions of this kind in the nation's concrete political mind. We must now assign and define terms to describe cleavages of this order.

In what follows, *ideology* will be used to denote the ideas, the forms of consciousness, which enable Americans to act politically, while *myth* denotes the ideas, the forms of consciousness, by which they understand and proclaim what they are doing. This usage is being stipulated for present purposes. While not unrelated to usage in some academic circles, it bears little or no relationship to certain other common usages.

The usage being developed here for these terms implies no ethical judgments whatsoever. The reader is asked to make a consistent effort not to associate these terms with such value-laden, accusatory remarks as "That's pure myth!" and "That's nothing but ideological thinking!" Instead, the reader is asked to make refinements of the following sort.

Karl Marx defined ideology as the stock of ideas, ". . . the legal, political, religious, aesthetic, or philosophic — in short, ideological — forms in which men become conscious of this [class-war] conflict and fight it out."[10] That is to say, in the class war there was a Bourgeois ideology and a proletarian ideology, and each would excite approbation or opprobrium depending on the partisan commitments of the observer. The usage of ideology being coined for this book is narrower than that of Marx, for the interest here is more exclusively with politics. Yet it would follow Marx in having ideology denote those conceptual forms by which men become conscious of their action situations and in them pursue, even fight hard for, things they want. The meaning given ideology in this book thus ranges over the whole field of operative political institutions, much

10. "Critique of Political Economy," in *Marx and Engels: Basic Writings on Politics and Philosophy*, ed. L. Feuer, Doubleday, New York, 1959, p. 44. In *The Manifesto of the Communist Party* Marx, of course, claimed that his own ideas "merely express, in general terms, actual relations springing from an existing class struggle. . . ." *Ibid.*, p. 20.

political philosophy, and considerable amounts of political symbolization. The only restriction is that ideology must be concerned with defining actual wants and specific, reasonably consistent ways of obtaining them. Omitted from this definition are all the pejorative and partisan connotations Marx associated with the term.

In this book, to say a nation has an ideology is to state merely that it has political capability. To observe this fact is to compliment the nation on having such capability. Of course, it can be further observed that the nation acts in terms of its particular ideology. This will raise questions about the nature and limitations of its particular political capabilities. These may be shown, on given ethical criteria, to be poor. In the chapters that follow, it will be argued that the United States has powerful ideological commitments. There is in that assertion no denigration whatsoever either of the United States or of the notion of ideological commitment. All that is asserted is that the United States can act politically. On the other hand, it will be argued that America's particular ideological commitments are narrow, that they lack key elements that would encourage political adaptability and that, above all, they are largely and inherently unresponsive to elementary demands of social justice. That kind of comment is certainly critical and proceeds from a particular ethical point of view, but it stems from judgments upon the content, not the fact, of ideological commitment.

Ideology is being used here to denote a very broad range of social phenomena. Nevertheless, the limits on this usage should also be clear. Ideology is not being used to refer to the totality of social memory and understanding by which a society identifies and organizes itself as a communal whole. Ideology denotes only that portion of the totality of social memory and self-understanding by use of which the society organizes itself for *action*. In this sense, ideology is an abstract from the historical materials and refers not to what was done and by whom, but to *how*, and to how only in the political realm — to that range of social action involving deliberate and authoritatively maintained action.

Finding out an operative ideology such as that possessed by the United States by the critical method is not easy, but it is possible. Our most important evidence will be the nation's basic documents and the operative political institutions these created. We will want to go behind these to determine underlying philosophical understandings about the nature of political life and action. To this end, consulting the great texts that guided the thinking of the nation's founding fathers will be instructive. But we will also need to go beyond these basic sources to observe actual political practice, and, almost as important, to read the daily press and listen to the candid talk of active politicians. Often we will hear them say things like, "That's all right in theory, but if you want to get something done, you have to be practical." The logic-clashing qualities of such statements should alert us to the fact that the speaker is trying to shift our attention — our minds — to the modes of consciousness by which we Americans get things done in politics.

What the critical approach will reveal about the ideological element in the American political mind will unfold in the chapters that follow. One general finding will be that the American operative ideology is a remarkably self-consistent whole.[11] That is partially because any ideology must be relatively self-consistent or it will generate intolerably confused political action. Beyond this and despite some appearances to the contrary, the American political ideology is very probably one of the most intellectually and operationally self-consistent ideologies in the historical record. But the primary reason we will find the American ideology highly self-consistent is that for purposes of analysis we have separated ideology from all the mythic elements of the American political mind.

The picture will change drastically once these elements are introduced into the analysis. Especially in America, but to some degree in all societies, myth contradicts ideology. This is a direct consequence of the primary social function of myth in generating communal cohesion in ways that ideology does not and cannot.

11. Compare this finding to those of public opinion analysts. See, for example, Donald J. Devine, The Political Culture of the United States, Little Brown, Boston, 1972. This book, a remarkable display of methodological ingenuity and thoroughness, is a deliberate effort to provide full scale "empirical" support for Louis Hartz's thesis that America's dominant ideology is an eighteenth century, Lockean Liberalism. The present essay, with its critical approach, in effect begins by accepting Devine's work.

The daily operations of a community's political system, its institutional patterns as much as the values they serve, are generally detailed, complex, mundane, virtually colorless. It is work that must be done if the society is to continue functioning. Even in the broadest of democracies, such work involves the direct participation of only a fraction of the society's total population. However, the governing fraction of the community, if it is to go about its work effectively and without undue interruption, will require from the bulk of the population some degree of positive and generalized acquiesence.

This problem plagues all governments, ancient despotisms and modern democracies alike. Moreover, the solutions all follow a common pattern. In one way or another, the ruling element of a community must set up modes and avenues of communication with the bulk of the population. It must then seek to persuade one and all, including most of its own membership, of two things. First, the ruling element must persuade the community at large that it is indeed a community, a social unity capable of sustaining in self-image and then in fact a common identity and life. For this purpose, materials drawn from every aspect of the community's cultural resources, its literature, historical memories, religious beliefs and practices, traditional manners, rituals, and symbols will be molded together into a single legend. In terms of this legend the people can come to see themselves as actors in history, as a nation among nations.

Second, the ruling element must persuade the community that it is the nation's proper governance. They will seek legitimization not just of themselves as persons but also of their system of operation, their regime. For this purpose, the ruling element will have to explain to the populace what they are doing and how their activities conform to the community's developing sense of itself. Even in the best of circumstances, this explanation by the minority to the whole mass of the population cannot be continuous, direct, and complete. Therefore, over generations of time, rulers will resort to simplified explanations and more or less straightforward or devious rationalizations. To ensure that these arguments are persuasive and generate awe, they will be decked out with all kinds of traditional symbols, folktale references, and other legendary allusions.

To the degree that it assumes permanent, ongoing form, the content of this two-phase explanatory process can be called the society's myth.[12]

It is essential in thinking about myth to keep in mind its origin in the dialogue between rulers and ruled. Rulers create the myth, and impose it for their own purposes, but they do so by drawing on materials indigenous and vital to the ruled. But it is also essential to keep in mind that myth is functional in the relationship between rulers and ruled and for the society generally. A people may share all sorts of beliefs, some based on fact, others clearly fanciful, that the world is flat, that blondes have more fun, that furry caterpillars with broad stripes portend a hard winter, that this man in history was a hero, that one a traitor, and so forth. But unless such culturally shared beliefs have been drawn into the ruler/ruled dialogue and elevated into the definition of communal identity and the legitimization of the regime, they cannot be labeled elements of the community's political myth.

Two further points must be made immediately about myth viewed in this light. The first is that while myth is socially functional in the ways indicated, it is not "operative" in the direct sense that the possession of a shared ideology permits those who run a society to go about their work. Myth tells us who we are and who are our proper rulers. But it does not tell us how to act or how to get things done. Thus, in a modern national representative democracy, the complex of electoral processes and connected institutions of government may be put to the general populace as a system of "popular government" through which "the people rule."[13] These mythic slogans may be effective and pardonable simplifications of what actually happens. But they are not operative. They neither describe exactly nor constitute and control what happens. In no direct sense, even in the most advanced modern democracy, can it be said that the people rule. What actually happens is con-

12. Compare this account to Plato's discussion of the "noble lie" in *The Republic*, tr. Allan Bloom, Basic Books, New York, 1968, pp. 93–94. Note especially Bloom's comments on this section in pp. xiv–xv and 365–369.

13. C. W. Cassinelli, *The Politics of Freedom, An Analysis of the Modern Democratic State*, University of Washington Press, Seattle, 1961, pp. 108–112.

trolled by the ideology of representative government, a very different business.

The other point about myth which must be promptly noticed here is that our discussion of it has already exposed the primary source of the inevitable contradiction between ideology and myth. Any effort at simplification, even the most straightforward, involves a degree of distortion and hence of contradiction. Consequently, any society in which the mythic and ideological elements of the communal political mind have developed permanent form harbors a permanent source of possible social tension.

This original and inevitable gap between a society's ideology and its myth can be greatly exacerbated by historical developments. Any nation's concrete political mind is not only a cultural artifact of its origins but is also built up over time. Each age will deposit, as in archeological layers, its own record of experience and aspiration, but none will dare blot out the nation's originating mythic sense of social identity and the attendant legends, cults, rituals, and symbols. That is precious, fragile stuff to be treasured through all time because of its extraordinary power to evoke broad feelings of association and commitment. As generations pass, the distance between a nation's mythic sense of historic selfhood and what it is actually accomplishing in present circumstances can widen greatly.

For example, the ancient Hebrews were originally nomads, and their patriarchical legends are all cast in these terms. But the people went on to enter into a promised land where life was more agricultural and settled and to an increasing degree dominated by urban centers and commercial modes of life. Even within the Bible itself the strains between ancient memory and the process by which Israel became a nation like others around it are sharply evident. But these conflicts pale before what the modern Jewish community experiences in trying to reconcile its sense of centuries-old Biblical identity to a worldwide environment.

Comparable patterns could be cited in the histories of Athens and Rome and in such modern nations as Britain, France, and the Soviet Union. America also shows these patterns of conflict, as the nation developed from a seaboard colonial community, through continental expansion, to a world power whose cultural patterns have been transformed by economic and technological changes. But the American example also reveals something else, an even more radical source of possible contradiction between ideology and myth. As will be argued hereafter, the American political mind was sundered congenitally by the accident of having been endowed at its very birth with myths and ideology that were in their particular contents fundamentally opposed.

The general consequence of all these observations is that the relationship between ideology and myth in any actual society must be construed not in static but in dynamic, even dialectical, terms.[14] What happens between myth and ideology in a particular society will depend on the content given these elements of the society's political mind in that society. Determining the content of a nation's myth is considerably more difficult than working out its ideology. Myth works best with sweeping generalizations encapsulated in slogans, or in vivid legends which incorporate but rarely explicate moral principles, or in symbols often endowed with systematically ambiguous meanings. The volume of these materials is usually very extensive but without clear delineation. Nevertheless, grasping and rendering this amorphous mass intelligible is not impossible, especially if the effort is made systematically and, above all, critically. Findings about American political myths will be presented subsequently, but a preliminary comment is possible now. The myths of American politics, viewed separately from the accompanying ideology, make up a remarkably self-consistent whole.[15]

14. ". . . it is the nature of myth to mediate contradictions . . . the function of myth is to portray the contradictions in the basic premises of the culture. The same goes for the relation of myth to social reality. The myth is a contemplation of the unsatisfactory compromises which, after all, compose social life. In the devious statements of the myth, people can recognize indirectly what it would be difficult to admit openly and yet what is patently clear to all and sundry, that the ideal is not attainable." Mary Douglas, "The Meaning of Myth," in The Structural Study of Myth and Totemism, ed. E. Leach, Tavistock Publications, London, 1967, p. 52.

15. The self-consistency of American political myths becomes all the more remarkable when their essentially Protestant character is pitted against the highly variegated ways in which American religiosity has found doctrinal and institutional expression. America, adage has it, is a nation of churches. Yet persons deeply familiar with the problem report what common impression can confirm, that at the level of genuinely operative practical belief

This is an interesting finding, but its significance must be all but overridden by the one which follows it and which our general discussion of the relationship between ideology and myth has prepared us to state in a summary way. That finding, the dominant theme of this book, is that though American ideology and myth are mutually supportive in important ways, the contradictions and tensions between them are radical and irresolvable.[16] They issue into conflicts that are more often socially destructive than constructive. Nevertheless, these two elements of the American political mind remain locked in intimate symbiosis, however unhappy.

There is a pattern in the ways in which myth and operative ideology interact in times of crisis, those often-repeated moments in American history which, whatever their particular form, seem always to promise that, at last, something definitive will happen, something of substance will be accomplished, if only we can weather the storm. A major purpose of what follows will be to elucidate that pattern. A mass of preliminary material will have to be presented first, but it may be useful to have from the outset a schematic outline of this myth/ideology cycle of crisis interaction. Because the sense of promise and achievement is so strong in America's moments of crisis, we must be prepared to explain them.

In the first (and what may be regarded as the normal) stage myth and ideology work side by side. Americans think they are one sort of people accomplishing in politics a certain

---

and aspiration, there is an extraordinary uniformity to American religious life. See Will Herberg, *Protestant, Catholic, Jew,* rev. ed., Doubleday, Garden City, N.Y. 1960, but also H. Richard Niebuhr, *The Social Sources of Denominationalism,* (1929), World Publishing, New York, 1957. Niebuhr's work is much earlier than Herberg's and written from a different perspective. Yet he, too, stresses the "Americanization" of especially the immigrant churches, and states emphatically, "The tendency toward conformity with the new civilization is, strangely enough, responsible for much of the denominationalism of America" (p. 213).

16. ". . . While 65 percent of our sample were liberal on the Operational Spectrum, only 16 percent were either completely or predominantly liberal on the Ideological Spectrum. Conversely, while only 14 percent were conservative on the Operational Spectrum, half were in one or the other of the conservative categories on the Ideological Spectrum. This discrepancy between operational outlooks and ideological views is so marked as to be almost schizoid." Lloyd Free and Hadley Cantril, *The Political Beliefs of Americans,* A Study of Public Opinion, Rutgers University Press, New Brunswick, 1967, pp. 32–33. (Compare footnote 11.)

set of goals, and they effectively conceal from themselves that their operational situation is quite different. The fit between the mask and the actuality, however, is never tight enough, the concealment never perfect. Even at this stage there is always a good deal of random strain, contradiction, tension, and outright cynicism. The situation is essentially unstable, and almost any untoward event can upset it.

The second stage develops when such an event occurs. The mask slips, and the contradictions between self-understanding and action are exposed to direct perception and comment. The result is outrage. Something must be done. But myth, in both definition and fact, is inoperative. Moreover, American ideology is incapable of responding constructively to the kind of grand challenges typically mounted by the imperatives of American political myth. The rage engendered by the resulting standoff must either subside impotently, or burst out into mindless vehemence, overt violence, or some other form of political paralysis.

The spill into violence or other forms of political breakdown constitute the third stage of the cycle. Here the mythic and operative tendencies of the American political mind thrash at each other senselessly until horror, exhaustion, or distraction still the combat. If the battle has been sufficiently extensive or dramatic, as in a civil war, widespread rioting, or a presidential assassination, the paralysis stage will typically end with some authority figure, a learned professor, a national commission, or a formal institution like the Supreme Court coming forward and solemnly reassuring us all that — "Yes, Virginia . . ." — there was no conspiracy, the violence was mere inadvertence, the presidency is a grand office still, — ". . . there is a Santa Claus."

The way is thus prepared for the fourth stage of the American myth/ideology interaction cycle, which is the recovery and the return to stage one. Comforting myths are rebelieved and old practices resumed. This is possible because the old practices are the only available ways in which American citizens can conduct practical life and because it is easy to rebelieve the myths. It is not in the nature of myth to be falsified by experience. Whatever falsifying experiences did show up in the earlier stages of the cycle, no matter how glaringly, are simply ignored.

We have sketched here only a pattern, hardly even a hypothesis. Its most important utility will be its capacity for identifying, assembling, and ordering without distortion large clumps of American political experience. Nevertheless, if this myth/ideology cycle can persuasively absorb major stretches of American political experience — and if it is not required to omit other significant areas as exceptional — then it will irresistibly point to important conclusions.

These can be briefly summarized by saying that the myth/ideology interaction cycle constitutes a neutral equilibrium, such as that of a cone lying on its side on a teetering plane, or a marble in the bottom of a rocking bowl. Energy abounds and motion too, perhaps of dizzying speed, but the tendency is to go nowhere, to return always to the beginning point. In other words, if the sketched myth/ideology cycle holds, it can be strongly suggested that the American political experience, for all its tensions, agonies, vehemence, and frantic pulsations, is overall one of stability and sterility.

The matters touched upon in these discussions will be treated systematically and extensively in the following chapters. What the present chapter has primarily attempted is to move into view the conception that the American political system, with its underlying philosophical constructions, its overt institutions, and its patterns of symbolization, constitutes a totality. That totality is a comprehensive, historically developed formation of political consciousness, a national political mind, by which we Americans understand ourselves as political actors, organize ourselves for political action, and drive ourselves onward toward political goals. Additionally, this chapter has suggested some ways in which the American political mind contains divisions that rend it. Finally, we have tried to develop methods of approach, conceptual tools, and patterns by which these divisions may be identified, analyzed, and evaluated.

But what all this points to ultimately is the possibility of answering an overriding question: have the bombast and failure that litter the American political past, recent and distant, been the consequence of mere historical accident, or are they better viewed as the nearly inevitable consequences of a defective political mind?

AMERICAN
LIBERALISM

THE PROTESTANT-
BOURGEOIS
SYNDROME
LIBERALISM
THE AMERICAN
ENVIRONMENT

THE PROTESTANT-BOURGEOIS SYNDROME

The American political mind is modern. That is to say, it displays few pre-modern (European-feudal) characteristics. It also displays few of those characteristics found in the political minds of nations which, having experienced civilizations comparable in quality if not degree to the American, have gone on, whether by revolution or other route, to further developments.

The western European nations are the relevant standard of comparison because America's seminal stock of peoples and ideas came from them. Most of these nations are, like America, modern communities. Nevertheless, they retain unmistakable evidence of their feudal pasts, and not just in assorted tourist landmarks. Significant bits and pieces of ancient patterns crop up everywhere in their legal systems, political institutions, class structures, religious organizations, and economic life. On the other hand, all of them have experimented seriously and extensively with what can be termed post-modern techniques of providing social welfare services, organizing economic processes, and so forth.

By contrast, America not only has no feudal past to speak of, it also has a scattered, tentative, and self-defeating record of experimentation in post-modern areas. Like the western European nations, the American nation is equipped with a predominantly modern political intelligence, but ours is the most purely, or some would say the most merely, modern.

Of what does this modernity consist? It is not to be confused with facts of extensive industrialization, technological advancement, and urbanization. Rather it is the set of attitudes about man and his possibilities in this world which underlies and accounts for those facts. In politics, modernity achieved its fullest expressing in the creed of Liberalism in the nineteenth century. But long before that, modernity grounded itself in the two most powerful movements involved in the shattering and transformation of medieval Europe, Protestantism and capitalism.

Protestantism and capitalism had separate, even antithetical, origins and their creeds are clearly distinguishable. Yet they were irrevocably joined, contradictions and all, as the operational faith for daily life of the ascendent Middle Class of northwestern Europe, the so-called Bourgeoisie.[1] This class bears prime responsibility for having made over the modern world into what it is today. Modernity is thus the final basis of belief and action for a whole structure of historical development whose complex of motives are mostly known by other terms. Since the American political mind is so exclusively modern, modernity is the ultimate root of American political conduct.

The fundamental tenet of modernity (and the one by which it most decisively turned against medieval thought) was anthropocentricism. Man-centeredness in general philosophical orientation was translated into radical individualism in practical ethics and politics. This was as true of modernity's Protestant emphasis as it was of its Bourgeois emphasis. On both sides, ego was preeminent. Society was an arena, a space to be guarded and stabilized to be sure, but essentially a stage on which "I" may act.

But within modernity, the motives, behavior, and interests of the "I" who acts were variously defined. To use significant American examples, Jonathan Edwards and Benjamin Franklin were at one, profoundly, in presuming in everything they wrote and did the active, self-directing ego. But the face Edwards put on that ego in his sermons was very different from the face Franklin put on it in his *Autobiography*.

Those differences will be tabulated shortly. They constitute a paradox because both Franklin and Edwards are authentic American types; in fact they represent different sides of a common, national character. Paradoxically, antagonistically, Franklin and Edwards, the one supremely Bourgeois and the other supremely Protestant, presume each other. As symbols, they are one figure, not two. Together they are the epitome of the American Protestant-Bourgeois syndrome.

---

1. The argument that follows, in the present chapter and throughout the book as well, proceeds from that presented in R. H. Tawney, *Religion and the Rise of Capitalism*, Mentor, New York (1926), 1947. Tawney derived much of his analysis from Max Weber, *The Protestant Ethic and the Spirit of Capitalism*, tr. T. Parsons, Scribner's, New York, 1958. With important reservations, both he and Weber were working in the wake of Marx and Engels. It was the genius of Marx and Engels that focused modern scholarship on the broad revolutionary impact on the modern world of the North West European middle class. See, for example, Engel's discussion of religion, materialism, and revolution in his "Socialism: Utopian and Scientific," in Karl Marx and Frederick Engels, *Selected Works*, Foreign Languages Publishing House, Moscow, 1951, Vol. II, pp. 86–106.

To go to the root of that syndrome one must leave American examples and return to the sources of the American political mind in Europe. Indeed wherever the Protestant-Bourgeois syndrome appears in the modern world, it is rooted in instabilities that go back through Western civilization all the way to Greek and Hebrew origins. But for our present purpose we need carry our direct examination only to Martin Luther[2] and Thomas Hobbes,[3] the first great spokesmen for the tortured contradictions of the modern political mind.

It is important to distinguish the spirit of Martin Luther's writing from the immediate historical actions which he and his church went on to perform in German political life. That spirit, the essence of evangelical Christianity of the sort that predominated in the religious life of Bible-reading nineteenth century American Baptists, Methodists, and the like, is vividly expressed in the opening page of Luther's "A Treatise on Christian Liberty."

Many have thought Christian faith to be an easy thing, and not a few have given it a place among the virtues. This they do because they have had no experience of it, and have never tasted what great virtue there is in faith. For it is impossible that anyone should write well of it or well understand what is correctly written of it, unless he has at some time tasted the courage faith gives a man when trials

2. Luther is preferred over Calvin as spokesman for the Protestant pole of the modern mind, because his type of radical, evangelical pietism was much more influential in the development of American religious feeling than was Calvin's more doctrinal theology. Calvin's influence in America was largely confined to New England and even there was much diminished by the eighteenth century. In addition, Luther's conservatism in economic and political matters, the natural consequence of the impotence of his pietism before problems in these areas, underlines the fact that the contradictions in the Protestant-Bourgeois syndrome were present from the beginning. See the discussion of Luther in Tawney, *Religion and the Rise of Capitalism*, pp. 72–91.

3. Hobbes is the preferred spokesman for the Bourgeois pole of the modern mind over such later figures as Locke and Smith, because his political radicalism is more extreme and purer than theirs. See the discussion of Hobbes in C. B. Macpherson, *The Political Theory of Possessive Individualism*, Oxford University Press, Oxford, England, 1962, Part II.

The frequent labeling, even in serious academic literature dating back to Weber himself, of the Bourgeois ethos by such phrases as "The Protestant work ethic" is both a misnomer and a major slight to the actual Protestant (Christian) spirit of communal love. However understandable such confusions may be, they must be scrupulously avoided if the real tensions in the Protestant-Bourgeois syndrome are to be revealed.

oppress him. But he who has had even a faint taste of it can never write, speak, meditate, or hear enough concerning it. For it is a living fountain springing up into life everlasting, as Christ calls it in John 4. For my part, although I have no wealth of faith to boast of and know how scant my store is, yet I hope that, driven about by great and various temptations, I have attained to a little faith, and that I can speak of it, if not more elegantly, certainly more to the point, than those literalists and all too subtle disputants have hitherto done, who have not even understood what they have written.

That I may make the way easier for the unlearned — for only such do I serve — I set down first these two propositions concerning the liberty and the bondage of the spirit:

A Christian man is a perfectly free lord of all, subject to none.

A Christian man is a perfectly dutiful servant of all, subject to all.[4]

The most obvious point where this statement helps to usher in the modern age is when Luther remarks, in an aside, that he speaks to "the unlearned — for only such do I serve. . . ." Gone in Luther's mind are the barriers the medieval age used to divide men into hierarchies of religious orders. He now grasps his fellow men by a mode of consciousness in which all men appear without distinction.

The concept of "all men" (a concept made so familiar to Americans by their Declaration of Independence that it might almost be rendered as one word, "allmen") has origins antedatting Luther and the Protestant Reformation by a thousand years, going back not only to the beginning of Augustinian Christianity but well into the Roman Stoic tradition. But Luther's use of it implicitly in this famous passage and throughout his religious teaching was in his day revolutionary. Moreover, the way he used it was truly new. Not only would he grasp all men into a company with himself, a single congregation without regard to the extent of their learning, but he also would talk with every one of them about the most profound matters of the spirit. The natural law tradition had always held every man to be a person, endowed with rights and the powers of reason by which to exercise them. The most ancient Christian tradition had held all souls to be equal in the eyes of God. But declarations of that sort are high abstractions compared to Luther's new willingness to draw all men into a dialogue with himself. In contemporary terms, Luther's spirit of congregationalism

4. The Muhlenberg Press, Philadelphia, Pa., 1947, p. 5.

heralds not just modern democracy, but modern participatory democracy as well.

This is the tone which should be read into the two italicized propositions in Luther's statement. Otherwise both are absurd, the first by seeming extreme arrogance, the second by excessive servility. But when these propositions are read in the spirit of a mutually responding brotherhood, their meaning is plain and unpretentious. The two propositions can now be seen as reverse images of a single vision in which men meet and treat with each other in a spirit of absolute egalitarianism, without a shade of reference to hierarchy, in a kind of loving, mutually supportive anarchy. The lines depict nothing less than a company of saints, and the vision of such a company as a utopian ideal has powerfully inhabited the Protestant conscience from Luther's time to this day.

The mountainous energy which this vision of the company of the saints presupposes in each of its members is a vitality which stems from faith. In the first paragraph of the quotation, Luther talks at length of faith. The word *faith* can be used in two dominant ways, and Luther's use of the term is confined to one. Faith can mean acceptance of propositions as true on grounds other than empirical evidence, rationality, or authority. It is "faith that" as in the phrase, "I took it on faith." The other kind of faith is "faith in" and it is this kind that concerns Luther.

"Faith in" requires an object or person human or divine to whom love, trust, and service can be pledged. Thus this conception of faith presupposes that there is in the self an energy, a stored power of will, which seeks outward expression. On the other hand, the object of true faith, Luther promises, will bestow upon the faithful "courage," the strength to endure all life's trials.[5]

Luther's testimony to the strength of the man of faith is his declaration of the priesthood of all believers. By this doctrine, Luther wished to deny both the need of the ordinary man for, and the right of the church to, a specialized, sequestered priesthood. His declaration has radical positive dimensions, for it asserts that any man, through faith, can reach God. This claim is monumental. The natural law tradition had implied

5. In the words of Luther's hymn, "A mighty fortress is our God. . . ."

that in each man there was a spark of reason by which the ethical order of nature could be perceived and known. But Luther is asserting that each man can gain his own salvation through the strenuous dynamics of a life of faith.

The image is of Job and of much else in the Bible, especially in the New Testament, and in ancient Christian teaching generally. But the Lutheran spirit is centrally Hebraic, in precisely the sense that sees the Hebraic mental cast more purely revealed in certain books of the Old Testament than in any books of the New, and also centrally personal, in precisely the sense that sees Job as the most personal of all the books in the Bible. The Jobian paradigm has dominated the heart of the Protestant experience for nearly five centuries.

The unspoken situation surrounding the book is that Samaria has long since been taken, Jerusalem has fallen, and the best of its people are in exile. In this situation, comparable in so many ways to that of modern men everywhere, Job is a Jew without a nation, a man alive and alone. But still God pursues him, and Job complains.

> What is man, that thou dost make so much of him,
>> and that thou dost set thy mind upon him,
> dost visit him every morning,
>> and test him every moment?
> How long wilt thou not look away from me,
>> nor let me alone till I swallow my spittle?
> If I sin, what do I do to thee, thou watcher of men?
>> Why hast thou made me thy mark?

7:17–20 (R.S.V.)

Job's problem between him and his God is profoundly personal, and its substance is beyond society and all its orthodoxies. In the range of his vision, he alone is being tested by the "watcher of men."

Job's response to this personal confrontation is full of emotion, and his moods dominate the poetry of the book. Truculence does not appear among those emotions. More remarkably for the modern viewpoint, stoical nobility is also absent. What is present, and constantly so, is an audacious sense of self. More than once Job turns on his interrogators, his speciously comforting friends.

What you know, I also know;
    I am not inferior to you.
But I would speak to the Almighty,
    and I desire to argue my case with God.
As for you, you whitewash with lies;
    worthless physicians are you all.

13:2–4 (R.S.V.)

Regularly he challenges God directly and puts into his rage an expression of self that verges on the blasphemous.

Oh, that I had one to hear me!
    (Here is my signature! Let the Almighty answer me!)
    Oh, that I had the indictment written by my adversary!
Surely I would carry it on my shoulder;
    I would bind it on me as a crown;
I would give him an account of all my steps;
    like a prince I would approach him.

31:35–37 (R.S.V.)

This willingness to approach God personally, this feeling that "There is no umpire between us" (9:33), is the prime thrust of the book and it leads, as much as Luther's promise that each man can be his own priest, to a final resolution.

I had heard of thee by the hearing of the ear,
    but now my eye sees thee . . .

42:5 (R.S.V.)

There is a promise in these words beyond the grand assumption that any man can be ushered into the very presence of God. The direct promise, broad and deep in its full implications, is that man, if full of faith, can endure life even to the point of death. In long days of joy and laughter, but also of pain and loss, man will not just hear of God but can also find him, "see" him, and be led on by him. Man is alone but God is with him. Each man's personal experience can teach him faith, for the faith that saves is not a truth to be learned from a book or heard from a teacher. Not a truth at all, it is a strength of the soul. It is gained by cultivating the divine which each man, if he will, can find and put into the story of his own life.

By recovering Biblical Christianity's concern for salvation achieved through a personalized confrontation between man and God, Luther outraged the medieval world. He threatened not only that world's theological principles but the substructure of its social order as well. But Luther's conceptions of man and his tasks in this life went beyond even these threats. Luther was revolutionizing the very quality of the self's being. A man who could declare, "Here I stand! I can do no other!" is doing more than braving the wrath of popes and princes. He is putting his fist into the wind. He is subjectifying the self. He is radically proclaiming the absolute responsibility of the self for the self. After Luther, in the modern age, autobiography comes first. The course of nature, the story of man, the histories of societies, and all their excitements and demands are secondary to the claims and the life of conscience.

The dramatic self, as it might be called, is the root which Protestantism gave the modern age and its prevailing individualism. But much the same conception lies beneath the other pillar of modernity, the Bourgeois spirit. The earliest and in many ways the most vivid and consistent expression of Bourgeois philosophy is to be found in Hobbes.

> Hereby it is manifest, that during the time men live without a common power to keep them all in awe, they are in that condition which is called war; and such a war, as is of every man, against every man. . . . Whatsoever therefore is consequent to a time of war, where every man is enemy to every man; the same is consequent to the time, wherein men live without other security, than what their own strength, and their own invention shall furnish them withal. In such condition, there is no place for industry; because the fruit thereof is uncertain; and consequently no culture of the earth; no navigation, nor use of the commodities that may be imported by sea; no commodious building; no instruments of moving, and removing, such things as require much force; no knowledge of the face of the earth; no account of time; no arts; no letters; no society; and which is worst of all, continual fear, and danger of violent death; and the life of man, solitary, poor, nasty, brutish, and short.[6]

As much as in Luther, statements of this sort assume far more than they assert. Hobbes is concluding, after an argument which has been straightforward and mostly analytical, that,

6. *Leviathan*, ed. M. Oakeshott, Blackwell, Oxford, England, 1951, p. 82.

men being competitive, fearful, and vain, life without a sufficiently awesome government would be deprived and miserable.
But a reading of this paragraph in simply those terms conceals
its explosive revolutionary quality readily sensed by Hobbes'
contemporaries, especially the kings and priests among them.

For such readers, Hobbes dangerously discarded reference
to almost all the characteristics of medieval society which they
still held dear. His argument suggested that *only* a sufficiently
awesome government is required to bring men out of their
natural, warring state. No mention is made of the divine right
of kings, obedience to bishops and other officers of the church,
or any other theologically grounded defense of authority. It is
enough if governments, by whatever means, inspire awe. Furthermore, Hobbes apparently cared very little for the conventions, myths, rituals, and social trappings by which medieval
society sustained princes in their powers. He did include society
in his catalogue of the losses that a state of nature imposed,
but the term is undefined and ranks behind letters, arts, chro-
nology, geography, engineering, architecture, overseas commerce and navigation, and agriculture. First on the list is "industry" and "the fruit thereof."

That these rankings are an accurate reflection of Hobbes'
general state of mind is corroborated by further reflection, for
Hobbes did more than let the medieval social world vanish
from view. The medieval mind put the social world and all its
marvelous traditional and legal intricacy first. The individual
came into that world and *found* his identity, status, and life
work in it. Hobbes wholly reversed that emphasis. Man comes
into the world to *make* it something for himself. He is already
an *ens completum*, self-motivating, self-defining, self-identifying. In the beginning was man, and man was alive.

Hobbes was essentially a utilitarian, but his utilitarianism
follows from his egoism. For the same reason, Hobbes believed
in industrialism, technology, agriculture and all the arts by
which man confronted and subdued his environment for his
own use. When Hobbes argues, at the end of the quotation,
that life in the state of nature will be "solitary, poor, nasty,
brutish, and short," he refers directly to man's life, and Hobbes'
assumption is that the argument will be overwhelmingly persuasive because it is so narrowly and so onesidedly an appeal
to personal self-interest.

Clearly Hobbes began his thinking where Luther did, with energetic man. It is also clear that Hobbes, like Luther, pictures man in a personalized, confronting relationship with existence. In this sense, both Hobbes and Luther are, at a very profound level, existentialist, nominalist, and modern.

Yet there is a world of difference between the two men. This is not because Hobbes, in contrast to Luther, was somehow an irreligious man. Hobbes was enormously learned about religious matters. His familiarity with the Bible was intimate, and much of his thinking, especially about the nature of sovereignty and power, follows Biblical patterns. Beyond that, Hobbes' sensitivity to personal religiosity of the sort of greatest concern among Protestants is evident throughout much of his work. But Hobbes did not view energetic man the way Luther did.

The difference between the Hobbesian man and the Lutheran man is the difference between the contexts of secularism and pietism, between worldliness and godliness. The men envisioned are actually the same, for both men confront their existence as a task to be accomplished. It is the tasks that differ.

The task of the pious man is to find, meet, and come to terms with that which is wholly other than the self, namely God. The terms are absolute adoration and service to God and absolute abnegation of the self. To meet these terms requires total dedication of the self to the search for them. Even then they are not found until, at the point of despair, all faith in self is lost and through the intervention of grace faith in God is granted.

The task of the secular man is much more concerned with the power of the self. Life is an opportunity to demonstrate personal potency and subdue nature. The secular man is a materialist in the sense that his material product records his progress best. In other words, what really matters is not the measure but the man, not the product but the producer. Hobbes was profoundly a materialist in this sense. So too was Marx long after him, for such materialism is the keystone of secular modernity to this day.

The difference between the Lutheran and Hobbesian conceptions of the tasks of man seems plain and uncomplicated.

One holds that the self must be denied by the self, the other that it must be asserted by the self. But further reflection will soon show that this difference is not simple at all.

For one thing, the unworldliness of the pious man is not, in the Protestant tradition, some kind of otherworldliness. The Biblicalism in which that tradition was rooted did not distinguish between this world and some other, supernatural one. There was but one world, one life, and the worldly and unworldly inhabited it. Nor was the secular man, even in the raw Hobbesian version, without his pieties. Hobbes well knew the costs and tests of life and armed himself with an iron rectitude against them. He said of himself that he was born in the year of the Spanish Armada (1588), and in that year, "My mother brought forth twins, myself and fear." To live was to triumph, a tribute to personal courage and prudence. Hobbes died at 91 in comfortable circumstances, no mean feat for a famous man in seventeenth century England.

These confusions were amply expressed by the actual historical situation. In northwestern Europe, most Bourgeois men were Protestant in their religious persuasions, and most Protestants made their livings, or hoped to, in the Bourgeois style. Moreover, Bourgeois men endowed the Protestant churches with powerful financial, social, and political support, and the churches reciprocated by preaching the virtues of strength, industry, and courage which Bourgeois men needed in their daily ordeals. Historically, Bourgeois technological science and narrow utilitarianism went hand in hand from the seventeenth century through the nineteenth century with Protestant asceticism and pietism.

Since they are inseparable, historically as allies and logically through shared commitments about the nature of the individual, it is reasonable to talk of a Protestant-Bourgeois syndrome. The phrase describes a single ideological construct powerfully active in the making of the modern world. It said that man can and must act. But the contrasts we noted earlier between what the two members of that syndrome said man must do persisted. To reconcile the conflict, Protestant-Bourgeois man twisted two ways. He sanctified profit taking and put a price on his soul. Luther proclaimed, ". . . as the soul needs only the Word for its life and righteousness, so it is

justified by faith alone and not by any works."[7] Hobbes, as if
in reply, asserted "a general inclination of all mankind, a perpetual and restless desire of power after power, that ceaseth
only in death."[8] Centuries later Andrew Carnegie, in a true
Protestant-Bourgeois blend of moral anthropology, insisted that
". . . civilization took its start from the day that the capable,
industrious workman said to his incompetent and lazy fellow,
'If thou dost not sow, thou shalt not reap,' and thus ended
primitive communism by separating the drones from the bees."[9]

LIBERALISM

When modernity expressed itself politically in Liberalism,
it carried forward not only its basic commitments but also its
internal contradictions and anxieties. These all can be seen
in the tradition that begins with Hobbes and extends through
Locke, Adam Smith, and Bentham. The tradition branches on
the one side into the American Liberalism of Madison, Calhoun,
and Sumner, through John Dewey to our contemporaries. On
the English side, it branches into the reformed Liberalism of
John Stuart Mill, T. H. Green, the Fabian Socialists, A. D. Lindsay, and the rest. During this development, the essential commitment to the needs of individual morality and self-resolution
is maintained. But contradictions, confusions, and innovations
(especially in the later English developments) can also be found
in abundance.

The history of Anglo-American Liberalism is long and complex. Our task is to abstract from the whole story a general
understanding of the Liberal philosophy. It is important to do
this because American Liberalism, our final concern, must be
seen for what it is: not a unique and indigenous American product, but rather a truncation of the general European and
particularly English Liberalism that was cut off in the emptiness
of the virgin American environment.

7. "A Treatise on Christian Liberty," p. 8.

8. *Leviathan*, p. 64.

9. "Wealth," in *Democracy and the Gospel of Wealth,* ed. Gail Kennedy,
D. C. Heath, Boston, 1949, p. 3.

The main tenets of Liberalism are an overriding assertion of the claims of the Protestant-Bourgeois individual, the purely consequential rights and obligations of governments, and an elusive conception of society. But these concerns were articulated, certainly at the outset and more or less continuously thereafter to almost the end of the nineteenth century, by spokesmen of a class who fervently believed they were leading a revolution, a social and historical process by which an old world would be transformed into a new.

The early Liberals were aware, at least politically, that for all their universalistic phrasings they spoke for only a segment of society. Locke is notorious in this regard. Much of his argument is wholly abstract in both assertion and form. And yet Locke never forgets that he is a controversialist. Today, Americans especially tend to write off his attack on the medieval-minded Filmer as uninteresting and unimportant. Locke did not see the matter in that light. Filmer was the direct object of his attack in the whole of the first of his two treatises on government, and the implicit target of the second.

The partiality of the early European Liberals is important to any balanced understanding of their actual words. Being controversialists, Liberals concentrated their fire on issues in contention, and they freely stated, even overstated, their concerns. Issues not in dispute they let lie. Locke asserted the rights of the individual and used in his arguments whatever defenses he thought would be persuasive to his audience, most notably the extra-social doctrine of natural rights. This is not to say that Locke was unaware of man's social situation or the impact of social factors on every man's mind. Much of his *Essay on Human Understanding*, a purely philosophical work, is built on that kind of awareness. But in his political writing Locke believed that there was nothing to be gained — and perhaps much to be lost — by raising issues about man's sociality. Burke, at core a Liberal almost as much as Locke, found himself in a politically contrary situation one hundred years later and accordingly reversed all of Locke's political arguments and emphases.

Similarly, when Locke wrote of the tasks of government, he advanced a favorite Liberal thesis, that "The great and *chief end* therefore, of Mens uniting into Commonwealths, and putting themselves under Government, *is the Preservation of their*

Property."[10] In an age when many powerful people still held
the functions of government to be more concerned with the
preservation of traditional authorities and the defense and prop-
agation of true religion, Locke's doctrine was as revolutionary
as anything to be found in Hobbes. But when Locke discussed
the actual operations of government, he never departed far
from the extant British system as both he and his opponents
understood it. Like all Liberals, he wanted a lawful, settled
government, and his argument demonstrated a clear Liberal
bias to legislative supremacy. But he never questioned the
existence of a separate executive or doubted that it had some
independent powers, among them the right to convoke the
legislative assembly.

The significance of these examples of partiality in Locke
will become evident in the next section when they are placed
in the American environment, where Locke's influence was of
transcendent importance but where his partialities were not
systematically noticed. We must now discuss the way Locke's
specialness of view reveals much about the early Liberals themselves and their understanding of themselves as members of a
new, revolutionary class in an old society.

Two chapters in the Second Treatise are particularly useful
in this regard, one on property and one on paternal power.
Both are disproportionately long, and both are redolent with
commonplace examples and arguments Locke obviously felt
would be familiar and persuasive to his readers. But for modern
readers what is especially interesting about all this material is
the way it reveals a powerful elitist bias behind Locke's general
doctrines. Locke was sincerely a Liberal, but he certainly did
not understand himself to be a common man, a peasant, a
member of what Mill later called the uncultivated herd, and he
did not write for any such persons.

In Hobbes man is alive, alone, and afraid. Those elements
appear in Locke's conception of man, but they are enveloped
in a newfound social status and security. When Locke writes
of the family, he envisages a *pater familias* endowed with wife,
children, nurses, servants, wine and fine cloth on the table,
and much property to be protected. It is assumed easily that
children may have tutors (Locke himself was a tutor in the

10. *Two Treatises of Government,* ed. P. Laslett, Cambridge University
Press, Cambridge, England, 1960, pp. 368–369.

Shaftesbury household.) Throughout his discussion, Locke is properly Liberal: the burden of his argument is to establish that parental power is to be qualitatively distinguished from the political power of a monarch, that it stems exclusively from the "infirmities" of the condition of childhood, that it therefore resides as much in the mother as it does the father, and that it ceases when "Age and Education" have brought the child "Reason and Ability to govern himself."[11] But it is apparent throughout this discussion — nowhere more so than in the extended insistence that children owe honor to their parents throughout their lives — that Locke has an intense interest in the family as a solid social unit. And what he envisions is something very much like what we would now call the upper middle-class family.

Locke's ambiguities of interest and expression are even more apparent in his discussion of property. Once again, the main burden of the discussion is properly Liberal, to define and defend the concept that property can and should be privately held, despite the acknowledgement that all property in origin is a gift of God to all mankind in common. Already he has eliminated from his concern, for example, the more communal interest of the landed aristocrats and the peasants who inhabited their estates. Locke's focus is on those who had the means and the minds to distinguish, if only by dotted lines on maps, between "yours" and "mine." It never occurs to him that criss-crossing a society with distinctions of this sort might have serious consequences — and not only for the general communal spirit. A sense of alienation is visited upon the individuals affected, whether by their being granted exclusive rights in the use of some things or by their being deprived of opportunities for common ownership and use of other things.

Locke enormously reinforces the psychological as well as the legal thrust of his position by his individual arguments in its behalf. The most important of these is his insistence that the foundation of private property is in the labor of the primitive man in appropriating from nature what was necessary to his subsistence. In this view, what is mine is purely consequent to my act. Locke argued explicitly that the validity of that act lies in itself, and not in any social acknowledgement.

11. *Ibid.*, p. 327.

And will any one say he [primitive man] had no right to those Acorns or Apples he thus appropriated because he had not the consent of all Mankind to make them his? Was it a Robbery thus to assume to himself what belonged to all in Common? If such a consent as that was necessary, Man had starved, notwithstanding the plenty God had given him.[12]

No argument can shade or qualify this doctrine into other than what it is, a law of seize, have, and hold. Moreover, its import becomes even plainer when it is set on its premise, about which Locke is even more explicit: "The Earth, and all that is therein, is given to Men for the Support and Comfort of *their* being."[13]

We can speculate that in conjuring up this concept of rapacious man, Locke, speaking both his own mind and the social mind he shared with his class and culture, had taken too seriously the first of Luther's propositions that the Christian man is a perfectly free lord of all, subject to none. Locke is arguing for more than that savage man must eat and will. He is arguing that through the labor of taking and eating, savage man has created for himself and posterity a proprietary claim to be observed, whether we like it or not, by all the rest of us. God gave all in common. Savage man, by his labor, transformed the natural order of possession into another order, his own. That is to rate the anointing power of the sweat of the primitive palm very high indeed.

In other words, there is a monstrous element at the heart of Locke's conception of man, just as there was in Hobbes. It persists in the Liberal conception of man to this day. How else are we to account for the utterly unfeeling behavior of contemporary ghetto landlords, corrupt politicians, and businessmen who despoil the streams, pollute the air, and lay waste the land, all in pursuit of profit?

The monstrous, rapacious element in his formal conception of man undoes every effort Locke made to articulate consistently a theory of society and communal cohesion. In a world in which avarice is the only motive, affection and duty can have no place. All human relationship must be reducible to mutually

12. *Ibid.*, p. 306.

13. *Ibid.*, p. 304 (italics added).

satisfying payoffs, transactions in which *quid* for me matches *quo* for you.

But is not this rapacious Lockean man, related only in avaricious transaction with his fellow man, a contradiction of the Lockean conception of the head of household who respects his wife, educates his children, and is a generous, thoughtful master to his servants? There are many contradictions in Locke's political writings, and on a literal reading of the text this would certainly be one of them. But it is so absorbed into the environment in which Locke wrote that it became commonplace. Locke was writing to, for, and about, men of substance in England, about how they related to each other and to the nature they felt summoned by God to subdue. He assumed the remainder of the human race would not read or hear of what he wrote. They all had their own things to do, wives mothering, children prating, maids waiting, servants doing their rounds, and so forth. Locke also assumed that the conduct of such other persons with each other and with the head of house, and the conduct of the *pater familias* toward them, would be governed by well-established Christian canons of charity, honesty, and service, canons radically different from those Locke was developing for the dealings of the men of substance with each other.

In other words, Locke was assuming that the ethics of business and political life were one thing and the ethics of family affection quite another. That many people, perhaps the bulk of Locke's readers even today, make this same assumption should not obscure its significance. That Locke made it so easily underscores the partiality of his political writing. It is also direct evidence of those tensions in Protestant-Bourgeois culture which were noted earlier.

A final point remains to be made about the men of substance for whom Locke wrote. Axiomatic for Locke (as it was for Hobbes) was the natural equality of men — at least of the men who matter in political life. But unlike Hobbes, who buttressed his argument by observing that what one man might have in superior strength another might make up for by craft, Locke seriously qualified his position.

Though I have said above . . . *That all Men by Nature are equal,* I cannot be supposed to understand all sorts of *Equality: Age* or *virtue* may give Men a just precedency: *Excellency* of *Parts* and *Merit* may place others above the Common Level: *Birth* may subject some, and *Alliance* or *Benefits* others, to pay an Observance to those to whom Nature, Gratitude, or other Respects, may have made it due; and yet all this [is consistent with] . . . the *Equality* I there spoke of, as proper to the Business in hand, being that *equal Right* that every man hath *to his Natural Freedom,* without being subjected to the Will or Authority of any other Man.[14]

The significance of this passage is that it reduces egalitarianism to equality in claims to freedom, and on the basis of this alone it may be concluded that Locke, like Liberals in general as their very name implies, cares more for freedom than equality. In fact, it may be supposed that Locke values highly those traits he lists which make men factually unequal. And in the chapter on property, Locke reveals the most important way men differ.

That chapter begins with a discussion which almost makes it appear that men have a right to appropriate from Nature's bounty only more or less equal amounts of private property, enough, that is, to subsist upon. But then, after a tortuous and not wholly consistent discussion of the invention of money, the chapter concludes on a different and powerful note.

But since Gold and Silver, being little useful to the Life of Man, in proportion to Food, Rayment, and Carriage, has its *value* only from the consent of Men, whereof Labour yet makes, in great part, *the measure,* it is plain, that Men have agreed to a disproportionate and unequal Possession of the Earth, they having by a tacit and voluntary consent found out a way, how a man may fairly possess more land than he himself can use the product of . . .[15]

Locke is exposing wide areas of his thought, some of it perhaps inadvertently, but the central message for the men of substance who read him was plain and simple. Given a society based on commerce and money and themselves rapacious, competitive, and self-serving, they could go all out to win, because Locke assured them that winners, by a right that antedates all formal civil and political society, can keep the spoils. Thus was the law of unlimited and unequal accumulation of private wealth unleashed on the modern world. Unleashed also was the

14. *Ibid.,* p. 322.

15. *Ibid.,* pp. 319–320.

revolution which modern men would bring first to Europe, then to America, and finally to the whole world. The specific doctrines according political protection to the pursuit of personal wealth can now be enumerated.

The first of these is the absolute, pre-social claim to "life, liberty, and the pursuit of happiness." What that happiness consisted of and how it was to be pursued should be clear. The claim to life and liberty amount to the absolute sovereignty of the self over the self. There can be no surrender of the self's powers or its freedom to employ them to its own advantage except by consent, and this consent can only be won by direct appeal to personal interest.

The early Liberals pass almost without pause from this doctrine to assertions that governments are instituted among men by their consent for the better protection of their rights, or, as Locke puts it again and again, for the preservation of their property. This haste for a long time concealed enormous difficulties which, when finally exposed, fatally undercut the Liberal argument for virtually any government at all.

The basic Liberal argument for establishing government is that it is neither in my interest nor yours to endure a state of nature in which the burden of self-protection is carried by each of us alone. Such a condition, if not one of perpetual misery as Hobbes contended, would certainly be highly inconvenient. Therefore, the Liberals concluded, it is in the interest of each for all to join in creating an umpire — the word is Locke's — to administer the equal protection of all. But that is too fast an argument. It is certainly in my interest to be protected from you. But is it as surely in my interest to have you protected from me? Certainly it is in my interest to have you compelled to keep your promises. But will it not be more to my advantage if you are compelled to keep your word and I am allowed to break mine? Would it not be almost a Liberal heaven, *for me,* to have all *save me* forced to abide by the law? There can be no satisfying answer from Liberals to such questions. Their fundamental equations had set them an impossible task: to found on private interest alone a theory of public authority.

In some ways, Hobbes' attempt came nearest to success. He threw logic to the winds and settled the argument by force: ". . . covenants, without the sword, are but words, and of no

strength to secure a man at all."[16] No mere promise can bind
the ego, which is absolute sovereign on its own behalf. Therefore, to contain that first sovereign, a political sovereign is
created, with the balance tilted in his favor by absolute possession of the sword. So far, so good. But what if the sword
wavers? What if it serves only he who holds it? Hobbes admitted that in fact it would not serve otherwise. And what if
the cost of obeying was prohibitively high or disobedience
absurdly cheap? In such cases, Hobbes effectively admitted, do
what you can get away with. In other words, the war of the
state of nature goes on, and Hobbes' argument has only apparently changed matters. Fundamentally, his problem was that
against the absolute sovereignty of the individual he posed the
absolute sovereignty of the state, each always to act in terms of
its own interest. But only one of these two sovereignties was
natural, man. The state was, in Hobbes' own words, a "mortal
god." Hobbes left it mortally wounded, however much he tried
to arm it — and it alone — with the sword.

Hobbes' successors in the Liberal tradition were never able
to do more than bandage the wound. No more than Hobbes
could they explain why I should obey the law when it is not in
my interest to do so, in all the tough, dangerous cases which
occasion the establishment of laws in the first place. What
argument could they make to persuade me to put the gun
down once I see that my interest is in picking it up? The final
absurdity to which Liberalism is forced by this primacy of
commitment to individual sovereignty can be seen in Adam
Smith, whose overall argument in defense of what he called the
system of liberty can be summarized as follows: if each of us
pursues, without restraint, what no one else wants, namely our
own particular satisfactions, then we will all get what none of
us is pursuing, namely the wealth of the nation.

The argument is as incredible practically as it is logically
impossible, and Bentham improved on it not at all by trying to
equate the old egoism, through enlightenment, with altruism in
ill-conceived talk about "the greatest good of the greatest
number." (What if that good is best met by decimating the
minority, be they German Jews, American Indians, or hosts of
others?) But one of the oddities of early Liberal experience is

16. *Leviathan*, p. 109.

that their philosophical problems did not hurt them much in practice. The probable explanation for this is that the early Liberals were again and again saved by their environment. In theory, they vastly overstated the rights of the individual. In social fact, they could assume and sometimes state that his individualism was complemented by an awareness of his identity as a member of the community and of his need to preserve that communal identity, even through what otherwise might appear to be personal sacrifices.

This is plain even in Hobbes. The state of nature in his account is in the end not wholly a warring, anarchic state. Here and there are hints that natural man aspires to family life and is willing to deal fairly with others on an economic, transactional basis. Reflection on Hobbes' argument in this light prompts the suspicion that the true objective of Hobbesian man was security in and for a system of self-satisfactions wherein the system, more than the self, defined what was satisfying. This suspicion is reinforced by rereading Locke. He not only assumes that his rapacious primitive man would quickly become in social fact a proper English middle-class gentleman. He could also assume that besides thinking himself the lord of all, this factual individual would heed from time to time Luther's other proposition to dutifully serve all. In other words, Locke could assume that his raw, explicitly Bourgeois man would never go too far, that his avaricious transactionism would be bridled by both asceticism and a sense of social membership. Much the same kind of social knowledge is in Adam Smith's "hidden hand." But beyond talking about the need for public roads, monuments, common currencies, and the like, Smith had no need to discuss these matters. Englishmen, even middle-class Protestant-Bourgeois Englishmen, knew instinctively about such matters. And Burke would make them all thunderingly clear in a few short years, in any event.

THE AMERICAN ENVIRONMENT

Unfortunately for Americans, Burke came too late. They were born with Locke and little else. Furthermore, cut off and provincialized, they read him literally, word for word. When Locke talked of every man, they thought he meant every man.

How were they to know he really meant every middle-class English gentleman? What could they know of the social context he assumed?

The literal rendering of the fundamental language of Lockean Liberalism was by no means a straightforward process. As we have seen, Locke's work contains important contradictions and ambiguities. When these are read literally, the result is not simplification but exaggeration, often to the point of outright absurdity.

The most important example of this process is the way in which the Americans took Locke's prime declaration that men are naturally equal, a point he put mainly in abstract terms, and stretched it into an absolute declaration of egalitarianism. There was little in their provincial environment to preclude their attempting this, and there was much in their Protestant and unpretentious middle-class heritage that encouraged them in this direction. Nevertheless, the American environment was not without its own complications. Besides the men of the sort who signed the Declaration of Independence, it contained large numbers of other persons: women, children, indentured servants, black slaves, and Indians. The dominant class of men were not prepared to admit these other people as politically equal to themselves. From the outset, the question of what was to be done ideologically with these people, who after all comprised the bulk of the total population, was acute. In his environment, Locke had an older, comfortable, even if contradictory, ideology by which he could have subsumed such persons into categories below the one reserved for himself and his friends. But the express doctrines of his treatises gave colonial American Liberals no such options. All they could do was ignore persons outside their own circle, or, which was the same thing, deny that they were "men." This explains the ruthlessness of the American system of chattel slavery, in its absolute denial of the legal and political person of the slave the most brutal of all systems of servitude in recorded history.

Failure to resolve problems ideologically because of a simplistic reading of great philosophy also explains much of what occurred after the excluded groups were originally denied political existence. As these groups came to political consciousness, they too became Liberals, there being no other ideological heritage in America. Under the Lockean banner, they demanded "in." The excluders fought back, but since they, too, harked to the Lockean creed, they had little ideological equipment to justify — or limit — their resistance. The immediate result was a series of simple ideological collisions. The end results have never been more than products of a contest of wills, messy at the least, catastrophic at the worst, ranging from casual insults to systematic and absurd legal exclusions, and on to outright violence, an extraordinary incidence of rape, murder, and other violent crimes, plus massacres and even civil war on an unparalleled scale.

What an analysis of the ideological factors in this situation shows is that demands for equality of treatment for the members of a class subsumed within an extant and complex social structure, which is what Locke stood for in England, are essentially moderate and containable. The demands of Americans for a universal and unqualified recognition of a natural equality, on the other hand, voice an impossible ideal, one so wholly opposed to all social structures as to be anarchistic.

> I heartily accept the motto, "That government is best which governs least"; and I should like to see it acted up to more rapidly and systematically. Carried out, it finally amounts to this, which also I believe: "That government is best which governs not at all."
>
> The only obligation which I have a right to assume is to do at any time what I think right.
>
> There is but little virtue in the action of masses of men.
>
> . . . any man more right than his neighbors constitutes a majority of one already.
>
> I was not born to be forced. I will breathe after my own fashion.[17]

That these statements come from an enormously popular essay by one of America's most distinguished men of letters is important. They reflect deep American convictions. But read in the light of the requirements of even the most unsophisticated of political and social theories, these eloquent, belligerent, and nobly individualistic statements are irretrievably absurd. You can have an ideology like that, if you are stuck with it. But the difficulties encountered in trying to run a society on such a basis are not easily overcome.

17. Henry David Thoreau, "On Civil Disobedience," in The People Shall Judge, Vol. I, University of Chicago Press, Chicago, 1949, pp. 646, 647, 649, 651, and 654.

Further difficulties flowed from the American provincial, truncated commitment to Lockean Liberalism. The most important centers on the Bourgeois character of the individual which Lockean Liberalism, in the American literal version, sets free, and in its conflicts with the Protestant heritage to which it was inseparably connected. These will be examined shortly. Another source of anxiety and irresolution in the American reading of Locke must be examined first, in order to outline the political context of what follows.

Whatever the pain and cost, it cannot be denied that American Lockean egalitarianism has come a long way in the United States. Relative to other nations, America is democratic in both ideological commitment and practice at the fundamental level of interpersonal life. Not the least remarkable feature of this achievement is that it has been gained under a system of government which is basically undemocratic, although still very much a creature of Locke's teachings.

Locke was a Liberal, not a democrat. He believed only vaguely in the sovereignty of the people and not at all in popular government and majority rule. He strongly believed in "mixed government," and his reasons for doing so were fundamentally Liberal and undemocratic.

These reasons stemmed from his formal understanding, which he shared not only with Hobbes but also with the Liberal tradition generally to this day, about the nature and uses of power and the problem it posed for government. Power was to be feared. The difficulty with the state of nature was that all men in it had power, their own. That meant war. The fundamental problem of governmental theory was to find a way to take that power from the people without putting it somewhere worse, such as in the unrestrained hands of a monarch. It did not occur to Locke to push the argument that power might sometimes be sought as a positive possibility, a resource by which a whole people might move to build a cathedral, go on a crusade, mass the resources of a nation for community betterment, or the like. For Locke the problem was negative, the challenge to remove power from its ultimate source in the people and to marshall it to the simple end of stabilizing the environment, so that he and his kind would be left free to go about their personal business.

Locke allowed that a dissatisfied people could "cashier" their governors. But the right to impeach and remove usurpers from office is as far as his widely noted "right of revolution" goes. Moreover, its use in the Lockean arrangement of things would always be unlikely. Citing the dangers of the Hobbesian solution of what to do with the mass of political power in a community, Locke advocated dividing it, albeit unequally, between the legislative and executive branches of government. Even as it eliminated the possibility of tyranny, that step effectively put political power beyond the reach of the people. It created a nearly impenetrable barrier between a class of men with access to some political power in the government and all the rest, who had no such access. Locke viewed with equanimity this division between the powerful and the powerless for two reasons. First, such a division conformed to his personal tendencies toward elitism. Second, as an Englishman he felt assured that the diverse holders of power would be bound by a sense of constitutional and conventional restraint and would seek to cooperate reasonably with each other in carrying out the several functions of government.

But once again Locke's American readers missed the saving assumptions of context, took his teachings literally, and stretched his theorems to the verge of absurdity. They predicted war among the branches of government. They wrote a constitution that did no more than set the stage within which one man's ambitions would be pitted against those of all the rest. While Locke assumed a relatively coherent community with a "mixed government," they assumed a permanently factionalized community in which the only possible government was one dominated by separation of powers and a system of checks and balances. The logic of Locke's system was a hope of cooperation among functionally delineated branches. The logic of the American reading of his words was every branch of government for itself, and the devil take the hindmost. This logic prevails even today.

A theme of internal governmental strife is neither positive nor hopeful, and as a system of *self*-government, it is downright degrading. But the situation becomes even more complex and negative when this theme, central to the operation of American political institutions, is set on its base, the American political citizenry. Owing to the way Americans read their Locke, the American political citizenry did become increasingly democratic and egalitarian. To the same degree, it became increasingly at odds with the persistently libertarian governmental structure which rested upon it. If Americans were able to democratize Locke's fundamental premise, why could they not do the same with his strictures on governmental organization? Why did they allow the strife within the government to be further exacerbated by putting the government into warfare with its people?

The answers to these questions are contained in points already made, especially Locke's granting the people a right of revolution. The American political experience verifies the proposition that this right is an empty gesture under a Lockean constitution. Such a constitution will permanently deprive the people of their "natural" power. The power is lodged instead in a governmental structure which history shows to have been, in its own terms, an extraordinary success. Hoarding power, it has an exceptional capacity for ensuring its own stability. As the nation's wealth and power have grown, the gap between the Lockean "Liberal" constitution and the Lockean "democratic" citizenry, between the powerful and the powerless, is greater than ever before. There is no reason to believe the situation will change short of total breakdown.

The techniques by which the American political system contains all these contradictions and strains within itself, and the massive frustration of it all, will be the subject of later chapters. Our immediate task is to place at the center of this picture of the Lockean American commonwealth its most powerful source of tension, the American citizen himself.

In his ideological structure and the political consciousness by which he understands himself as a political actor and by which he sets out to meet and treat with his fellows, the American citizen is the pure embodiment of the Protestant-Bourgeois syndrome. He was that when he came here, and being alone during all the years he was setting down a fixed and enduring political culture for himself and his descendants, he was never able to measure himself against alternatives or think in terms of being different from what he was. Moreover, although he was subject to enormous internal tensions, they were non-creative ones. Even if he had wanted to change, he lacked the intellectual/ideological equipment to do so.

On the one hand he was Bourgeois man, and in the American environment there was virtually no stopping him. The land awaited his coming and the laws and government were made for him, a man on the make, to use Woodrow Wilson's words. The record of his reckless achievement in this country is amazing. So is the cost. And this has not been lost on him, because wherever Bourgeois man went, his Protestant shadow went also. Like Bourgeois man, Protestant man found his way virtually unchecked in America and has likewise left an amazing and costly record. The achievements in that record cannot be denied. Despite the omnipresence of the corrupting, crass materialism of Bourgeois man, Protestant man, mostly by simple preaching and exhortation and without recourse to any rigidly structured hierarchy of the sort familiar in Catholic nations, made America the most thoroughly moralistic and pietistic of modern countries. The major cost of this achievement was that Bourgeois man was never fundamentally confronted and the tensions between him and Protestant man were never resolved.

They have not even been moderated, however much they are shifted from some topics and areas of human conduct to others. Frettings about pornography, permissiveness in child rearing, alcohol, and even instances of corruption are not the same thing as an attack on the avaricious transactionism at the core of Bourgeois life. American Protestantism has left that untouched.

American Protestantism could not get at it. The vital areas of Bourgeois man's life were magnificently defended by the nation's laws and political institutions, and from these sanctuaries Bourgeois man was consistently able to bribe Protestant man, if not into silence on central issues, at least into some dextrous sidestepping. Furthermore, Protestant man in America knew nothing but himself and could draw neither inspiration nor conceptual tools from alternative religious commitments. (The most prominent possible source of such alternatives, immigrant Catholicism, was either humiliatingly relegated to the ghetto or "yankeefied" into imitative behavior.) Finally, there were Protestantism's own structural weaknesses.

The most important structural weakness was that Protestant man shared with Bourgeois man a fundamental commitment to individualism and transactionism as the basic formula for human relationships. Taken as literally as the colonial American read Locke, the great commandments of the Christian tradition to love God and neighbor become simple imperatives about one-to-one relationships. Although the Protestant American could urge that the coin in the transaction should be love and faith rather than material interest, and that the emphasis should be on giving rather than receiving, he had not moved from the world in which the central question was always "What's in it for whom?" Committed to it himself, Protestant man was blind to Bourgeois man's basic misunderstanding of the nature of social man. How could he attack Hobbes for leaving man alive, alone, and afraid when such a man was Job, at least in the American reading?

This same flaw, the lack of a sophisticated social sense of man's identity with his neighbors, precluded all attempts by Protestantism to develop into a consistent, powerfully operative political force. To some degree, Bourgeois man had preempted the field of political organization, which meant that if Protestant man wished to enter the lists, he could do so only by accepting Bourgeois principles. This he often enough did with self-serving results ranging from the petty to the grandiose.

This initial Bourgeois advantage is only partly explained by the natural power of the Bourgeois appeal to self-interest. Men have often given their lives and fortunes in other causes. More to the point is the fact that in provincial America, Bourgeois man had the more intellectual conception of political organization, even though it was a rickety conception of uncertain foundations. Weak as that was, Protestantism's theories were weaker still. For one thing, while in the Lockean tradition Bourgeois man was allowed to enter a race in which some might win if not outright dominion over others at least a measure of privileged access to the government, Protestant man in the Lutheran tradition put all men directly before God. The resulting egalitarianism was absolute, for nothing in this life could change the nature of that first existential situation.

Second, reading not just Locke and Adam Smith but also Benjamin Franklin, Bourgeois man in America had an easily grasped theory for manipulating the behavior of neighbors by

appeals to self-interest. For his part, Protestant man was re-
stricted by his own versions of individualism to appeals to
personal conscience and loving sentiments. Exhortations of this
order can touch powerful springs to action, but they are inconstant and unpredictable in their effects. Best for engineering
crusades, they are nearly useless by themselves for organizing a
disciplined party bent on long-term reform of a nation's economic and social organization, its basic laws, and its political
consciousness. To effect deep-seated social change, it is not
enough to call on citizens to cleanse their hearts of evil
thoughts and rededicate their zeal to goodness.

Consequently, the attack of Protestant man on Bourgeois
life in America was scattered, effusive, often mainly sentimental,
and largely expressed in personal terms. Inevitably it was
politically superficial. American Protestantism built churches
and other private institutions such as schools and hospitals
without number. It moralized everywhere and lacerated the
conscience of Bourgeois man so that he could not find joy in
his selfish gains. From time to time it mounted crusades to
abolish slavery, prohibit drink, ensure civil rights, expose corruption, comfort the downtrodden, and combat poverty and
other social ills. Pathetically, with massive weakness, it con-
demned war and called for peace. But it changed no fundamental laws, it altered no established power structures, it imposed no new definitions of socially effective rewards and
punishments. It may be unfair but it is not far off the mark to
conclude that American Protestantism's efforts at political organization never got much beyond the church supper.[18]

This is not the end of the matter. The contest in America
between Bourgeois man and Protestant man is a draw. As a
result, the tensions between them go on, and in the thin

18. The political impotence of American Protestantism is illustrated by the
Social Gospel movement, in which such intellectually powerful figures as
Walter Rauschenbusch diagnosed with force and precision the roots of
America's capitalist ills. But Rauschenbusch prescribed only the standard
techniques of his religion for releasing the latent energies of society for
moral regeneration. "The force of religion can best be applied to social
renewal by sending its spiritual power *along the existing and natural relations of men* to direct them to truer ends and govern them by higher motives. The fundamental contribution of every man is the change of his own
personality. We must repent of the sins of existing society. . . ." *Christianity and the Social Crisis* (1907), ed. R. Cross, Harper and Row, New
York, 1964, p. 412 (italics added).

cultural environment of America they thrash, rage, and grow. Their tensions are not between opposing parties or opposing people. They are soul-racking tensions inside the national political mind we all inhabit. They are a persistent theme of our political-cultural life, as is evidenced by countless novels, plays, movies, and television productions. Moreover, their presence in our political life is direct and important, and not just by way of those Protestant crusades with political overtones.

The picture of the powerful politician with one hand in his pocket and the other holding a Bible is a familiar one. Lyndon Johnson, to pick on one political figure, was a man of personal piety, progressive instincts, and powerful dedication. He was also dangerously vain, deceitful, intransigent, and possibly guilty of personal corruption on a large scale while in government service. This is not to say that he was a knave or a fool. He was neither. He was an American, a man divided against himself, and in rather simple terms.

On the other hand there is the American citizen, the central figure in American politics. He also is a man divided against himself. But unlike the American politician, he has little power. He therefore works out his Bourgeois proclivities in his private occupations. In politics, he is free to be a saint. It is in the broad and relatively powerless democratic base of American politics that Protestantism, with its enthusiasm, hope, and despair, is given free rein. There it springs up eternally to castigate rascals, cheer champions, and dream of great works to come. When these are postponed, it despairs mightily — until new heroes, new hopes, and new causes arise.

Our picture of American Protestant-Bourgeois Liberalism is now complete, except for one last observation. So far, the picture has been developed by piling contradiction upon ambiguity upon anxiety. Surprisingly, the last element in the picture is a pervasive factor for stability and containment.

In Europe, Liberalism thrust its way forward as a revolutionary creed. In keeping with that spirit, it sent legions to America, and all who went there carrying the Liberal banner believed that the new nation would be a "citty upon the hill" and an example for all peoples. On the other hand, in America there was no revolution, really, to be fought, much less won. It went by default. By 1776, America had already long since become a free nation, and the so-called revolution that began that year was in fact hardly more than a holding operation.

To be given a permanent bye in the contest for freedom was unnerving for many Americans, and the paranoid invention of enemies boring from within has been a national political pastime from the days of the Salem witch hunts. Much more important was the perverse twist which this achievement of freedom without really trying gave to American Liberalism. It became conservative not in content but in form and intent. From the ironically titled "Revolution," it bent every effort to self-preservation, not advancement, to ensuring that utopia was retained, not gained. Originally the most progressive and humane nation of its time, America rapidly set into a cast that held it at its starting point. Internally it raged against itself. But even in hours of gravest desperation, its powers of self-containment greatly outweighed those of self-regeneration.

The overall tasks of the American political system must be interpreted in this light. They are not easily accomplished, but, in its own terms, the system has had considerable success. In one way or another, it has been able to paralyze what is here in a persistent pattern of strain, disintegration, crisis, and painful, costly recovery, while all the time proclaiming that the earth should be grateful for so fair, pure, and progressive a nation.

CONSTITUTIONAL IDEOLOGY

THE BOURGEOIS CONSTITUTION
MADISONIANISM

THE BOURGEOIS CONSTITUTION

The first task of American government is to see that the life of the Bourgeois man can go on. To this end it must guarantee in law freedom for his personal affairs; provide other, sometimes highly material, supports for his initiatives; and ensure stability in the environment so that he may hold his gains. Provision of this kind of wherewithal for Bourgeois man was the core intention of the American founding fathers. This is apparent from even a cursory inspection of their handiwork, the federal Constitution itself. To show that this is also profoundly true requires a more detailed analysis of that document.

Before we launch our analysis of the Bourgeois constitution, certain preliminary cautions against misunderstanding will bear repeating. We said earlier that the Protestant-Bourgeois syndrome did not divide Americans into opposing groups; it split and charged with tension the world of political consciousness which we all inhabit. Similarly, while the federal Constitution overall is profoundly Bourgeois and reflective of a general philosophy which can be labeled Madisonianism, the document also reflects Protestant aspirations in highly significant ways. The presidency especially, even while rooted in the Bourgeois consciousness expressed by the Constitution and reflecting that consciousness in its daily operations, has become the single most important articulator in American politics of the Protestant conscience and its inordinate tendency towards mythic beliefs. Comparable reservations have to be made about the rational/professional spirit, the latecomer to the American scene that is mostly expressed in the bureaucracy and the judiciary. This spirit, for all its special pretensions to purity, rarely appears unalloyed with other elements of the American political mind, and it often appears in the Congress and other places far removed from its usual home base.

All three elements of the national political spirit, Bourgeois, Protestant, and rational/professional, can claim certain aspects of the political system as especially their own. Nevertheless they all intermingle in various proportions throughout the whole system. This intermingling and the resulting challenge and counterchallenge generate the paralysis, tension, and anxiety which are the preeminent characteristics of American political life.

The Bourgeois element in the federal Constitution can be seen immediately in its mood and its words. There are fewer than four thousand of them. Fifty-six of these are "no" or one of its variants, "not," "neither," "nor," and "nay."

Recall in contrast the happy phrasing of the document's Preamble, the one section of it that lacks legal force:

We the People of the United States, in Order to form a more perfect Union, establish Justice, insure domestic Tranquility, provide for the common defence, promote the general Welfare, and secure the Blessings of Liberty to ourselves and our Posterity, do ordain and establish this Constitution for the United States of America.

In this sentence are at least eight words that most readers would count as having positive, uplifting connotations ("perfect," "Union," "Justice," "Tranquility," etc.), but of these only one, the almost neutral sounding "general Welfare," is used again in the Constitution's text. Instead the language there, when not merely prescriptive and colorless, is either negative or else filled with visions of evils to be guarded against.

The negations begin as early as the third paragraph: "No Person shall be a Representative who shall not have attained the age of twenty-five Years. . . ." The double negative could have been avoided by simply affirming the qualifications to be met by those wanting to be Representatives. But the negative, exclusionary slant of the Constitution's language is sustained not only in all the clauses specifying the qualifications of other officers but also where it is stated that representatives are to be apportioned among the States according to population.

Representatives . . . shall be apportioned among the several States . . . according to their respective Numbers, which shall be determined by adding to the whole Number of free Persons, including those bound to Service for a Term of Years, and excluding Indians not taxed, three fifths of all other persons. (Art. I, Sec. 2)

Blacks in America have long and resentfully pointed out that this counting of their people at the nation's beginning by a fraction is a persistent symbol of their effective status even today. Others will note the baldness of this early example of compromise between the contradictory principles that all men are created equal and that black slaves should not count at all. But the overwhelming emotive impression left by the Constitution's language is that black people are outside the company of those who count.

From this point on, the negations are scattered liberally throughout the document. Fifteen of its eighty-five paragraphs actually begin with "no" or "neither," and the Constitution contains almost as many restrictions on the use of power as assignments of it. More important is that the document as a whole consistently carries forward and deepens the impression that its composers were men preoccupied with, first, their sense of being on the inside surrounded by threats from without, and second, the suspicion that all kinds of disaster lurked within as well.

The fear of threat from without is obvious in the references to the need for "common Defence," "Piracies and Felonies committed on the high Seas, and Offences against the Law of Nations," "War," "Letters of Marque and Reprisal," "Captures on Land and Water," "Armies," "Navy," "Invasions," "the Erection of Forts, Magazines, Arsenals, dock-Yards, and other needful Buildings," and above all "Treason," a subject so much on the mind of the founding fathers that they not only devoted two paragraphs to it specifically but also mentioned it elsewhere on three occasions. Invasions are mentioned four times. But there are also forecasts of "domestic Violence," "Insurrections," "Cases of Rebellion," and of criminals and "Person(s) held to Service or Labour" fleeing from State to State. Perhaps we should read the paragraphs negatively specifying the qualifications for representatives, senators, and president in this context. The age, citizenship, and residence requirements for these offices can all be seen as crudely insuring that the outs would stay out. It is perhaps also in this context that the founders presumed that the houses of Congress would meet privately and the requirement that they publish a journal of their proceedings explicitly excepts "such Parts as may in their Judgment require Secrecy" (Art. I, Sec. 5).

Possible threats from within are even more vividly portrayed than those from without. Beyond a paragraph specifically authorizing the House to initiate impeachment proceedings, the subject is directly discussed in three other paragraphs of the Constitution and mentioned in passing twice elsewhere. Moreover the crimes for which impeachment is authorized include, besides treason and "other high Crimes and Misdemeanors," bribery, a crime presupposing personal greed. The same vice is presupposed in another stricture.

No money shall be drawn from the Treasury, but in Consequence of Appropriations made by Law; and a regular Statement and Account of Receipts and Expenditures of all public Money shall be published from time to time. (Art. I, Sec. 9)

The suspicions the founders had of their future governors were suspicions they had of themselves. It was obvious that many of those writing the Constitution would go on to hold positions of authority in the structures it might create. Yet this fact seems to have compounded their anxieties. They hastened to put down the assurance that members of Congress "in all Cases, except Treason, Felony and Breach of the Peace" were to be privileged from arrest (by whom?) while going to, attending, or departing sessions, and that, on the other hand, they could be compelled to attend, punished for "disorderly Behaviour," and even expelled. There are requirements that sitting congressmen are barred from appointments in the executive branch and are similarly barred, even after leaving Congress, from any office they might have had a hand in creating or increasing "the Emoluments" thereof. Likewise the president, after being assured that while in office his emolument cannot be tampered with, is barred from drawing salary for any other office he might hold in the federal government or in any of the State governments. Was it simply common prudence to spell out all these matters?

For whatever reason, the founders did spell them out, and more. Ominously, they included the now almost forgotten clause,

Neither House, during the Session of Congress, shall, without the Consent of the other, adjourn for more than three days, nor to any other Place than that in which the two Houses shall be sitting. (Art. I, Sec. 5)

Think of the imagination required to conjure up circumstances in which the Houses would have to be forbidden to do these things. The founders employed like imagination in detailing how the Congress, after receiving his written objections, could override the president's vetoes of their work, and in providing for presidential authority to adjourn both houses "in Case of Disagreement between them, with Respect to the Time of Adjournment."

Taking all this negative, forbidding language in sum, why

were the founding fathers so glum about themselves, their countrymen, and their common prospects? The language they used has far more the tone of Hobbes than Locke, yet none of them had firsthand experience with the kind of turmoil Hobbes personally underwent. We can venture that few of them had more than reading knowledge of many of the matters they chose to discuss directly in the Constitution, matters like impeachment proceedings, bills of attainder, treason trials, and piracies on the high seas. Some of them had more knowledge of governmental corruption and domestic violence, though hardly on a scale to merit major attention by historians. And a few of them had all too direct knowledge of that matter they tried most to avoid discussing at all, black slavery and "The Migration or Importation of such Persons as any of the States now existing shall think proper to admit. . . ." It is understandable that in the wake of the Revolution they would be concerned about armies and navies and have fears of wars and invasions. But was the unsettling experience of the Revolution, coming after a relatively long period of hard-won but extraordinarily successful colonial experience, enough to engender paranoia about human nature, not excepting their own?

A possible answer to this question lies in the notion that the founders were Bourgeois men, Protestant-Bourgeois men, but little else. That is to say that when they read Locke, they identified directly and literally with his rapacious man, grasping after property and restrained only by bleak Protestant conscience. Perhaps they even recalled the sentence in Locke's chapter on property beginning, "Thus, in the beginning, all the world was America . . ." and took it to be a teaching of their own closeness to an actual wilderness. Given this understanding of themselves, it would follow that they would write a constitution for savage, violent men, men with little sense of social membership and who could be impelled to do their duty only by fear of punishment.

This discussion has outlined the negative side of the founder's moods and intentions. The positive side of their work can be stated more briefly. Obviously the founders wanted a government that would work, a legislature that would "establish . . . uniform laws" (Art. I, Sec. 8), an executive that would "take Care" that they were "faithfully executed" (Art. II, Sec. 3), and a court system that would move surely through the process of "Indictment, Trial, Judgement and Punishment, according to Law" (Art. I, Sec. 3). In constituting a workable government, the founders further aimed to form that "more perfect union" of the thirteen colonies whose separatist tendencies had not been sufficiently contained by the Articles of Confederation. As obvious and unexceptionable as all this is, securing union through law is a very particular objective. The types of law the founders had in mind make their objectives more particular still. A modern fascist or communist movement will seek national unity through bringing revolutionary fervor or love of the fatherland to full throat in the mass of the people, and the prime instrument for achieving this kind of objective is invariably a highly disciplined, tirelessly active political party. That kind of thinking is a world away from the ideological minds of the founders. They had no thought of national unity of that sort. Like Hobbes,[1] their overriding intent was to guarantee through law "domestic Tranquility." They desired not national unity but national peace, a politics of nationwide stability through the firm establishment of a system of law.

What this suggests is that even in their positive aims the founders were negative in their attitude toward government. The Constitution provides no description of the president as an active national leader; it pictures him almost exclusively in his administrative capacities and says almost nothing about his general duties beyond the requirement that he see that the laws are faithfully executed. Only Congress is pictured as positively active, but notice in which ways. It was to have the power to make laws that would:

lay and collect taxes	organize armed forces
regulate commerce	borrow money
define bankruptcy	define naturalization
fix standard weights and measures	coin money
build a postal system	punish counterfeiting
define copyrights and patents	build post roads
declare war	define piracy
	build a court system
	build a national capitol[2]

1. See Frank Coleman, "The Hobbesian Basis of American Constitutionalism," *Polity*, Vol. VII, No. 1 (Fall 1974).

2. This list is a compression of the Constitution's Art. I, Sec. 8.

The list could have been drawn up by Adam Smith. As much by its brevity as by the particular items it includes and omits, it makes plain that for the founders the important work of society is done outside the political realm. That work is the industry, agriculture, commerce, and culture of the citizenry. Government does none of it. Even if allowances are made for functions left to State and local authorities, nothing on the list of congressional powers or elsewhere in the Constitution indicates that government specifically, or political life generally, had any primary or ennobling functions of their own. Obviously, a strong, stable government was indispensible, but its status in life taken as a whole was purely secondary.[3]

Ideologically, this fact is the most important feature of the federal Constitution and in long-term significance outweighs all others combined. This fact more than any other gives the Constitution its overwhelmingly Bourgeois bias. The founding fathers had no direct interest in nation building or in creating a political community. They were building a structure in law which would protect and release the energies of Bourgeois man, the man on the make. In twentieth century terms, they held that the nation's business was business. Of course the rawness with which they held to this proposition has been well concealed by national myth and scholarly commentary. But their primary intent is made plain not only by the words of the constitution itself but also by their most signal commentary upon it, the Federalist papers.

The evidence is abundant even in the first pages of that remarkable series. Locke had begun his defence of the English constitution yielded by the Revolution of 1688 with discussions of universalistic theories about Adam in Eden and then, even more abstractly, about men in the state of nature. Hamilton, in the first paper after a ferociously denigrating description of party debate in his day as essentially self-serving and irrationally motivated, cuts to the core of what he thinks will appeal to his readers:

> . . . I am clearly of opinion, it is your interest to adopt it [the proposed new constitution]. I am convinced that this is the safest course for your liberty, your dignity, and your happiness.

3. Martin Diamond, "Democracy and *The Federalist:* A Reconsideration of the Framers' Intent," *American Political Science Review*, March 1959, especially Part III.

The direct appeal to personal interest is sustained in the summary which Hamilton gives of the topics the papers are to cover.

I propose, in a series of papers to discuss the following interesting particulars . . . *The utility of the UNION to your political prosperity* . . . *The insufficiency of the present confederation to preserve that Union* . . . *The necessity of a government, at least equally energetic with the one proposed, to the attainment of this object* . . . *The conformity of the proposed constitution to the true principles of republican government* . . . *Its analogy to your own state constitution* and lastly, *The additional security, which its adoption will afford to the preservation of that species of government, to liberty, and to property.*

The appeal to men of property who want liberty to enlarge their prosperity within the framework of a strengthened union runs through the whole of the Federalist papers and provides substance for the more explicit and familiar arguments about the need for federalism and separation of powers to combat the threat of mass rule or, alternatively, anarchy. That the founding fathers, the writers of the Federalist papers, and their prime constituencies were all predominantly men of substance and commerce was long ago established. They also *thought* like Bourgeois men, and remarkably simple-minded ones at that.

Like all Bourgeois men, they trivialized politics in their thinking about it. At both the personal and social levels, they denied it the ennobling functions that the dominant strands of Western political theory from Plato and Aristotle to Aquinas and Rousseau had characteristically seen in it. But the American Bourgeoisie did more than elect to side with the minority of voices in the Western tradition who saw politics in dark and narrow terms (voices like Augustine, Machiavelli, and Hobbes). Beyond denying politics higher functions, they debased it. Of course, they said, politics is rooted in self-interest. But they then went on to characterize the normal self-interest of men in the meanest terms. "Why has government been instituted at all?" asks Hamilton, and then provides his answer: "Because the passions of men will not conform to the dictates of reason and justice, without constraint" (No. 15). Madison echoes the thought: "What is government itself, but the greatest of all reflections on human nature?" (No. 51) It would be hard to formulate a political idealism in more simple and self-debasing terms.

The political significance of this conclusion is large. It is sometimes thought that the founding fathers were more counter-revolutionary than revolutionary. It is said they were aiming to arrest an on-coming revolutionary surge located elsewhere in the national community. Certainly much of their language about democracy and anarchy indicates that such was their intent. In posture the founders were clearly counter-revolutionary — pinched, negative, and fearful. The difficulty with pronouncing the founders counter-revolutionary in fact is in locating the revolution they were seeking to arrest. The notion that the men of 1787–1789 were seeking to stem the revolutionary fervor of the men of 1776–1783 cannot be supported when in so many cases they were the same people. Washington, with Hamilton loyally at his side, was the pre-eminent public figure in both periods. More important examples are the three drafters of the Declaration of Independence: Franklin was active at the Constitutional Convention itself, Adams admired its work as he would his own, and Jefferson, after some initial doubts, vigorously supported its product. Any search beyond this group is equally fruitless. The antifederalists were generally even more conservative than the federalists, and those who were not were scattered and ineffective. Sam Adams and Tom Paine, however notorious, never spoke for a sizable and coherent following. Finally, the so-called democratic enthusiasms said to have rocked places like Rhode Island were both widely exaggerated and misinterpreted. And Shays' Rebellion, a matter very much on the minds of those who wrote the Constitution and supported its adoption, can in no way be cited as an example of revolutionary, democratic, egalitarian humanism radically at odds with the mood of the founding fathers themselves. As Hamilton wrote, "If Shays had not been a *desperate debtor,* it is much to be doubted whether Massachusetts would have been plunged into a civil war" (No. 4).

Our analysis is forced back to the self-image the founding fathers had of themselves and to the notion that in expressing distrust of others they were distrusting themselves. Once the matter is put this way, it is easy to see why they felt as they did. The source of distaste for self is conscience, and it is obvious that while in overt mood and act the founders were

Bourgeois through and through, in conscience they were something else. In conscience they were Protestants and democrats, every bit as much as Sam Adams and Tom Paine. All of them were appalled by what they knew of the slave trade, and few of them positively approved of slavery as an institution. That was on their consciences, both in the writing of the Declaration and in the composition of their Constitution. Moreover, for all their systematic denigration of democracy, they harbored powerful sentiments in its behalf. Kind, if rhetorical, references in its favor crop up all through the Federalist Papers and even in the Constitution. "We the People . . . do ordain . . ." is the way the Constitution begins.

That was myth in whole cloth, of course. The Constitutional Convention had no standing in law, much less any involving an electoral process rooted in the people. The people were only remotely involved even in the Constitution's adoption. But there at the head of the founders' Constitution is that brave, egalitarian rhetoric, as bland as it is brazen, a mere disguise of democracy. Yet it can be safely claimed that the founders put it there with assurance. If pressed, the founders would have argued for the right to put it there, citing theories of virtual representation, spokesmen-of-the-people doctrines, or other such scholasticisms. And they would have argued that without the people's mandate their work would have lacked an essential element of legitimacy.

It is easily verified that the founders' commitment to democracy, in the loose sense of government by and for the generality of the people, was sincere,[4] but it was mainly sentimental and sharply contradicted by more powerful convictions of other sorts. The overall cast of their work was undemocratic, and much of their argument in its behalf was positively antidemocratic. The Constitution's provision for the House of Representatives was, it is true, made explicitly to serve as the "popular" chamber rooted in the general electorates. But the three other major elements in the proposed government — the courts, the presidency, and the Senate — were carefully insulated from any direct involvement with the general electorates. And the Senate was granted exceptional duties in the work of the government which were pointedly not granted to the House.

4. See Diamond, "Democracy and The Federalist," especially Parts I and II.

The creation of the House as a popular chamber must be seen for what it was: a highly selective gesture in the direction of democracy, and one which carefully went no further than any of the States had already individually gone. But it was at least that.

In any event, the House quickly took on the coloration of the government as a whole and never developed an independent and characteristically democratic ethos. This was inevitable, as will be explained in the next chapter. It is sufficient for now to hear Madison state again the overriding purpose of his governmental design: "In the compound republic of America, *the power surrendered by the people* is first divided between two distinct governments and the portion allotted to each subdivided among the distinct and separate departments" (No. 51, italics added). Power surrendered that way and that far is not easily recovered, which is precisely what Madison and his colleagues wished to assure.

The founders' Constitution, then, is a Bourgeois, elitist document with nothing more than a Protestant, democratic tinge. But that is not the final conclusion on which we should leave the discussion of this matter. Rather we should note the ineffectiveness of the founders' conscience. Regardless of what their consciences preached, their work remained pinched, negative, backward-looking, fearful, and bleakly forbidding. Conscience did not lead to any positive regeneration in these dark views. It tagged lamely along behind the main effort. The significance of Protestant practical weakness in the face of Bourgeois practical strength will loom larger as our analysis continues.

MADISONIANISM

The interior logic of the governmental engine Madison and his colleagues created is founded on the theory that motivation for political action stems, before all else, from personal ambition. As a theory it cuts two ways: if we wish to move a political actor, we have to interest him personally in our project; alternatively, if an actor has moved and we wish to know why, we must search behind any appearance of altruism or dutifulness that may mask what he has done to discover the interest he satisfied by his action. Moreover, the literature of Liberalism from Hobbes to Adam Smith and beyond, from which this theory obviously comes, makes it clear what in fact will interest a political actor. He seeks material reward, the power to obtain it, or security in the enjoyment of it. Translated into a motto for life, the theory preaches, "Get Rich! Get Rich!"[5]

Americans, understandably, do not easily countenance the notion that their governmental system is fueled by so unadorned and raunchy an appeal to material avarice, and they mask the fact well. But Madison made plain what he and his colleagues were about. In a single page of Federalist Paper No. 10 he rejects both the idea that we can rely upon our governors being "enlightened statesmen" and the parallel notion that the populace might be restrained by moral or religious motives. More importantly, in Paper No. 51:

> Ambition must be made to counteract ambition. *The interest of the man must be connected with the constitutional rights of the place.* . . . In framing a government which is to be administered by men over men, the great difficulty lies in this: You must first enable the government to control the governed; and in the next place, oblige it to control itself. A dependence upon the people is no doubt the primary control on the government; but experience has taught mankind the necessity of auxiliary precautions. (italics added)

The reference in the last of these sentences to "dependence upon the people" is another of those democratic twinges to be found scattered all through Madison's work. It is clear even from its immediate context that what he called "auxiliary precautions" were in fact for him the primary ones. But even so, the reference has a technical significance we must pause to examine.

The phrase "dependence upon the people" could not have had a very precise meaning for Madison in the period of 1787–1789. The situation would have been very different had he been writing a century later, for by that time in England,

5. Rev. R. H. Conwell, "Acres of Diamonds," quoted by R. H. Gabriel, *The Course of American Democratic Thought,* rev. ed., Ronald Press, New York, 1957, p. 158. This interpretation of the content of Bourgeois "self-interest" does not rule out that Bourgeois individuals — and their observers — may be sometimes confused between means and ends and seek power for its own sake. But even where this happens, we can still ask, "Power to do what?" The answer is, power to command and manipulate, directly or through the service of others, human material product.

both the theory and institutions of what by then was called "responsible government" had received ample development. Much more was involved than broadening the franchise and organizing the electorate into equitable constituencies. Considerable advances had been made in these areas in the United States during the same period without significantly altering the general character of Madison's Constitution. The truly important development in England was a new theory of political motivation and new institutional patterns for its expression.

In their new theory of political motivation, the British remained in many ways as much Liberals as their American cousins. But while the Americans continued a constitutional pattern that basically related each political actor to his interest by the adage "Every man for himself," the British updated Sir Robert Walpole's emendation of that adage, "If we don't hang together, we'll each hang separately!" In the context of their parliamentary institutions, they evolved the idea that politicians could be coerced and cajoled into patterns of cooperative behavior and then into relatively permanent and cohesive organizations if a condition of their having power was that they must show broad, unified support in the majority of the electorate. More particularly, at the institutional level the ministers of the British government were allowed almost unlimited power — provided only that they could demonstrate, on almost a daily basis, that they commanded the confidence of a majority of the House of Commons. The rub was in how that kind of demonstration could be made. It was not just a question of winning each vote as it came up. Before those votes were taken, under the sharp operations of the tandem doctrines of collective and individual responsibility, British ministers were made to answer by a host of parliamentary devices for the use they had made of their power. To this day in Britain, responsible government has come to mean responsive government, responding government. Ministers must talk. If they do not do that well and cannot answer persuasively for what they have done, their government, their party, and their own ambitions all fall together.

Whether the British system works well or ill is neither here nor there in the present context. The point is that it is different. Its interior logic is radically apart from that of institutions constructed to the rubric which pits one man's ambition against another's. British government is unified, party government on behalf of the majority. American government is dispersed, personal government on behalf of individuals. Regularly Americans get confused about this by everyday language, by myth, by the misguided teachings of professionals of the stature of Woodrow Wilson. But American government is not, fundamentally, a system of responsible government dependent upon the people, however much and however often it may don that disguise.

In important ways Madison was after the reverse of all that the British were later to evolve. Instead of seeking to mass power and unify majority support behind it so that those who were responsible for its use would be clearly identified, Madison was terrified of anything on that order. Notice the harshness of his verbs:

Among the numerous advantages promised by a well constructed Union, none deserves to be more accurately developed than its tendency to *break* and *control* the violence of faction. (Federalist Paper No. 10, italics added)

By faction Madison meant essentially what we mean today by political party, any combination of persons, "whether amounting to a majority or minority of the whole, who are united and actuated by some common impulse of passion, or of interest. . . ." He specifically lamented that under the Articles of Confederation, ". . . measures are too often decided, not according to the rules of justice, and the rights of the minor party, but by the superior force of an interested and overbearing majority." Of course Madison also worried about minority factions but concluded that these, simply by being smaller, were less dangerous than a faction supported by the majority. In other words, those whom the British were later most anxious to cultivate and empower Madison regarded as the chief threat to freedom and the public good.

His fundamental perceptions about the nature of man forced Madison to conclude that there were no cures for the causes of faction. Because men are inherently passionate and self-centered, all societies are permanently factionalized. Genuine social unity is a utopian chimera and Madison would have scoffed at slogans like, "Bring us together!" Practical men would rather aim no higher than controlling the effect of faction, violence. The difference between bad government and good, for that matter between no government at all and any kind of civil order, is simply one of degree. Through politics men gain no qualitative change in moral status, capacity, or opportunity, and they remain as fragmented from their neighbors as ever. The Hobbesian war in the state of nature is simply moderated. The most that a well constructed polity can achieve is replacement of pillage and violence with patterns of "antagonistic cooperation"[6] and systems of shared security. Instead of transactions in blood we can hope for transactions in coin of the realm.

Even these improvements are not easily won. The fundamental trick which constitutional engineers must somehow perform is to ensure that all political actors (especially those who through possession of high status and large estates have much to lose and many to whom they might lose it) are securely situated in the political system with enough power to defend themselves. The first step toward this goal is to partition and disperse governmental power, and the second is to ensure that the partitions are permanent. This second step is the crucial one, and in his discussion of the doctrine of separation of powers as applied in the federal Constitution Madison reveals how he believed he had accomplished it. He proclaimed that ". . . each department should have a will of its own. . . ."

Separation of powers is not accomplished by giving each department some special function. On the contrary, functions are happily mixed. Separation of wills is accomplished instead by so constructing the departments "that the members of each should have as little agency as possible *in the appointment* of the members of the others" (Federalist Paper No. 51, italics added). Independence of recruitment, distinctness, and separateness of political base for each political actor is revealed as the key not only to Madison's understanding of the separation of powers but also to the general logic with which he imbued the whole of his constitutional structure. It was designed to be a system peopled throughout by political actors anchored independently of one another.

6. The phrase is actually William Graham Sumner's, but it is wholly congruent to Madison's thinking. "Antagonistic cooperation is the most productive form of combination in high civilization." *Folkways*, Ginn and Co., Boston, 1907, p. 18.

Separation and distinctness of the avenues of recruitment (election of the president by one route, senators and congressmen by others) and the dependence of no one election on the results of any other secure separation of wills in two ways. Negatively, they preclude the electoral triumph of any other. Positively, they compel each of the actors always to look out for himself, in fact to put personal survival ahead of all other concerns, if only because no one else can help or hinder him in his pursuit of it except through reciprocally useful alliances or other indirect arrangements. This is what Madison meant when he said, "The interests of the man must be connected to the constitutional rights of the place."

That the separation of powers and federalism of the Constitution so magnificently carried through his original intent, the separation of wills, is a tribute to Madison's constitutional engineering genius. It is also a tribute to the faithfulness with which the American people have clung to his original principles in the face of all kinds of countervailing pressures and distractions, and to the ingenuity with which they have extended both the scope and the application of those principles.

Once wills had been separated in basic construction and situation, Madison demanded that in their daily operation they face each other and mingle their work. Only then could the "policy of supplying by opposite and rival interests" be set in motion so that each of the several constituent parts of the constitutional machine, "by their mutual relations, be the means of keeping each other in their places" (Federalist Paper No. 51).

In the actual operation of the constitutional machine, especially in the course of contemporary crises in presidential/ congressional relations, it is natural that the various parties should mount extreme claims on their own behalf and insist not only on independence of will and base, but also on sovereignty of right in their respective theaters of operation and responsibility, functionally defined. Under the guise of doctrines of "executive privilege," presidents especially have sought to put the workings of their office beyond the reach of both Congress and courts. Madison and his confreres would have had to allow that such claims were to be expected as a natural expression of the conceits and fears of the wills so carefully separated in the government. But by the same token they would have denied such claims any validity. They deliberately involved the president in legislative affairs not merely by the veto power but by its contrary: no bill passed by Congress could become law unless submitted to the president for his signature. The president is thus involved in *all* lawmaking. Deliberately, they gave the president powers over various aspects of the legislative body's sittings. Deliberately, they involved the Senate in presidential appointment processes and treaty-making. A central concern of the founders was the need to involve the branches of government in a process of thrust and counter-thrust as representatives of factions in society at large. They tended to see the president as less politically significant than we do today, because for them he did not stand for any clear factional interest rooted in society at large. The two houses of Congress were designed to and did, and in their interactions the founders expected to see the most serious of society's factional wars moderated and contained.

That the founders intended a separation of wills and an intermingling of performances is most sharply revealed in their attitude toward the legislature. The two rigorously separated bodies shared the function of making laws. Note Madison's summary comment.

In republican government, the legislative authority necessarily predominates. The remedy for this *inconveniency* is, to divide the legislature into different branches; and to render them by different modes of election, and different principles of action, as little connected with each other, as the nature of their common functions, and their common dependence on the society will admit. (Federalist Paper No. 51, italics added)

The founders were thinking far more of separating powers in the literal sense than they were of distinguishing between functions. But there are even more important points to be found here, ones best approached by looking for the origins of the founders' philosophy of the separation of powers.

Those origins are more in Polybius and in Aristotle himself than in Montesquieu or Locke. As we have seen, Locke assumed for most of his argument the context of a coherent, structured society. His primary concern was not with the division of power between different elements of the government each rooted in a separate faction of society. It was to establish the legislature as a single body in possession of supreme power over the whole community. That established, his interest was in distinguishing between the legislature and the executive as functionally discrete. He agreed that the powers to discharge these functions are often and should always be in different hands,[7] but his argument in support and interpretation of these assertions was merely the sociologically and economically superficial contention that too much power in one place will lead to its selfish use. Montesquieu, whom Madison described as "The oracle who is always consulted and cited on this subject" of separation of powers (Federalist Paper No. 47), may well have been the source of the founders' explicit division of the federal government into legislative, executive, and judicial branches. (Locke distinguished only between the legislative and executive branches, assuming the judiciary to be a part of the latter.) Also, the author of The Spirit of the Laws saw that the capacity of the branches of government to check and balance each other arises from the constant intermingling of their workings. But Madison paid no heed to Montesquieu's overriding intellectual objective: to discover and define in broad sociological terms the comprehensive and organic unity between a community's history, people, geography, and laws — in a word, its national character, the veritable spirit of its life. Only in the context of that search can Montesquieu's discussion of the proper separation of powers, demonstrated for him by eighteenth century Britain, be understood. In that context, the doctrine is more one of coordinated and cooperative elements of a single body politic than what Madison had in mind.

What Madison had in mind, on the other hand, is strikingly similar to Aristotle's preoccupation, in Books III–VI of the Politics, with "stasis," the interruptions in the processes of communal life caused by jealousies between social and economic classes and the resulting civil strife. The terminology Aristotle used to discuss the political institutions which he felt could handle the problem of stasis and the specific governmental functions he assigned those institutions have inexact and misleading counterparts in modern political vocabularies. But this should not distract attention — as it usually has — from the fact that Aristole saw the central problem for con-

7. Locke, "The Second Treatise on Civil Government," Chs. XII and XIII.

stitutional government precisely as Madison did. While others concerned themselves with schemes to enable political leadership to integrate the various functions of government into patterns of positive social accomplishment, Aristotle, like Madison 2000 years after him, saw as his primary aim to catch and contain in a fixed constitutional cage that perpetual internecine strife inherent in all but the simplest of societies.[8]

Aristotle's theory is worth reconstructing from his scattered notes, because doing so will reveal his (and Madison's) extraordinary faith that a cage constructed merely in laws could catch and contain — "break and control" — social and economic forces rooted in the very nature of man.

The theory begins simply. It notes that some of the city-states of ancient Greece had one-man rule, in others a few governed, and in still others the many ruled. But Aristotle rapidly associated these numerical categories with social and economic ones. The many were invariably poor and also constituted what John Stuart Mill would later characterize as "the uncultivated herd." The few were moderately wealthy and were "people of the better sort," to use again the words of those who carried the ancient biases forward into modern times. When one man ruled, he would be drawn from the class of very rich men and would be an outstanding person by reason of either birth or personal achievement. This phase of the Aristotelian analysis concludes by associating with each of the numerical/economic/social categories a characteristic political institution. Obviously, one-man rule in the ancient world would be through a kingship, the few would customarily rule through a small council or senate, and the many would crowd into a massive assembly.

The symmetry in all this categorizing is a bit too neat. Even in Aristotle's day, there must have been instances in which the king was not one of the richest men in his realm, and there must also have been times when the poor did not significantly outnumber the moderately wealthy. But such empirical variations would not have dissuaded Aristotle or those who imitated his work down through the centuries. Awkward facts would

8. This does not deny the validity of the founders' claim (Hamilton, Federalist Paper No. 9, para. 4) to have advanced beyond ancient teachings. Specifically, they claimed to have added provisions for "checks" and "balances" to the original "mixed government" theory.

not have much embarrassed his theory because, as theory, it was more heuristically valuable than it was positively descriptive.

In any event, the next phase of the theory's development began with the hostility, presumed to be congenital and born of jealousy and fear, which the different classes had for each other. This inherent hostility assured two consequences, the second following always from the first. The first consequence was that suspicions between the classes prevented any communal sense a city might develop from ever lasting long. The second consequence was simply that the rule of whatever class was in power would, despite all initial idealistic attempts, degenerate into selfishness and cruelty. Thus the rule of the noblest king, a true monarch governing in the interest of the whole community, would predictably degenerate in time into a tyranny through either the corruption and hubris of the aging king himself or that of his offspring. Tyrannies, of course, are overthrown in time, usually by revolutions led by a few virtuous men, but the resulting aristocracy, ever exposed to the paranoia of the poor, must soon go the oligarchical route. And that degeneracy will itself have to give way, as its own weakness collapses before the march of the many led by leaders of Periclean proportions. But such events merely open the door, Aristotle gloomily concluded (like Plato before him and Cicero and Polybius after), to a final degeneracy: democracy. Rule by the mob in thralldom to demagogues ensues, blindly driven by passion and illusion, until rescue could come through a restoration of the original monarchy. And the cycle would begin again.

The bad name Aristotle gave democracy in the course of his description of the revolutionary cycle was a lesson Western culture took to heart until the mid-nineteenth century, long after America's founding fathers had done their work. But what they learned from Aristotle was far more important than that. Aristotle, a constitutional as well as a philosophical genius, was primarily remembered among students of politics for his teachings about how the revolutionary cycle could be moderated.

A trick was involved, superficially a simple one, but the very one Madison used: include in any proposed constitutional machine all three of the political institutions characteristically associated with each of the three economic-social classes found in all cities. The result will be a "mixed government" giving each class enough of a hand in the government to ensure both its own protection and its interest in the government's survival. But do not give any one class so much as to enable it to tyrannize the others.

Through the Aristotelian prism we can see what Madison was really getting at by employing a scheme of checks and balances. Aristotle's philosophical presuppositions are infused throughout his constitutional teachings, and as a result, for him the motive of "mixed government" constitutional engineering is more than a simple trick to harmonize the diverse interests of the various classes. The higher philosophical aim is to achieve oneness, wholeness, and a degree of political unity in a situation that, practically, represents social chaos. The Greek philosopher always aims to perceive in every object its *form*, its essence, the idea by conforming to which it became what it was.

Aristotle dreamed that each citizen in the ideal *polis* would perceive through reason his place in the unity of the whole community and perform accordingly. Notice how this idealism combines in one thought technically perfect concepts of, first, membership, and, second, participation. In unity each member participates; in the social whole each citizen has his function, and he fulfills his destiny by performing it. But such perfection of parts in wholes bound up in reason is not for men of this world. Blinded by selfishness and other passions they are too short-sighted to see either the higher demands of true citizenship or the real fulfilment possible in common life. So in this world we must settle for less.

A lot less. We must adjust to human meanness. The political unity we can achieve, the *form* of the practically possible state, will be less than noble. It will be nothing more than a cage. Tough and confining, no mere illusion of laws, mixed government would still constitute a city's political essence, the idea in terms of which it could become a whole. Therein lay the possibility of political unity where the conditions for social unity were absent.

That was the general point of Aristotelian (Madisonian) constitutionalism. There was also a particular point. Mixed government combined in one constitutional structure the institutions characteristic of each of the social/economic classes.

If we regard each of these institutions as expressive of the political essence of the class it was associated with, then we can see why Aristotle was so sure that mere inclusion of the appropriate institution in the constitution would guarantee the presence of the class in the political process.

Of course, Aristotle and Madison were not so mystical as to leave matters on so highly abstract a plane. Aristotle talked at some length of the practical advantages of a system of graduated property qualifications for the various offices of the state. And if Madison had carried through literally on this kind of thinking he would have specified not only differing age requirements for senators and congressmen but differing property and perhaps even educational qualifications as well. As it was, his sharply differing electoral routes (direct election for members of Congress, indirect election for senators, and selection via a special electoral college for the president) are clearly aimed at achieving the same result. Nevertheless that result, the material representation in the political process of differing social interests, is not comprehensible merely in terms of these technical matters. Only against the background of Aristotelian constitutionalism does the whole picture become plain. What we then see is truly a marvel: a theory that the chaotic forces of practical social life can be made into an overarching political unity by imposing a conceptual apparatus upon them. The constitution is a cage, but cage as concept is king!

To put the matter one more way, when Madison wrote the single most important sentence revealing the interior logic of his Constitution, "The interest of the man must be connected with the constitutional rights of the place," he was not just talking the language of baited mouse traps. Within the larger framework of general constitutional engineering principles, this sentence is fraught with a complex of meanings. Which men? What interests? Which places? To understand the words, we must understand volumes, or at least Books III through VI of Aristotle's *Politics*.

Two further matters need to be noted before concluding this review of the interior logic of Madison's Constitution. The first is that as a form in law, the Madisonian Constitution implies a conception of justice. This in no way belies the constitution's being rooted in the rapacious ethic of "every man for himself." As an encagement of all men so motivated, its principal assurance is that each one will get a fair shake at what he wants. For this Constitution, justice is fairness, individual fairness.

The Madisonian Constitution is a system for assuring the just satisfaction of private wants, and that is all that it is or even aims to be. In its logic, it knows nothing and can learn nothing of the problems and principles of social justice. Although there is a clear ancillary need arising from the demands of the system to be preserved as a whole, the system *qua* system knows and understands only the language of private satisfaction. No wonder then that Madison, American Bourgeois Liberal to the bone, was willing to work with it.

The second concluding matter is hardly more than a rephrasing and refocusing of the first, yet even more ominously it points to danger ahead. Madison's constitutional system not only allows for private satisfaction; it depends absolutely on the participants in the system pursuing their private satisfaction. Should they fail in that, should any significant proportion of them succumb, for example, to the spirit of charity and self-sacrifice, then the system would collapse. Self-interest is this system's lifeblood as much as love is the ideal family's. But hammering this point home forces a further fact into the open. An elitist implication in the system, present even in the original Aristotelian formula, is concealed behind discussion of other matters. All men, the system supposes, are self-interested and more or less troublesome as a result. If they are big enough to threaten real trouble, the constitution is designed to catch and cage them in the manner described. But what of the rest, the ones too small to pose a threat to others? In Aristotle's day there were women, children, slaves, aliens, and citizens too poor, too old, too sick, or too apathetic to participate actively in the political life of the city. For Madison, add Indians. And then the fact stares. To all these people, Aristotle and Madison speak only in paradoxes. They are weak? They need help? They should organize and become powerful enough to ask for it. Of course, then they would be strong and not need help. But they could and would get other things. In other words, the Aristotelian/Madisonian Constitution is for people who matter, the people who are big enough and bad enough to matter. The rest do not.

IDEOLOGICAL PRACTICE

THE AMERICAN BARONAGE
THE RULES OF THE GAME

THE AMERICAN BARONAGE

The limits of American politics were set by the logic which Madison built into its Constitution. Surprisingly, these limits and the logic upon which they are based have hardly changed to this day. Major changes took place almost immediately in the way in which the Constitution worked in practice. And there have been major changes in the nation's political environment because of geographic expansion and economic and technological advances. But to this day, the political system as such confronts only most awkwardly the problems of social justice and of the nation's dispossessed. To this day, it remains primarily what the spirit of Aristotle and the brain of Madison intended it to be: a rigidly stable system for guaranteeing the private satisfactions of those citizens that matter.

Nevertheless, the changes that took place after 1789 are important to any general understanding of how the system operates internally today, and we must describe them carefully in order to understand the way in which the original Madisonian logic was preserved.

These changes can be summed up by the word "individualization." They are largely the consequence of the fact that, in its extraordinarily uniform Bourgeois character, the American socio-economic environment offered almost no reinforcement for the distinctions upon which so much of Madison's thinking rested. The Aristotelian class biases simply were not there. The Constitution was therefore set to work in an environment so fluid that almost immediately its projected hierarchies and differences began to flatten and to blur.

This process is not to be confused with "democratization," a separate development largely engineered by the broadening of the electorate and one which will be discussed in the next chapter. Individualization involved a massive dispersion by which power was dispersed not to "the people," but to individuals, individual governments and individual politicians, all to operate within the context of the Constitution's system of laws. That is to say, the American individualization of the Aristotelian/Madisonian design did not compromise but rather carried to a literal extreme that design's essential impulse to multiply and separate distinct political wills within the all-containing legal cage.

In a sense, what the Americans did was to turn the Aris-totelian/Madisonian design on its side and then enormously complicate its internal workings. They converted a vertical arrangement of weights and balances involving relatively few elements into a vast horizontal maze all fitted out with a great assortment of one-way doors, roundabouts, hurdles, and chan-nels every one of which was attended by crews of latch, pully, and treadle operatives. For all that, the end result is not much different from the original intention: much activity and satis-faction for the operatives but little general consequence beyond a deadening stability for the system as a whole. Stasis is still the central problem and stasis is still contained.

Although most of Madison's intellectual concern (and the bulk of our own discussion so far) focused on separation of powers, federalism was also part of his scheme. It did to geo-graphy and separately constituted governments what separa-tion of powers did to departments within governments. The Americans picked up this logic and carried it forward formally and informally. They let the Constitution as a matter of accepted principle divide power between the national government, the thirteen original states, and the thirty-seven that have been created since. Remarkably, while the nation was transformed from a dispersed, agricultural, seaboard community into a con-tinental, industrialized, technologically bonded single economy, the basic divisions between these elemental fifty-one govern-ments in the system have persisted. In their operations they interact all the time. Sometimes the federal government, espe-cially in recent times, appears to have created a "new federal-ism" in which it is not so much partner as master calling the tune. Its budget, spending, and tax-collecting powers have grown enormously, not just in absolute terms but also in terms relative to those of the States. And it has enacted and drawn the States into a wide range of grant-in-aid programs in which it supplies the bulk of the money, selects the objectives, and sets the standards — and the States are relegated to doing the work. But the resulting relationships apply almost entirely to the bureaucracies of the governments involved. Politically, the States have maintained their separate identities, and their poli-ticians rise to eminence in their own right. Their power and distinctness of political will is still their own and comes not through any gift from federal masters but through the continu-

ing force of Madison's original commitment to the formal principles of federalism.

More important, talk about the new federalism should not
be allowed to disguise the fact that it is the informal extension
of the federal principle that most marks the continuing American commitment to it. At the beginning of the Union or as they
were subsequently admitted, each of the States created local
government systems in which sundry towns, cities, and counties were chartered and granted powers, functions, and jurisdictions as the State authorities in their wisdom saw fit. But this
is only the beginning of the story. Local autonomy is a powerful
instinct in the American environment and the dominant Bourgeois-Liberal ethos of individualism comprehensively reinforced
it. What custom warranted, usage and the entrenching powers
of skillful, long-lived local politicians hardened into effective
constitutional mandate. In the end, the relationships between
State authorities and local figures are indistinguishable in kind
from those between the State authorities and federal officials.
Even in those grant-in-aid programs which some think detract
from the federal principle because the federal government by-
passes the States and deals directly with local governments,
local government figures end up working with people in the
nation's capital just as they work with people in their respective
State capitals. The American environment thereby flattens all
the hierarchies between governments in the political system.

And this is not the end of the story. Under the cover of
the principle of "taking things out of politics" or because they
recognized the need to create authorities that could operate
across established local government jurisdictions, Americans
have created a host of special purpose governments. These are
as various as port authorities, bridge authorities, and even
mosquito control authorities. By far their most numerous type
is the independent school district. By being separately constituted and granted self-sustaining powers of revenue generation in addition to the particular responsibility they were created
to perform, they are as much distinct political wills as any
other local government authority. They are as susceptible as
the rest to the pressures to develop autonomy to the point of
virtual constitutional independence. And the overall result
combines the national government, State governments, all types
of regular local governments, and the myriad special purpose

authorities into an effective federal system of up to 90,000 units, a far remove from the original 14.

It may not always immediately appear that, for example, a small mid-western city applying to Washington for help in an urban renewal project is making that appeal from a position as a partner in a federal relationship. Equally, it may not at first appear that a minor local education board, buckling under to regulations promulgated by State authorities, is dealing with those authorities in a federal style. But in the first instance "the federal government," for all its sprawling size, is no monolith. Local governments often have considerable independent leverage upon this or that one aspect of it. In the second instance, closer knowledge of the situation will regularly reveal that however much local boards may complain about the high-handedness of State authorities, they in turn complain about their inability to discipline the local people. The truth in such situations is that in the give-and-take so generally characteristic of the American political process, one or another of the participants will be bigger, have stronger leverage, be able to cite a clearer mandate either in law or in politics, and thus get its way. And in this dealing back and forth all parties large and small are compelled, by sinewy custom if not by law, to recognize each other's existence and distinctness of political will as givens not to be denied.

A case in point. The New York metropolitan region is "governed" by more than 1500 local government authorities, ranging from New York City itself, the New York Port Authority, the Metropolitan Transit Authority, the Triborough Bridge Authority, and other similar special purpose authorities to a dozen or more county governments and a host of satellite cities, towns, and villages, most of which are rather inexactly paralleled by independent school districts. Regardless of their particular legal origins, every one of these 1500 authorities has long since developed a separate political will, and it is worth remembering that more than half of them have their own police forces. In addition, three State governments intrude powerfully into the area and they, in turn, are constantly rubbing shoulders with a broad array of federal departments, agencies, and regulatory commissions, some of which are just going about their nationally oriented business in the area but many of which are busy supervising, promoting, or actively supporting local government activities of one kind or another. Viewed in terms of its attempts to deal with broad regional problems such as crime, environmental protection, and general economic and cultural planning, the result is a complexity, a maze, or a federalist's nightmare. But it is certainly fulfillment of the Madisonian dream of creating a plethora of independently constituted political wills.

Thus, Americans have done wonders with Madison's federal concept. Other words would have to be found to describe what they have done with his doctrine of separation of powers. At the federal level, two changes from the Constitution's original design were effected immediately and with massive significance.

First, within a decade the presidency was politicized. Jefferson is usually assigned responsibility for politicizing the presidency, or it is seen as a consequence of the personal rivalry between him and Hamilton. But given the American Bourgeois-Liberal environment, the presidential prize could not have gone for long politically unpursued. The office had been intended as a Washingtonian *deus ex machina* which would, in a politically disembodied way, defend the nation from enemies without, supervise the class strife between the houses of Congress, and, taking care that "the Laws be faithfully executed," see to the efficient administration of government generally. Even Washington proved more politically embodied than expected, and by the time Jefferson took office it was readily apparent that no president would be able to perform even the office's minimal functions without political connections and the kind of influence they generate. The Constitution as written had left the presidency a political vacuum, one that would inevitably be quickly filled.

The politicization of the presidency is a process which must be kept in perspective. The next chapter includes an extended discussion of the cult that has grown up around the heroes who have occupied the presidency, and of the general involvement of the office in America's Protestant democratic mythic restlessness. But that, emphatically, is not what is under discussion here. What we are now discussing is how presidents, from the start of the Union, have had to find ways of making out on a day-to-day basis in the practical, Bourgeois world of American Liberal politics.

In other words, the politicization of the presidency does not refer to the process by which the occupant of that high office became, supposedly, the national leader of a massive political party and hero to an army of aroused Americans. That myth will be discussed later. The politicization of the presidency refers rather to the process by which presidents came to realize that far from being disembodied *machina* let down from on high, they had to act within the political context. The logic of system, as it operated in the American environment, dictated to each president as he came into office the lesson that he, as much as any other operative in the political system, must individualize his political will and look out for himself. The modern wisdom on the subject is contained in the most important work on the office of the presidency published since World War II.

> When we inaugurate a President of the United States we give a man the powers of our highest public office. From the moment he is sworn the man confronts a personal problem: how to make those powers work for *him*. That problem is the subject of this book. My theme is personal power and its politics: what it is, how to get it, how to keep it, how to use it. My interest is in what a President can do to make his own will felt within his own Administration; what he can do, as one man among many, to carry his own choices through that maze of personalities and institutions called the government of the United States.[1]

These words were written by a man with extensive experience on the White House staff. Beyond revealing how well the Americans have applied even to the presidency Madison's fundamental dictum that the interest of the man must be connected to rights of the office, they point to the inevitable consequence of the widespread use of that dictum. Even the occupant of so lofty an office as the presidency is but "one man among many," and all have some power of one sort or another in the Madisonian world of American Bourgeois politics. In a system centering in Washington but spreading out nationwide, the president is not deity or monarch, but baron — bigger than most and certainly most noticeable, but still a lesser noble and one of many.

To call the American president a baron is deliberately to coin a technical term. To see what it means, we must de-

1. R. Neustadt, *Presidential Power*, Science Editions, Inc., New York, 1962, p. vii.

scribe the general context of the Americanization of the Madisonian Constitution, beginning with the second of the major
changes effected at the federal level in the period immediately
after 1789. Both the Senate and the House of Representatives
were, like the presidency, politicized, that is to say radically
individualized in the context of the prevailing Bourgeois-Liberal
politics.

Because the societal biases that Aristotle and Madison
depended upon were absent from the American Bourgeois
environment, both houses of Congress flattened into headless
bodies. Unable to represent particular social classes, they not
only became indistinguishable, they grew into simple collections or clubs each of whose members represented a particular interest — his own and that of his respective (Bourgeois)
clientele group. In time, of course, as the houses met for business, some members achieved prominence because of social
position, personal wealth, talent, skill, useful connections, or
other attributes. Also, an inevitable bias in favor of seniority
developed. Finally both houses, but especially the more un-
wieldy House of Representatives, set up complex patterns of
internal organization which stressed strong committees and
tight rules of procedure. As a result, committee chairmen came
to have more power than ordinary members over such matters
as determining which bills would come up where, when, and
in what form. But none of this effort to knit the houses back
into organizations capable of doing business and getting it done
could wholly cover over the hard political fact that every
member must face by himself the problem of getting elected
the next time around. That was *his* personal problem and consequently, whether senator or congressman, whether widely
known and influential or unknown and weak, in the final
analysis he came to. Washington to tend to his own business
as best he could. The forces for individualization were overwhelming. Like the president, senators and congressmen became barons.

So far only some of the more prominent members of
the baronage have been identified. After all, are not some of
the State governors as prominent in national politics as senators,
especially when an open presidential campaign looms up?
Moreover, do not those governors, when they take office in
their respective States, face "a personal problem": how to

make the powers of *their* offices work for *them?* And is not the same true of the mayors of our cities? In fact, given the loose character of American political parties, are not all of America's half million or so elected officials pretty much on their own, scrambling with what help they can get to be and stay elected, scrambling to use whatever power and influence they have to get what they can and stay ahead of the game?

The empirical answer to these questions, verified year in and year out by the daily press, is an obvious affirmative, and the analytic reason is also plain. Madison's doctrine of separation of powers, reduced by the American Bourgeois environment to the single caveat, "Every man for himself!" has been extended to every level of the political system with extraordinary uniformity and consistency. All the States imitated the national government's pattern of separating the powers and wills of the executive and legislative branches of government, and then nearly all of them went the basic pattern one better. Insisting that most of the principal officers of the executive branch (not just the governor and his possible replacement) be separately elected, they splintered the unity of the executive branch into a collection of politically individualized wills. Almost all the cities, counties, and towns adopted this pattern, and even today, after decades of "enlightened" efforts at reform and consolidation, most of them still reflect it. And once the logic of individualization had gone this far, sheer momentum kept it dominant regardless of legal forms.

Thus most counties and most special purpose governments, whether of school, water, or whatever districts, are run by boards without separately elected executives. This is also true of those cities (about 2,000) and counties (fewer than 30) which have opted for the so-called council-manager plan. These boards and councils may sometimes reveal stronger patterns of coherence and "party solidarity" than legislative bodies elsewhere in the United States. But in almost every instance one or more of the members have achieved considerable individual prominence before joining it and use their membership to enhance that personal prominence. Only on the rarest occasions do these groups submerge such individuals into patterns resembling parliamentary government.

Paralleling their extension of the federal principle to the extreme of creating a plethora of special purpose authorities, the American people extended the principle of separation of powers by creating, with truly perverse abandon and at every level of their governmental system, independent commissions. Their responsibilities are enormous, diverse, overlapping, but always fragmentary. Each commission represents the separation of some fraction of executive power and responsibility and the entrusting of it to a semi-autonomous agency.

Think of the enormous responsibilities assigned — separately — to such widely known agencies as the Federal Communications Commission, the Interstate Commerce Commission, the Federal Reserve Board, and the rest of the independent regulatory commissions of the federal government. Think also of the large and extraordinary blend of administrative and quasi-judicial functions so long assigned, again separately, to the Atomic Energy Commission. But think too of the way in which the all-important local government function of planning is broken up in the typical suburban community between the town board itself, an independently appointed director of planning, a zoning board of appeals, and, most importantly, a planning board. The powers and responsibilities of this board are real and important. Its members, exactly in pattern with the distant federal models, are appointed for relatively long, staggered terms to ensure "independence" and "freedom from politics," to ensure impartial service to "the public interest." But think finally of the real effect of all this fragmentation of executive authority upon the American political system. Wholly apart from the dubious supposition that these commissions perform their avowed function of removing important administrative processes from "politics," their real effect is to reinforce the tendency of American politics towards the individualization of political power.

This effect can be observed vividly in the commissions themselves. As politically embodied in their individually appointed members, they obviously are individualized. Many commissions may have members who work harmoniously as coherent groups. If so, such harmony and group coherence are the product of skillfully contrived agreement among the members, never of policy imposed by an outside and publicly responsible master. More often commission memberships are divided, this way on one issue, that way on another, as each of the members jockeys and bargains in behalf of his personal sense of interest and mission. On the other hand, the original executive authorities from whom these commissions have been hived away are left with diminished responsibilities and powers. And they are increasingly isolated by the need to do what they can with what they have left in their own behalf.

The Madisonian doctrine of separation of powers has been extended, in fact or in effect, through every level of America's political institutions. There has been a radical dispersion of power assigned in bits and pieces to a host of individual officers. But once again, this is not the end of the long, long story. Any principle so systematically applied and extended, especially when allied to the principle of federalism, will have impact far beyond the immediate area. In two major areas the individualization of power in the nation's formal political institutions has had a consistent, shattering, scattering, mirror impact. The first is the nation's governmental bureaucracies, and the second, the political interest groups which, while privately operated, actively attempt to influence the administration of government activities in a wide variety of ways.

Bureaucracies are normally thought of as organized in decisively hierarchical patterns, and in form all American federal, State, and local bureaucracies are so structured. The hierarchical pinnacle is nominally occupied by some chief executive, whether president, governor, mayor, town supervisor, or council. But it is precisely the pinnacles of governmental authority that separation of powers has most thoroughly fractured. As a consequence, legislative bodies, themselves effectively headless, especially in Washington, lose their memberships in frantic and highly individualized competition with the nominal executive authorities for control of the bureaucratic apparatus. But their aim is to "control" not the "government" but those particular portions of special interest to this or that particular legislator. And this lateral penetration of the bureaucracy by legislators is duplicated by the urgent activities of representatives from other governments in the system, of the private interest groups, and of elements of the bureaucracy itself working on each other.

The overall effect of these patterns is more than a flattening and scattering of bureaucratic hierarchies and the replacement of much of the formal chain-of-command structures with an intense amount of personalized back and forth activity on largely horizontal planes. Consider the effect on the attitudes of the bureaucratic officers themselves. With the identities of their effective masters hopelessly confused, many of them chart their own courses with increasing skill over the years. They act for themselves personally and for the particular agencies and clientele assembled under their sway. The autonomous power of some such men can become notorious, as in the case of J. Edgar Hoover and similar figures in various State and local jurisdictions. More typically, bureau chiefs of long standing, watching their nominal executive superiors come and go over the years as electoral fortunes ebb and flow, quietly become men to be independently reckoned with. We must add to the long list of "barons" in the American political system a large but indefinite number of bureaucratic officers who have accumulated some bit of power in their own right.

Also to be included on that list are a large number of private figures — persons who, while usually holding no position in government at all, can nevertheless greatly influence government activity through their leadership of private interest groups. Once again, these persons cannot be thought to bear massed banks of private power down on the centers of public authority. The private interest groups of America, however powerful in aggregate, are as scattered and personalized in their leaderships as the governmental structures they seek to influence, and the prime reason for this is the dispersion and individualization of power in the political system itself. Some of the private interest groups have massive sounding names, such as the National Association of Manufacturers or the AFL–CIO, but such organizations are in fact umbrella structures, loose confederations of autonomous individual units. Rarely can they wield the full force of their whole membership in a unified effort. As a rule, the elements of such confederations have long since established their own on-going relationships with such portions and personalities of the total governmental apparatus as concern them individually. These relationships depend on who the leaders happen to be. Once again, the overriding rule of American politics holds true, and when the government deals with some one of America's interest groups, the process goes forward best when baron meets and deals with baron. This is as much the case when an aircraft manufacturing company wants to renegotiate a contract with the Department

of Defense, or a broadcasting company wants to renew its
license, as it is when a labor union wishes favorable intervention in some dispute by the NLRB; or a foundation applies for
tax-exempt status with the IRS; or some private group, working
through a congressman, seeks a change in the law or its application by an administrative agency.

This survey of the general character of the American political system as a constitutional system modified by practice has
put us in a position to summarize the major characteristics of
a political "baron." The term was first applied to the president
but is now being applied to almost any figure of importance in
or to the American political process. In this light, barons have
three major characteristics.

A baron is an independent political personality. He may
or may not be a member of a political party. If he is, that fact
will have a particular significance to be weighed along with
much other information about his various organization memberships and social and political relationships. The point of the
matter is that if he is a baron of more than casual significance,
whatever party membership he may have will be useful to him
only as it enhances or at least protects his personal stature. At
no time does a baron, whether president or sheriff, let his party
membership submerge him into the anonymity of mere party
worker. In its Madisonian, operative aspects, American politics
is personality politics. Only in myth is it a politics of party and
party contests.

As a personality, what is important about a baron is who
he is, what is his name, where did he come from, who are his
friends, what does he owe them and they him, what are his
talents, what is his present status, what has he done, and what
can he do? Above all, how clearly does he see his own opportunities in other men's needs?

The baron's identity, its history and its prospects, his expectations, and those others have for him are crucial. The
personalized character of this identity is heightened by the
second major characteristic of a baron: he must have a bailiwick, a political base upon which to stand as a political personality. Usually, but not always, this is centered in the office(s)
he holds, especially as his holding that office is seen in the long
term. The office is important in the first place because through
it the baron acquires the formal power to do something about

government activity. But possession of particular office is if anything more important for the way it focuses and defines the baron's identity as a political actor, as an official member of America's political elite, as part of the baronage. Out of office a baron drops rapidly from the sight of the general public; he also slips off the round of activity which before filled his life with his brother barons. They may still feel a strong personal loyalty to him, but meanwhile they must deal with his successor.

Extending outward around the baron's office, his political base will include his personal entourage, his clientele, and his "public." The different ways he relates to these different groups are matters of supreme importance to an understanding of American politics. We will discuss them in due course. But first, the third characteristic of an American political baron: as a part of the political system major or minor, national, state, or local, he is encaged by it. In fact, the cage was built for him so that somewhere within it he could have, keep, and use a bit of power in his "personal problem" without disturbing social stability as a whole.

THE RULES OF THE GAME

Perhaps a million encaged persons of power, some nationally prominent, most hardly known outside their particular jurisdictions, some located centrally in the system, others on its furthest fringes, are the barons of American politics. That the political system requires each to exercise a separate political will, while at the same time placing them within a sharply limiting, intricately constructed system of laws and conventions, forces on each of them the role of contestants in a game.

As distinct from a game, the objective of a task — domestic chore, surgical procedure, or engineering job — is to complete the work in the most efficient way commensurate with achieving a satisfactory result. In a game, however, contestants vie to *win* within a contrived situation defined by the rules of the game. There are tasks which the American political system is expected to perform, work defined by historic and contemporary commitments. But the Aristotelian/Madisonian/Americanized Constitution has turned the performance of these tasks, for the barons who operate the system, into a game, just as a parent anxious to get little children to eat might call out, "Let's see who can finish first!" Such is the inevitable result of the radical individualization of power.

In the context of the Protestant-Bourgeois heritage, the American political system requires its barons to play two games in varying combinations and often with much overlapping and stress. One game is what the barons play with their "publics" in their respective bases of support. The archetypal player of this game is clearly the president, the name of the game is "democracy," and it will be discussed at length in the next chapter. Senators and members of the House of Representatives are consummate players of the other game, by which the political system operates as a governmental process. It is mostly a private game played by the barons amongst themselves with, or on behalf of, their various clienteles. Its essence is the same "avaricious transactionism" that we found earlier at the core of Locke's Liberalism.

The rules by which the barons play their version of avaricious transactionism within the constitutional structure of American politics cover three related areas: the baron as a personality type, the nature of the political process the barons operate, and the payoffs they can expect from that process.

A recent Speaker of the House of Representatives, a man whose long career demonstrated that this office can be the single most powerful baronial office in the political system, not excepting even the presidency, is quoted as having told a younger colleague that in Washington politics, "To get along, go along." Encapsulated in this maxim is the notion that the successful baron must be an agreeable and approachable fellow. More profoundly it assumes, with good warrant, that to advance his own interests and those of his political base every baron will need help. Given the complexity and longevity of even the simplest political process in American government, that help must come from many sources and be forthcoming over a long period of time. But given also the massive individualization and horizontal character of American politics, not even a Speaker of the House of Representatives can command that it be supplied. It must be begged, borrowed, or perhaps stolen. In any event, it must be arranged for — and paid for — sooner or later, one way or another.

Practicing this kind of wisdom is not easy. Politicians are actors on the public stage and few of them avoid developing proportionate egos. In the American Bourgeois environment that sense of their own importance must be still further enlarged. Added to this is the isolation the political system invariably imposes upon them. Too, while the contests among America's political barons are fierce, prizes so endlessly divided become suprisingly small. Finally, the atmosphere in which bargaining and contesting is conducted is one of sustained cynicism and hard-learned distrust, especially of allies. Yet for all this, the ideal performer in the primary game of American politics remains the genial, agreeable fellow, always ready to spot an advantage, find an ally, help a friend, close a deal, and ". . . go along."

Although the successful American political baron's personality has been described in detail in many canny novels, it is rarely revealed in the daily press. But it does happen. The governor of New York State recently attempted to impose his own choice for mayoral candidate on the local leaders of his party in the city of New York. The governor was exceptionally powerful, the local leaders relatively weak. But by American standards, the governor's action was an extreme affront to local autonomy and was resisted strenuously, in a struggle which forced the whole scrabble into public view for a few days. Among other things, newspaper stories developed around the personalities of the governor's local protagonists, men otherwise unknown to the public. One of these men was especially interesting. Of the lot, he was the oldest, most experienced, and most successful. He was on intimate terms not only with the principal figures of his own party throughout the State, including the governor himself, but also with all the leaders of the notoriously strife-ridden alternative parties in the State. However fraught with political implications and connotations, all these relationships were truly personal ones. The man really *was* everybody's friend. To underline this point, it was recorded that he had a conversational habit of addressing all his colleagues without distinction, from the governor on down, by the single appellation, "Sweetheart!" More significantly, the man had the habit of invariably ending his conversations with his many friends with the phrase, "Ya owe me one."

The political process conducted by the barons is complex.

Such close observers of it as novelists, biographers, and journalists all report that what matters in the American political
process, as much at the local as at the national level, is the
intricacy of its detail. Good barons have good memories, sharp
eyes, and careful psychological imaginations. Who said what to
whom? What debts remain uncollected? What can tempt whom
to do what? These are the important questions. The broad
ideological or philosophical ones almost never come up. The
American political process is an endless, intricate, intercon-
nected negotiation among busy, self-willed, self-interested
barons, each going his own way while the whole complex
process slouches forward from one day to the next. His im-
mersion in this kind of world requires the baron to be an
agreeable fellow at least in appearance, easy to work with,
tough but compromising, ever ready to go on, one meeting to
the next.

The meetings barons attend are the structural points of the
political process. First there are all the formal meetings, sessions
of Congress, of its committees and subcommittees, meetings of
the president's cabinet, the National Security Council, policy-
making sessions of bureaucratic councils, executive sessions of
the great commissions, and similar meetings all up and down
the State and local government scenes. But the good baron will
regard these formal governmental meetings differently than an
ordinary citizen. The baron will respect such meetings when he
has an interest at stake in them or fears their possible outcome.
But he will do his best to reduce them to "mere formalities."
He prepares rigorously for them in advance, and after them he
moves swiftly to follow up his advantages well before reaching
the next formal hurdle.

The skillful baron prepares for, recovers from, and follows
up formal meetings by participating in a very much larger
number of informal meetings, caucuses of interested parties
held before and after the formal meetings. The persons who
attend these caucuses are diverse. Imagine the history of a bill
going through Congress. The first caucuses about it, those in
which the bill takes form as a simple proposal, may well not
include any members of Congress at all. Most bills nowadays
originate in the bureaucracy and probably grow out of some
interaction between bureau chiefs and the professional lobby-
ists of private interest groups or State and local government

figures. But even when a serious proposal is ready for pre-liminary drafting at this level, the approach to Congress may still be delayed while the White House and other groups are sounded out. Just as often the White House is not approached until after a foothold for the bill has been well mortared in the legislature. Equally, the decision whether to seek general sup-port from the public through the national and/or selected local press must be taken carefully. Due thought is given to whether certain persons and groups are to be enlisted in the cause, neutralized, ignored, or boldly confronted. It must be stressed that often enough, depending on the subject of the proposed legislation, what "the public" thinks or could be made to think is simply irrelevant to the calculations of those trying to push the bill forward.

A long, long trail awaits a proposed bill before it is actually passed into law over the signature (or not) of the president. Its application or misapplication through the admin-istrative process is equally complex, to say nothing of possi-ble involvement with the judicial process. Surveying the whole political policy-making process, we notice a number of other important features of the practical world of baronial politics. A most significant element is the constant interaction between the formal meetings, with their designated memberships and defined authority, and the informal caucuses, with their diverse, often confused memberships recalling floating crap games. Especially in meetings of the latter sort, there is a constant need for compromise, both "additive," as allies are "bought in," and "subtractive," as opponents are "bought off." Moreover, the fluidity and *ad hoc* quality of the process must be apparent throughout. In this kind of world, a proposed bill might evolve over the months into something quite different, so much so that the original sponsors drop away, to be replaced by quite different interests. In the same light the fluid, flattened charac-ter of the process means that one project's development spills over into the stories of others. And there will be constant inter-mingling, especially in the caucuses, of legislative and execu-tive interests and of national, state, local, and private group interests. But however fluid the whole process is, it unfolds within the overall structure of the political system. To satisfy this requirement, the American political game has been con-strained to develop the principle of "concurrent majority."

This doctrine holds, first, that in the development of any project all relevant interests must be consulted. It holds, second, that if it becomes clear that the project threatens adversely the *vital* interests of any one of the participants, then that participant may veto the whole project. This doctrine clearly reflects the two prime realities upon which the American political process is built: that the community as a political whole is splintered permanently into a multiplicity of diverse, self-centered, and self-activating interests, and that no grouping of these interests can or should be allowed to "tyrannize" over any of the rest. This doctrine so clearly epitomizes the nature and mood of the American political process that it is worthwhile to quote from John C. Calhoun's original formulation of it.

> . . . To prevent any one interest or combination of interests from using the powers of government to aggrandize itself at the expense of the others . . . [there must be adopted] . . . some restriction or limitation which shall so effectually prevent any one interest or combination of interests from obtaining the exclusive control of the government as to render hopeless all attempts directed to that end. There is, again, but one mode in which this can be effected, and that is by taking the sense of each interest or portion of the community which may be unequally and injuriously affected by the action of the government separately, through its own majority or in some other way by which its voice may be fairly expressed, and to require the consent of each interest either to put or to keep the government in action. This, too, can be accomplished only in one way, and that is by such an organism of the government — and, if necessary for the purpose, of the community also — as will, by dividing and distributing the powers of government, give to each division or interest, through its appropriate organ, either a concurrent voice in making and executing the laws or a veto on their execution.[2]

The notion that Calhoun was an aberrant, sectional spokesman for a South that would see its principles dashed by the force of arms collapses before the revelations in this, the most important single paragraph he wrote. All the fundamentals of Aristotelian Madisonianism and of the spirit in which the Americans have put those fundamentals to work are here. Calhoun wrote as an American politician, as a baron in behalf

2. *A Disquisition on Government,* ed. C. G. Post, Liberal Arts Press, N.Y., 1963, p. 20.

of his bailiwick, and he said no more than any other baron would who had the wit and analytic power to articulate his needs. His proposals for a dual presidency would have done no more to that office than what Madison had succeeded in doing to the legislature in 1789. Moreover, Calhoun himself recognized that "sections" are divisible into all kinds of internal rivalries and attain an apparent unity only in the face of external threat. If he had carried his analysis further, he would have seen what perhaps only our modern homogeneous culture now makes plain, that American politics is neither sectional nor "interest group" politics, but a personality politics in which barons can seek support in every corner and crevice.

Nevertheless, even the doctrine of concurrent majority, the fundamental rule of the Bourgeois game of avaricious transactionism, is not uniformly observed. It is a norm, but departures in actual political practice are widespread. Instead of open politics almost to the point of participatory democracy, which the doctrine clearly calls for, much of American baronial politics is exclusionary, secretive, even conspiratorial. Moreover, despite much propaganda to the effect that they are all "professionals," barons often fail in their various projects, go to jail in droves, and are otherwise banished from political life. They do not always play by the rules, and often as not they pay penalties accordingly.

One important reason for these failures is the very difficulty of baronial politics. Just as it is hard to constantly be an agreeable fellow, is it hard for an American baron to touch every base in developing a project. On occasion, even to try might be to court disaster. Often the best possible strategy may be to bypass affected parties until a *fait accompli* has been achieved. And then even the best possible strategies may not work. And, finally, American politicians are no smarter or courageous on the average than other humans. Stupidity, ignorance, and cowardice appear in American politics just as in human events generally.

But there are other reasons for the high incidence of baronial failure in American politics. These arise from the nature of the payoffs which the system puts the barons to seeking. Most startling, perhaps, is that failure itself is one of the probable payoffs, something that the logic of the system presumes will happen to a majority. Baronial politics is in some ways like a game of musical chairs in which only a relatively few players are able to stay in for a long period of time. For every long-term city boss, for every octogenarian congressman who has been in the House since before most of the rest of us were born, for every senator and governor who makes it back term after term, for every career politician who has climbed over the years from one office to the next toward the biggest baronies of all, there are countless others, little known and quickly forgotten, who have had their careers prematurely halted by losing a critical election or failing to pick up a sustaining bureaucratic appointment. This is an inevitable consequence of the individualized and competitive character of the system. But it etches a truth in the minds of every baron. As one of them is reputed to have said, "Winning isn't everything, but losing isn't anything."

Another source of baronial failure, even more directly related to the payoffs the American political system and its underlying Bourgeois ethos set the barons to seeking, is corruption. How prevalent corruption is in American government is impossible to say with precision. Incidents recounted in newspaper stories about government officers found guilty of corruption can be safely multiplied, through the same reasoning that convinces farmers that for every rat they see there are ten more concealed. One can guess with confidence that while American government may not be as corrupt as that of Liberia, for example, it is very much more corrupt than the governments of Britain and the Scandinavian countries.

More interesting is the analytic evidence suggesting that generalized corruption in American government is virtually inevitable in the light of the nature of its political processes and their underlying Bourgeois ethos.

The problem begins with the fact that the Aristotelian/ Madisonian Constitution puts as its first presumption the notion that political operatives are corruptible and dangerous. That is why they have to be encaged. The act of encagement presumes the energy and motive to lawlessness. The consequence of this kind of thinking is that Madison's basic principle of constitutional engineering, "The interest of the man must be connected with the constitutional rights of the place," is the virtual equivalent of a dictionary definition of corruption as "the violation of a public trust," or "the use of public office for personal advantage." The end result for the barons, in their daily operation of the system, is that they cannot define in moral, qualitative terms the difference between a corrupt act and a legitimate one. Avaricious transactionism is the name of the game.

These considerations are greatly reinforced by the Bourgeois ethos which sustains the system and sets its general tone and objectives. In Bourgeois life, economics articulated in monetary terms is the central mode. A parallel political life will inevitably ingest the same mode, and money will become in some degree the medium of exchange in both. The assumptions of the political system say that no politician will act unless tempted by an appeal to his interest; in the language of economics, he must be bought. Can there be any wonder that in American political life, rooted as deeply as it is in American economic life, the price that will move a politician is so often set in cash?

The validity of this analysis of the origins of American governmental corruption can be seen in two ways. For all its prevalence, corruption does not seem to threaten the stability of the system. When it becomes truly rampant, as it has many times in various cities, there may be a perceptible drop in the efficiency with which public services are provided, with consequent public outcry and eventual replacement of regimes. But in none of these cases has the nature or the stability of the system's structure been challenged, a fact that should impress those political scientists who make stability the hallmark of good government. In fact, such stability is a kind of marvel in the light of what is known about the large-scale subversion of local government law enforcement authorities all across the country by syndicated criminal elements in defense of gambling, prostitution, and narcotics operations. The only possible explanation of marvels of this order is that they are not marvels after all, but ordinary events. We should reverse our usual thinking about corruption in American government. It is not a force burrowing from without. It is the system expressing its real inner logic. Avaricious transactionism is working well when *everyone* who matters is getting his piece of the pie.

The other way of demonstrating the validity of our analysis of corruption is to note how the system moves against those whom it chooses to punish for corruption. Such moves are usually made tardily, hesitantly, even spasmodically, and are almost always accompanied by torrents of rhetorical exaggeration about the evils being uncovered. The barons do not move decisively against one of their number for ordinary, everyday corruption. If one is to be convicted and politically ruined, it must be for outrageous crimes, for having finally gone "too far." Reflection suggests what the point is that spells "too far." When the offending conduct is so extensive and blatant that it at last appears to threaten, not public morals but the cage itself, and the sense of confinement that restrains all the rest of the barons, a line is crossed. An "impeachable offense" is bad conduct that looks as though it might break up the game.

Even so, the penalties the system imposes upon the corrupt are extraordinarily mild. By ideal standards, it might seem that corruption is one of the most dastardly of public crimes, outright treason against the public order. But American barons hesitate to do more than push corrupt fellows off the field. Vice-President Agnew's conduct was egregious. But he resigned, pleaded *nolo contendere* to one count of tax evasion, and drove away from the courthouse in a government limousine with secret service protection (which he continued to use, along with much governmental office support, for months thereafter). Implicitly the prosecution accepted his defense, that he had merely followed prevailing custom in his systematic acceptance of bribes and that his only crime was to have been caught. He had "gone too far" beyond the edge of the cage and had been caught outside.

It may seem perverse to conduct a discussion of what the barons expect from their participation in American politics with such emphasis on the negative payoffs. But in the perspective of their lives, of their chances as they calculate their futures, the emphasis must be on the dangers, the sudden halts, the uncomfortable exposures. If mishaps do not occur, what does the American political system hold out for the barons? What can they "win?" At best a comfortable life, material rewards in good measure, and ample ego embellishments. There may also be guilts of the sort reviewed in the next chapter. Nevertheless, unless they "go too far" as barons in a Bourgeois world, they should be all right.

More specifically, if they leave taking initiatives largely to others and are content to push along within reasonable limits, they will get a share of what is going. These days, there is a lot going. The broad policy objectives set by the mythic heroes — to hold back communism, salvage the dollar, combat mental illness, succor the poor, employ the unemployable, stamp out poverty, cure drug addiction, blast crime in the streets — will require more or less comprehensive programs of bureaucratic action. Best of all are programs to send men to the moon, prepare the national defense establishment for wars never fought, and build highways from here to there (alternatively, restore railways from there to here). All these programs and hundreds like them require huge amounts of money to set up this training program, to conduct that study, and above all to let out this, that, and another contract — all to friends owed or to be made. The goals are general, and may even do a little good. Much more to the point, so far as the barons are concerned, the deals have been made, the favors tendered, the debts collected (or held over), and the whole process of baronial life, negotiating and developing through caucus and meeting and caucus again, has inched forward from this day to tomorrow.

This analysis of the life and labors of America's political barons will end with an example that pulls together many of the points made throughout the chapter and puts special emphasis on one in particular, the negative notion that American government is not "responsible" government. This emphasis will be useful in moving from the present chapter on the operative realities of American government to the next, which deals with its hopes.

In 1946 Congress passed and the president signed into law the so-called Employment Act. The act has been hailed as belated recognition by the American federal government of what has become a commonplace among other governments of modern industrial nations, that "full" employment is a reasonable objective even for "free," capitalist societies, that the problems involved are as much political as economic, and that national governments must accept responsibility for "managing" their economies to ensure that full employment is reached and maintained. The act's somewhat fulsome rhetoric to these points is significant.

It is the continuing policy and responsibility of the Federal Government to use all practicable means consistent with its needs and obligations and other essential considerations of national policy, with the assistance and cooperation of industry, agriculture, labor, and state and local governments, to coordinate and utilize all its plans, functions, and resources for the purpose of creating and maintaining, in a manner calculated to foster and promote free competitive enterprise and the general welfare, conditions under which there will be afforded employment, for those able, willing, and seeking to work, and to promote maximum employment, production, and purchasing power.[3]

To accept a responsibility meaningfully presupposes at least the possibility of discharging it, however well or ill. But the most important "machinery" the act created was a Council of Economic Advisers located in the Executive Office of the president. This council at least gave full employment to three economists. More seriously, it focused ill-founded hopes on the presidential office. For the plain fact of the matter is that the American federal government lacks almost all meaningful capacity to "manage" the American economy.

There are well-known levers by which well informed governments willing to plan and coordinate their actions can influence, even "manage," free economies, and many foreign governments attempt to do so, though they may not succeed. But a review of these levers in the American context shows, first, that authority to regulate the supply of money and interest rates is divided between the Treasury and the Federal Reserve Board. Both jealously defend their independence of each other; both are subject to a wide variety of conflicting pressures. Moreover, these matters can be strongly influenced by other agencies of the government over which the Treasury and Federal Reserve Board have only distant control. Second, changes in tax policies, which should be taken sharply and comprehensively to be effective, require action by Congress. In the past this process has taken years, often for reasons remote from issues of national economic management. Finally, control over the federal government's spending programs, both as to overall size and as to patterns of spending, is gross at best, despite the efforts of the president's Office of Management and Budget. And to suggest that the federal government might control the spending programs of all the State and local authorities across the country is to speak the final absurdity. The sum

3. Quoted in S. K. Bailey, *Congress Makes a Law*, Columbia University Press, New York, 1950, p. 243.

of the situation is that from time to time the federal government can and does give the national economy a well-placed and powerful shove. Quite apart from the question of whether the motives for such shoves might bear economic inspection, scattered shovings are a long way from "management of the economy." The American (eighteenth-century, Bourgeois-Liberal, Madisonian) Constitution was designed for very different objectives, and therefore it is nonsensical to hold it "responsible" for performing such modern tasks as managing the national economy.

The 1946 Employment Act demonstrates the non-responsible character of the American political system in another way even more germane to this book's main arguments. The story of how that act was passed, a "narrative [that] has no real beginning and no clear ending," has been told in exhaustive detail in one of the classics of American political science, S. K. Bailey's *Congress Makes a Law*. Everything is there, how and by whom the first proposals were developed and in response to what pressures, how senators and congressmen were drawn in, the role played by the president, various bureaucrats, and private interest groups. The story demonstrates that the passage of this bill was a classic example of "incrementalism" in legislative policy making, although in this instance the "increments" gradually rendered what was at the start a moderately strong bill into an admittedly weak bill, after many intervals in which it came perilously close to being no bill at all. But the most interesting feature of Bailey's book is the conclusion he himself draws from his tale. He asks who was responsible for the bill's passage, and then ticks off the possible answers.

Certainly President Truman cannot be held responsible. . . .

The political parties cannot be held responsible, except in the negative sense that their weakness made irresponsibility inevitable. . . .

Can responsibility be placed on the pressure groups? Not in any meaningful political sense. . . .

Who remains? The individual Senators and Congressmen?[4]

Bailey absolves even them. His final conclusion about the passage of the bill is that:

. . . legislative policymaking tends to be fought out at the level of largely irresponsible personal and group strategems and compromises

4. *Ibid.*, pp. 237–238.

based upon temporary power coalitions of political, administrative, and non-governmental interests. . . .

Put in its baldest form, the story of S. 380 adds up to the fact that majority sentiment expressed in popular elections for a particular economic policy can be, and frequently is, almost hopelessly splintered by the power struggles of competing political, administrative and private interests, and is finally pieced together, if at all, only by the most laborious, complicated, and frequently covert coalition strategies.

. . . . the fact remains that the American voter could not and cannot hold any recognizable group, interest, or individual responsible for the Employment Act of 1946.[5]

But is Bailey bragging or complaining? In the Madisonian (Aristotelian/Bourgeois/American) perspective, a government so disconnected from the whims of the ordinary citizen could be said to qualify as ideal.

5. *Ibid.*, pp. 236–237.

DEMOCRATIC
MYTHS

EGALITARIANISM
POPULAR GOVERNMENT
PRESIDENTIAL GREATNESS

EGALITARIANISM

The second task of American government is to conceal itself from itself. Its success in this task over the years has been uneven, but sufficient. Though they are tattered and worn threadbare by calamitous events, American government still wears its myths persuasively for most of its citizens.

In our (Protestant) hearts, we know that we are not, in our actual (Bourgeois) political life, what we would like to be. Sometimes this grieves us mightily, and the air reverberates with calls for reform, even "revolution." The barons of the system can be disturbed and forced to cashier some of their number. But mostly they and other system-sustaining agencies, such as the mass media and educational institutions, react to uproars of this sort by setting out to repersuade us that we are not what we are, that the nation's actions have not defined us, that our true identity lies rather in our aspirations, our myths. This task is eased by the nation's aching need to believe. The truth about our practical greed, corruption, and political impotence in the face of social crises is repulsive; the myths are wonderfully comforting. Even the barons come to believe them, so we and they accept them again and are all happy once more with being Americans.

But believing these myths causes trouble. Deluded about ourselves, we undertake actions beyond the actual capabilities of our Madisonian political institutions. The results are worse than failure. After failure and the connected personal tragedies come mythic disillusionment, self-doubt, mutual distrust. Beyond that, often enough, comes violence, pointless, mindless, chaotic, exhausting. Myths are not just quaint beliefs and funny stories about ancient folk heroes. They are permanent, massive, functional parts of the overall political system. In some ways they are not only comforting but also ennobling. Mostly, however, being myths, they are dangerous.

Exposing political myths is not easy. They are tenaciously believed, and pinching the comfort they provide invites ridicule and anger. Nevertheless, no account of the American political system can be complete without an effort to remove its masks.

In contrast to its operative ideology, which boils down to the rules of the game played by the barons and their immediate clients, the myths of the American political system are mass phenomena. We all are compelled almost hourly to respond to their symbols and declarations. The symbols are multitudinous: flags, seals, emblems, pictures, fables, songs, slogans, ritual exercises, imposing buildings and monuments; and they appear everywhere. Then there are the speeches, sermons, editorials, and articles composed for our urgent attention, which apply the meanings of the symbols to specific situations. What we have learned, we must learn again. What we believe we must profess. We must both be and seem American, to ourselves and to each other.

Although myth and ideology are different, and although these differences are especially great in America, even in this country myth and ideology are never far apart. This is true even in the physical sense. The most apt illustration of this fact is none other than America's supreme political symbol, the Constitution itself. As we have seen, the content of this document is in essential ways antidemocratic. It represented the nation's incipient barons' plan for organizing and operating the country's operative political institutions. Whether from guilt or shrewdly perceived political need, when they offered this plan for general adoption they decked it out in the democratic costume of "We the people. . . ." They even offered it as the symbol and definition of national unity and identity. The offer was readily accepted, and to this day the nation, with extraordinary misunderstanding of the principles it contains, treasures the document as a sacred relic. It is sealed, guarded, and protected by every conceivable technological device, especially during the dark hours of night, as if it were the Holy Grail itself.

America's political myths are largely Protestant in origin because Protestantism has been locked into Bourgeois life as its conscience. But surprisingly, the myths that conceal but challenge our daily practice are still, despite a growing universal secularism, expressed largely in the language and images of nineteenth century Protestantism's King James version of the Bible, with a predominant emphasis on the Old Testament. That book may not be as familiar to us as it was to our grandfathers. But because it was so very familiar to them, and because they built its tongue into the political thinking they bequeathed to us, the Bible's imprint is strongly upon us even as we cease to read its text.

Noticing that American political myths often imitate Biblical forms makes it simpler to make out their shape as coherent wholes among the symbols and declarations in which they are expressed. For analytic purposes the major myths of American politics can be grouped under the following heads: first, the myth that the American people have been chosen out of history to reveal a great truth, humanistic egalitarianism (this might be called the identity or covenant myth); second, that the American people have congregated into a progressive democracy dedicated to the achievement of truth and justice both at home and abroad (this might be called the crusade myth); and third, the myth that the American people have been led in times of crisis into transcendence and tragedy by heroes, their "great" presidents, and that such men will come among them again (this might be called the savior myth).

We will analyze each of these myths as mass phenomena characteristically expressed in modes with a strong Biblical flavor, especially the first and the third. And we will relate each myth to those aspects of the operative political system which it conceals.

The myth that the American nation is a congregation of humanistic egalitarians consists of two parts, one formal, that we are a unified national community, and the other substantive, that what unifies us is the commitment to humanistic egalitarianism. The second of these parts took root at the outset of the colonial experience. Every father came here with the conviction that in this new world was a new life, an unsullied opportunity for himself and for his son to express personal potential and faith. This was as true for the Puritan divine as it was for the ordinary commercial adventurer, and it can be supposed true even for the indentured servant. With perseverence and faith, all hopes could be realized. Only blacks and Indians, the first because enslaved as a beast, the second because slaughtered or driven off the land, remained untouched by the dream of expressing ego's will. And we have been taught to believe that what men believed for themselves, their women believed also, if not for themselves then at least for their men.

At this level, the interaction between myth and operative ideology is so close that the two elements are almost indistin-

guishable, and they are powerful in mutual reinforcement.
Bouyed by faith and confident in the doctrine of the priesthood
of all believers, the self marched forth to test the moral fiber of
the soul in Liberalism's marketplace and to return with a just, if
material, reward. From Franklin's *Almanacs* through the Horatio
Alger stories, "The Message to Garcia," and beyond, personal
Protestant morality and Bourgeois avarice intertwined to make
up the core sense of American self-identity.

   Nevertheless self-doubt, telltale sign of incomplete synthesis and tension, was apparent almost from the start. In 1774,
the First Continental Congress declared:

> That the inhabitants of the English Colonies in North America, by
> the immutable laws of nature, the principles of the English constitu-
> tion, and the several charters or compacts, have the following rights:
>   . . . That they are entitled to life, liberty, and property. . . .[1]

Tactfully, less than two years later, the Declaration of Independence changed the last word to "happiness."

   How tact could be served by such a change is a question
we should press. This tact concealed a contradiction in the
developing American political mind which no one was willing
to face or to modify by de-emphasizing one or the other of its
polarities.

   On the one hand, in the years before the break with the
mother country, the leading colonists wished to define and
defend what they had, a society in which relatively large numbers of men, especially those with something in the way of a
preliminary material start, had enjoyed extraordinary practical
freedom to exploit the available economic opportunities in
agriculture and commerce. But because of its very liberality,
this kind of society generated and magnified inequalities, first
in wealth and then in social status, cultural benefits, and leisure.
Such inequalities were visible proof of personal success. If all
were to win equally, who could say he had won at all?

   On the other hand, when the break with Britain came the
Americans were compelled to assert a different principle. To
establish a plane of argument with the mother country, egalitarianism was essential. So, reaching back to the "spirit" of the
American provincial (Protestant) experience, they declared
themselves in good conscience the equal of the British sover-

1. *Journal of the Continental Congress, 1774–1789*, Washington, 1904, p. 64.

eign and of all other men, too. This was, of course, a "self-
evident" truth. It had to be. All the factual evidence contradicted it.

Jefferson claimed that in writing the Declaration in 1776,
he intended it "to be an expression of the American mind."[2]
But its enunciation of egalitarianism was neither a description
of the facts nor a goal for political action. The economic, social,
and political distance separating the Hudson River patroon
from the black field slave in Georgia, considering the elevation
of the former and the degradation of the latter, was as extreme
as anything known in Europe. That fact stands, even if a disproportionate number of American white males were of the
typically provincial, middling sort. Moreover before the Revolution, during it, and in the years following it, there existed no
concerted and widely supported plan for doing anything about
the new country's economic, political, and social extremes, let
alone black slavery. Egalitarianism represented the "mind" of
America rhetorically, not in any operational sense. Operationally, in those early days, the guiding lights of the nation were
exclusively libertarians.

Yet it cannot be denied that these same men "believed" in
egalitarianism. They also believed that their commitment to
this doctrine most marked them off from the European societies
where systems of honor and privilege were imposed. It seemed
to all that the spirit of democratic egalitarianism truly made
America a "new" nation. There could be no more backing off
from this commitment of selfhood than there could be from
the opportunities of a free, competitive economy. Hence the
Declaration, a proclamation as much of identity as of independence, tactfully drew the veil over a Liberal society's
inequality and put on instead the mythic mark of "happiness"
and egalitarianism.

The myth that the truth of egalitarianism was specially revealed to the Americans has become the basic political myth of
the nation. It asserts that our society is alive with a spirit of
equality of the sort Tocqueville noted:

In America, where the privileges of birth never existed, and where
riches confer no peculiar rights on their possessors, men unacquainted

2. In a letter to Richard H. Lee (1825) quoted by Carl Becker, The Declaration of Independence (1942), Vintage Books, New York, 1958, p. 26.

with each other are very ready to frequent the same places, and find neither peril nor advantage in the free interchange of their thoughts. If they meet by accident, they neither seek nor avoid intercourse; their manner is therefore natural, frank, and open; it is easy to see that they hardly expect or apprehend anything from each other, and that they do not care to display, any more than to conceal, their position in the world. If their demeanor is often cold and serious, it is never haughty or constrained; and if they do not converse, it is because they are not in a humor to talk, not because they think it their interest to be silent.[3]

As a European of aristocratic background, Tocqueville was startled by the egalitarianism he observed in American manners. As twentieth century Americans looking back on what he said, we can argue that he exaggerated what he saw. But there is no denying the fact of what he saw or the perceptiveness, almost clairvoyance, of his reportage. In their egalitarianism, Americans had become a certain kind of people. Neither pretentious nor servile, the Americans, at least in manners, had become open, friendly, and natural. The evidence now is even stronger: in self-image, Americans are trusting, loving, and generous to a fault.

This evidence (alongside all that contradicts it) is everywhere. We are a nation of givers, and private charity (tax deductible) is for many a way of life. We are also a nation of joiners, especially of clubs which exclude all except our own kind. And our soldiers, symbols of the nation's highest commitments, give chewing gum to the urchins of the world, before and after "protecting" them and their families with weapons of advanced technological design.

The most persuasive evidence of the American self-image, however, is to be found in the field of commercial advertising. Working in this field are men and women of outstanding acumen and sensitivity. They are acutely conscious of the need to address their work to the aspirations of potential customers, to what we all would like to have and be, and to how we like to think of ourselves. In the images of ourselves which they spread before our wanton eyes in TV commercials, advertising copy in the press, and elsewhere, we appear healthy, beautiful, and virtuous. More subtly, we are portrayed as cheerful, afflu-

3. *Democracy in America*, ed. R. D. Heffner, Mentor, New York, 1956, p. 222.

ent, gregarious, trusting, loving, and generous. This is ironic, for those who portray us thus are straining every artifice and talent, every resource and sinew, to manipulate us into actions that will bring them personal profit. It is all outrageous flattery. But the advertisers know their targets, and there is no more irony in their endeavors to reach them than in the law which requires "In God We Trust" to appear on our money of all places, both paper and coin.

The great myth of American friendly egalitarianism, which most conceals what it most contradicts, an avaricious transactionism breeding every kind of suspicion and inequality, came to the nation by national presupposition and direct teaching. We were and are egalitarians immediately. But as the nineteenth century progressed, especially in the wake of the Civil War, egalitarianism came to be seen more and more as the content of a desperately craved national unity. The Declaration had dealt with the principle by stating it as a philosophical truth. Now it was seen coming to us, as in Biblical stories, through a shared baptismal experience in a clearly delineated national and historical context. Our truth was revealed to us in and by our Exodus, and our Exodus across the oceanic voids and through the hard years of continental development prepared us as a nation for our truth. From scholarly tome to the most childish of toddler's history books, the facts and stories were knit together into the legend of how America became the first "new" nation through a sanctifying experience.

The germ of this mythic truth-through-history process was put down as early as the Revolution itself. In 1782 Crèvecoeur asked, "What then is the American, this new man?" and answered his own question.

He is an American, who, leaving behind him all his ancient prejudices and manners, receives new ones from the new mode of life he has embraced, the new government, and the new rank he holds. He becomes an American by being received in the broad lap of our great *Alma Mater.*

Here individuals of all nations are melted into a new race of men, whose labours and posterity will one day cause great changes in the world. Americans are the western pilgrims. . . .[4]

4. "Letters from an American Farmer," in *Living Ideas in America,* ed. H. S. Commager, Harper, New York, 1951, p. 20.

However, Crèvecoeur's germ was little cultivated until Civil War divisions in a horrific present put a premium on finding unity in our origins. Intellectually, the most systematic effort to find such unity to this day is Frederick Jackson Turner's so-called "Frontier Thesis."[5] Turner claimed that the nation was less divided between North and South than unified by a common experience with the western advance to the Pacific. We should notice the mythic element in Turner's account of this process.

The frontier is the line of most rapid and effective Americanization. The wilderness masters the colonist. It finds him a European in dress, industries, tools, modes of travel, and thought. It takes him from the railroad car and puts him in the birch canoe. It strips off the garments of civilization and arrays him in the hunting shirt and the moccasin. It puts him in the log cabin of the Cherokee and Iroquois and runs an Indian palisade around him. Before long he has gone to planting Indian corn and plowing with a sharp stick; he shouts the war cry and takes the scalp in orthodox Indian fashion. In short, at the frontier the environment is at first too strong for the man. He must accept the conditions which it furnishes, or perish, and so he fits himself into the Indian clearings and follows the Indian trails. Little by little he transforms the wilderness, but the outcome is not the old Europe, not simply the development of Germanic germs, any more than the first phenomenon was a case of reversion to the Germanic mark. The fact is, that here is a new product that is American.[6]

This charming passage should be read twice. Only on a second reading is it plain that its charm derives from its absurdity. Whatever became of that railroad car? Was it simply abandoned in one of the Indian clearings while its passengers went whooping into the woods? More significantly, can we seriously entertain the thought that the benighted Indian, slaughtered or driven from the land like an animal, was nevertheless some kind of parent to the developing American culture?[7] Much more could be said for the alternative hypo-

5. See the Appendix, "The Study of America."

6. *The Frontier in American History*, Holt, New York, 1920, pp. 3–4.

7. The question is rhetorical. Nevertheless Richard Slotkin, in *Regeneration Through Violence, the Mythology of the American Frontier, 1600–1860,* Wesleyan University Press, Middletown, 1973, takes an opposite view, although without reference to Turner.

thesis that the exploitation process by which American civilization advanced westward, its destruction of Indian cultures, and its land, forest, and mineral development practices are best described as rapacious Bourgeois egoism feasting with little restraint upon a rich and almost defenseless environment. But the real significance of this passage from Turner lies in how it fitted into his overall argument, an argument which did far more to respond to and foster myth than it did to further the cause of historiography.

Turner assigned a radically disproportionate influence to the frontier because he also wanted to assert that "the slavery question is [only] an incident"[8] in American history. He assigned to the frontier a constant and continuing influence in the development of American culture because he also wanted to assert that "The economic and social characteristics of the frontier worked against sectionalism."[9] Above all he assigned to the frontier a permanent and powerful influence because he wanted to assert that "the most important effect of the frontier has been in the promotion of democracy here and in Europe."[10] But the kind of democracy Turner felt the frontier had helped so greatly to develop was a very simple thing almost to be equated to mere individualism. He argued that

... the frontier is productive of individualism. Complex society is precipitated by the wilderness into a kind of primitive organization based on the family. The tendency is anti-social. It produces antipathy to control, and particularly to any direct control.[11]

Turner went on to applaud the notion that during and after the Revolution "individual liberty was sometimes confused with absence of all effective government." Or as he put it in another place,

American democracy was born of no theorist's dream; it was not carried in the Susan Constant to Virginia, nor in the Mayflower to Plymouth. It came stark and strong and full of life out of the American

8. Turner, *The Frontier in American History*, p. 24.

9. *Ibid.*, p. 27.

10. *Ibid.*, p. 30.

11. *Ibid.*, p. 30.

forest, and it gained new strength each time it touched a new frontier.[12]

The point in all this is not that Turner was wrong, though obviously he was. Actually American government is and was from the beginning an enormously complicated affair and a product of intellectual theorizing almost without parallel in the practical formation of working constitutions. The central point about Turner, however, is how powerfully he reinforced the American citizen's dream, the sacred myth that his democracy was a pure, simple thing, an absolute egalitarianism.

Turner's intellectual significance can hardly be exaggerated in any account of America's political myths. As social symbol, however, he is vastly overshadowed by other figures, and most importantly by Abraham Lincoln. The Gettysburg Address is an oracular statement of American national self-understanding by its leading prophet. It states the myth of American democratic egalitarianism in all its fullness, without a trace of distortion, and incidentally in a profoundly biblical form. The Address is a replica in exact detail of an ancient Hebraic covenant renewal ceremony, and given the predominance of Bible reading in nineteenth century America, this derivation made the Address not only a speech to the American people but also a powerful prophetic testament on their behalf.

From the Address's very first words, Lincoln adopted the Hebraic style of total reliance on shared memory in the search for the meaning of events. Others might argue in syllogisms. Lincoln, much like Hosea recalling when "Israel was a child," conjured up national beginnings and the authority of the patriarchs. And what he claimed them to have done was not the discovery of truths but the commitment of the "new" nation to a covenant. The image is of Moses at Sinai in the Book of Exodus.

And he sent young men of the people of Israel, who offered burnt offerings and sacrificed peace offerings of oxen to the LORD. And Moses took half of the blood and put it in basins, and half of the blood he threw against the altar. Then he took the book of the covenant, and read it in the hearing of the people; and they said, "All that the LORD has spoken we will do, and we will be obedient." And

12. Quoted in Henry Nash Smith, *Virgin Land*, Vintage, New York, 1959, p. 295.

Moses took the blood and threw it upon the people, and said, "Behold the blood of the covenant which the LORD has made with you in accordance with all these words." (24:5–8 R.S.V.)

When Lincoln said that it was the brave men who struggled on the Gettysburg battlefield, who bled and died there, who truly "consecrated" it, he alluded, however unconsciously, to the symbolism which blood had for the Hebraic imagination. Blood was life, and to be joined in blood was to be joined in life, by the most solemn of bonds, to shared memory, common experience, and a communion of anticipation.

Lincoln's central teaching becomes that by *their* sacrifice *we* are bound to their burden, that of carrying forward the test of whether "any nation so conceived and so dedicated can long endure." The words of Lincoln summon us today as strongly as they did in 1863. His image is of old Joshua, anxious to lay down his share of the load, calling together the people, recounting to them the history of Israel, and then thundering to them, "choose this day whom you will serve. . . ." (Joshua 24:15, R.S.V.)

All over America Lincoln's aspiration that this be one nation indivisible with liberty and justice for all is still recited. For the purposes of our present argument, there is rather more point than in Turner's case to showing how far off the mark of operative fact this high aspiration is. That distance is not in the mere fact that national egalitarianism is an aspiration. Aspirations, at least in the sense of intentions, are the stuff of all politics. Nor is there any absolute error in claiming national unity. In matters of political mind, believing is being. If we assert sincerely that we are one, then one we are. In self-image, we really are a nation dedicated to humanistic egalitarianism, and we prove the reality by the anguish we characteristically display when confronted openly with our failures. The difficulty here is that the Lincolnesque aspiration is only aspiration, mere declaration. It is myth, a whole myth, but essentially false in both its formal and its substantive aspects.

Americans believe they are one, and they are one in that belief, especially in the uniform commitment to the totality of the Liberal, Protestant-Bourgeois ethos. But the belief conceals that this very Liberalism fragments the nation into a host of competing interests and that the nation's operative Constitution both presupposes and fosters fragmentation. More directly to the present point, Lincoln asserted the ideal of national unity on the battlefield of civil war, while himself engaged in directing an effort to restore national union in law by force of arms and at terrible cost. His doing so may be understandable in human terms, but in no way can it be said that he was confronting the facts. And the most important of the facts he did not face that bleak November day at Gettysburg was that the unresolved moral issue which brought on the war would not be resolved by the war either. It is not resolved to this day. The divisions between black and white in this country, patched over here and there by constitutional amendments, court decisions, and all sorts of programs of governmental and private action, rend us still.

But the fact that the dream of national egalitarianism remains a dream is not what proves the Lincolnesque aspiration a myth. The clinching argument is that the American people have no realistic intention of turning the dream into reality. In pragmatic terms, Americans have only the most ambiguous commitment to egalitarianism at the operative level, either in specific terms of the race issue or on general principles. At the operative level, Americans are libertarians and are therefore not just tolerant but encouraging of inequalities of every kind. Lincoln's personal vacillations and hesitations on racial issues were characteristically American. After all *Uncle Tom's Cabin,* the most famous if not the most important of the Abolitionist tracts, is redolent with the presupposition of racial superiority, and its author was an active proponent of the notion that America's blacks would be best off if shipped back to Africa, despite the fact that even in her day the vast majority of them had been in this country for generations.

In the second place, even if the Americans had a realistic commitment to egalitarianism, they possess no institutional machinery for achieving the kind of social transformations necessary to its practical application. To put the point again directly to the present case, Lincoln claimed in the Address, as a second great principle of Americanism, that this nation is a monument to government of, by, and for the people. It is difficult to take his statement of this principle other than rhetorically, difficult, that is, to give it serious analytic attention. In a sense all governments, regardless of form, are sustained by general consent and must be if they are to endure. In another sense, government by the people is a contradiction in terms, for the very meaning of government is that it enables the few to lead the many. But if Lincoln's phrases are taken, loosely, to suggest that we have in the United States something approximating "popular government" of a sort which could marshall the energies of the whole people in massive efforts at social accomplishment (such as would be required to realize egalitarianism as a practical ideal), then he is simply wrong. America has no such government.

On the other hand, by asserting that America does have a system of popular government, Lincoln was accurately expounding the myth that we do, a matter to which we must now turn.

POPULAR GOVERNMENT

The ground upon which the second of America's great political myths rests is nothing more than the first myth. For a nation of humanistic egalitarians, only a system of absolutely popular government would be appropriate. Nevertheless, the second myth is distinguishable from the first and in some of its aspects even contradicts it. It is also much more closely and intricately related to the operative aspects of the political system, being itself an elaborate theory of government, albeit a largely inoperative one bereft of institutional realization.

This second myth is that the American people, burdened with their sacred truth of egalitarianism, have been massed and organized for political action, a veritable crusade for the achievement of socially progressive goals. This basic assertion can be broken down into three intertied elements: statements of high principle, supposed institutional patterns, and summations of grand problems, achievements, and prospects.

It should be noted at the outset that most of the evidence upon which this exposition of the myth of American popular government is based is drawn from work by scholars, especially political scientists, as they have sifted and interpreted the rhetoric and lives of practicing politicians and citizens. These political scientists published their findings in widely used textbooks for high school and college courses in American government. In doing this work, they should be viewed not so much as scholars (although no denigration of their personal academic credentials is implied), but as high priests of the system, teachers who propound the truths and glories of American democracy to the young and thereby generate and sustain its myth. Interspersed in their restatement of the myth are scholarly observations on the realities of American politics. But the two kinds of material are rarely systematically distinguished, and students must find it difficult to keep them apart. In fact, it often appears that the authors of those endless tomes with titles like *Government by the People, American Democracy in Theory and Practice, The Democratic Republic,* and so forth, are themselves hopelessly confused about their priestly and scholarly functions.

The first principle of the myth of American government is "sovereignty of the people." Those who assert this Rousseauean concept, a true "general will" notion, as basic to American government never seem to notice that it has no place in the operative constitutional mechanism Madison erected — and could not have except by shattering Madison's logic from top to bottom. Nevertheless, not only do the textbooks often list sovereignty of the people as American democracy's first principle, they often blithely put as a second principle of our political system that we have a government of laws not men. Sovereignty of the Law, or "Cage as concept is king!" is the foundation upon which Madison built. But what the textbook writers fail to point out is that building this principle into the constitutional system precludes all practical realization of sovereignty of the people except as powerfully evocative rhetoric. Logically, both principles cannot be sovereign; it is either the people or the people radically fragmented and restrained by the law. But there is also the practical fact that cage-as-king government has a fundamental elitist bias; it is government of, by, and for those that matter.

None of this is to suggest that the American people's belief that they have been ensconced as the sovereign voice in their government is unimportant. Myth masks. Despite a continuous outpouring of statistics and stories from scholars and investigative reporters showing how little popular opinion counts in the daily round of governmental decision making and administration, people still imagine themselves sovereign.

More directly, the myth of the sovereign people has had an important impact on the way in which American government operates. In their business rounds, the barons have not been greatly disturbed, but they have been compelled to wear the dress of democracy. Besides avaricious transactionism, they must also play electoral politics with every appearance of earnestness and at great expense. They usually win at this second game, more often than not, easily. In America, a very high percentage of incumbents, at all levels of government, are returned or go on successfully to higher office. But there are ample challengers willing to try and try again. Electoral politics is a game incumbents must play; sometimes they lose.

Electoral politics is a serious business. It determines who will get to play — or go on playing — the political system's primary game of avaricious transactionism. Nothing could be more important than that for the players personally. For them it hardly matters that American election campaigns are filled with bombast and meaningless and/or irrelevant debate, that the contests are essentially personality standoffs in which the main emphasis is on trivial factors, and that the outcomes are largely predictable. Most important of all, they are themselves too bemused by their rhetoric to notice that, in terms of broad social policy directions, it hardly matters who wins elections, Republicans or Democrats, right, left, or center. Avaricious transactionism will go its socially aimless way regardless. All that matters to the players in America's electoral raffle is whether they personally win.

Within these narrow confines, the limits of which were all preset by Madisonian constitutional engineering, American electoral politics took root early. Carrying forward something of the spirit of the Revolution itself and the squabbles with British governors which led up to it, early American electoral activity took on a style in which "the people" were pitted against "the government." The fact that the Madisonian Constitution put the one popular element in the whole, the House of Representatives, virtually at bay before the rest furthered this mood. And it can be seen in the battle for the adoption of the Bill of Rights and in the contents of those amendments to the Constitution as well. Most of the amendments clearly presuppose a flat and dangerous opposition between citizens and those in authority.

The explanation for this sense of contest between government and people lies in the loose fit between myth and operative ideology. The people believe that this is a democracy and that their voice is law. But often they sense or can be brought to fear that such is not the case, and there has been hardly a politician from earliest times to the present who could refrain from playing on these suspicions. All candidates for public office are friends of the people. All are enemies of the "bosses" and vested interests, hobgoblins of American electoral rhetoric far more durable even than "aliens" and "subversives" because, unlike the latter, they are not imaginary.

Sending this friend of the people to Washington rather than that one could not make much difference in favor of government for the people under our system of radically frag- mented power. Even so, the myth of the sovereign people and its demand that only the people's friends have a right to power has resulted in a progressive democratization of the electoral base of American government. The barons quickly realized that it is dangerous to seem to oppose the people and relatively harmless to support claims to increase the electoral rolls. All voters can be swayed, and there might well be safety in num- bers. Moreover, giving out more votes is in no sense giving away power. So, with a great show of democratic revolutionary zeal, the franchises of American electoral arenas have been widened to include all adult males, women, blacks, and now even eighteen-year-olds. Some might think that the outer limit of this gradual extension has now been reached. However, in view of the level of intelligence presupposed in the electorate by the most modern of election "merchandizing" techniques, there would seem to be room for further advances. In any event, the American political system now has at its base a mass electorate fully serviced by mass media facilities of every de- scription. Through that ocean of votes the barons must wade to reach their offices.

To organize this recurring journey, the barons have created in myth an institutional elaboration of popular government. Far and away the most important element in this elaboration is the notion of "the two party system." No such "system" actually exists at the operative level of American politics, because at that level no parties, in any recognizable sense of the term, do or could exist for long. In a practical world where the funda- mental rule is every man for himself, only temporary alliances for momentary convenience are possible. The first obligation of sensible operatives in that kind of world is not to large organizations but to themselves, to defining their own public images and relationships with their own supporters and electorates. If walking under the mythic banner of this or that "party" helps in that endeavor, then it is done with appropriate vigor. Often it does not help, and the spectacle of politicians keeping a discreet distance from their nominal party allegiances is a familiar one in American politics.

However, at the level of myth, the felt presence of the great American political parties is virtually overwhelming. Of course they "exist." There they are, tumultuously assembled in their quadrennial conventions, in the soaring rhetoric of their anointed candidates, the headlined victories and defeats. There they are again, marching to take over State houses, dominate city councils, and organize and "control" the houses of Congress itself. More concretely, perhaps, there they are in their national, State, and local committees, and in all the State and federal laws which control the operations of these bodies, their financing, primaries, and so forth. Finally, there they are in the work of the scholars, especially in those facile generalizations which seem so quickly to fit the facts: the Republicans are the party of business and of white, middle-class, Protestant, establishment Americans, whereas the Democrats are the party of labor, ethnic groups, and reformers.

To say all this is to speak the language of myth. Again, that is not to say it is unimportant; its importance in specific ways will be noted below. But the actual operations of American politics are determined by other, non-party factors.

Let us go over the ground again. Think in logical terms about what a "system" is, the orderly combination of parts into a whole according to a clearly articulated principle. Next put into that conception the notion of a party as a possible element in a system, and define party as a group of people organized to gain control of government by the election of their candidates to public office. The key word here is that a party is *an* organization. Now, how can a *system* of two-*party* interaction be read into a Madisonian constitutional structure of power fragmented down to the last extreme, the last individual baronial officeholder?

Or think empirically. Are either the Republican or the Democratic parties single organizations in the same way that the General Motors Corporation, the United States Army, a New England college — to say nothing of the nationally organized British Labour Party — are single organizations? Is not the Democratic party simply a historically haphazard collection of disparate groups, each of which owes more of its identity to its local base than to its national title and colophon? Even at the State level there is little disciplined "organization," and each of the State committees are collections of personalities with political standings of their own. In fact, is it not the personality factor, the alliances between individuals seeking opportunities in other people's needs, that gives to the parties, local, State, or national, whatever unity they may achieve at any particular time?

These facts are well known. So why all the talk, even among learned, sophisticated scholars about the American two-party system?

The first beneficiaries of such talk are the barons. It would not be helpful to them to be forced to go before "the people" and say boldly, "I'm in this for myself." It is far easier to claim that they are marching shoulder to shoulder with other selfless men and women and under the banner passed down by the founders of a great organization. The myth of the two-party system wonderfully masks baronial egos.

The myth is also comforting to the ordinary citizen. It masks the emptiness of his vote. Rather than choosing between two personalities more or less effective in the game of avaricious transactionism, the citizen, distant from the centers of powers, impotent and frustrated before social problems of every kind, can be led to believe that he is choosing between causes. His vote now becomes participation in a crusade.

But most important, via the two-party myth American electoral politics becomes generally meaningful, both immediately and in the longer term.

Immediately, the barons of the system have persuaded large segments of the American electorate that at each election they have an opportunity to hold their governors responsible for the discharge of their duties during the preceding period of office, *as measured against party principles and stated programs.* Given the actual fragmentation of the system, this is absurd. Any baron without the wit to shift responsibility for all failures except the most egregious personal ones from his own to other shoulders, while claiming responsibility for all successes, does not deserve to stay in the game. This point holds true no matter how many barons may on occasion leave political life by this exit. Nevertheless, even respected and influential political scientists make serious talk of responsible party government in America.

Government by the People, a leading textbook on American government that has been on the market with great success for more than twenty years, opens a major section titled "Policy Makers for the People," with this "problem guide" statement:

> The main problem posed by Part Five is *responsible leadership.* By "leadership" we mean the readiness and ability of officials to act effectively in meeting the problems facing the country. By "responsible" we mean the ability of voters sooner or later to hold these officials accountable for their actions.[13]

The text goes on to point out the difficulties which actual American government presents to getting clear answers to this problem. Nevertheless, it persists in holding that they are reasonable, meaningful questions in the American context, and presumably have so convinced untold thousands of young Americans.

A more serious, though older and less broadly influential, example of this kind of purveyance of persistent myth is the classic publication of the American Political Science Association titled "Toward a More Responsible Two-Party System," which was put out in 1950. This is an important document because it was the product of a four-year collective effort by some fifteen leading lights of the profession, directly aided and advised by as many more. Moreover, in preparation for the writing of the report, the authors consulted widely with all kinds of persons "engaged practically in different segments of the political process." In the end, they were able to write of their preparatory work that "A conscientious effort has been made to get hold of every strand of thinking on the American two-party system."[14] But the document is also important because it so clearly speaks for the reformist conscience of pro-

---

13. James MacG. Burns and Jack W. Peltason, 5th ed., Prentice-Hall, Englewood Cliffs, N.J., 1963, p. 369.

14. *American Political Science Review,* Sept. 1950 (Supplement), p. vi.

fessional students of politics in America. And what it speaks is myth.

As close students of American politics, the authors of the report were well aware of the problems "popular government," as they repeatedly call it, faces in the United States. Nevertheless, as much as the standard textbooks, they persisted in thinking that it is meaningful to worry about how popular government can be improved in this country. The central problem as they saw it was that:

Historical and other factors have caused the American two-party system to operate as two loose associations of state and local organizations, with very little national machinery and very little national cohesion. As a result, either major party, when in power, is ill-equipped to organize its members in the legislative and the executive branches into a government held together and guided by the party program. Party responsibility at the polls thus tends to vanish. This is a very serious matter, for it affects the very heartbeat of American democracy.[15]

The authors of the report were optimistic that much could be done about the problems they identified, and they listed many recommendations, ranging from complex proposals for building and tightening party organizations on a national scale to changes in the Presidential Electoral College and in the terms of congressmen, to suggestions that there should be a single National Election Day, preferably set on a convenient Saturday or Sunday.

It would be pointless to evaluate these specific suggestions now. Moreover, the major flaws in the committee's thinking were amply exposed within months of the publication of their report by other members of the profession. In a brief but trenchant comment published in the *American Political Science Review* less than a year after the appearance of the Committee's report, Austin Ranney pointed out that American political parties are highly resistant to change and have remained, organizationally, as they now are for as far back as careful students have investigated them. This condition has persisted despite repeated calls for reform. Ranney's argument was especially effective because in support of it he was able to cite unimpeachable authority:

15. *Ibid.,* p. v.

Fifty-odd years ago, A. Lawrence Lowell suggested . . . [an] . . . explanation of the resistance of American parties to change which the authors of the *Report* might well ponder. His thesis was that American parties are the way they are because they are entirely appropriate to the kind of government the American people want. He developed it thus: Unified, disciplined and responsible parties are appropriate *only* to a government which seeks to locate *full* public power in the hands of popular majorities. England is the leading example of such a government. . . .

In the United States, Lowell continued, the people want majority rule only up to a point and within very definite limits.[16]

Again the issue is not that talk of popular government in America is wrong. Nor is it the absurdity of claims advanced by the barons themselves or professional political scientists that in America parties can or should be held "responsible" for the conduct of their members who hold public office. All that is beyond argument once it is noticed. The problem is to get it noticed. The blinding myth-talk about the two-party system and responsible leaderships goes on and on. The American people, in conscience, ache to have government broadly responsive to social needs and especially to the wants of the weak and the poor. What they have instead is the very opposite and small chance of ever changing it. So they pretend, or half pretend, or hope, that somehow they have or will one day have a real democracy, a system of popular government.

A final illustration of this kind of talk is a contemporary one with roots going well back into the history of the nation's reform enthusiasms. Common Cause, a massive independent citizen's group, is currently attempting to muster broad support for a proposal decades old that the congressional seniority system be abolished. This proposal is part of a general plan for attempting to revitalize American government's least respected branch (the Watergate affair's damage to the presidency notwithstanding). But those who would do away with the seniority rule should think seriously about why this rule was adopted in the first place and followed so consistently thereafter.

The problem the seniority rule solves is the question of who shall have the coveted chairmanships of congressional committees. The rule giving the chairmanship of each commit-

16. June 1951, p. 495.

tee to its senior member from the majority party is a model of simplicity. The rule is protested because it is unfair to the voters, inconsistent in its implications for policy, and obviously biased in favor of those whose primary virtue is age, often extreme age. Alternatives would have chairmen picked by the members of their committees, a caucus of majority party members, all the majority party members of the parent legislative body, or the majority party leadership. Whatever the specific alternative, the object would be to have chairmen picked with some respect for "merit," a variously defined combination of personal talent, knowledge of the appropriate subject matter, parliamentary skill and fairness, and loyalty and identification with the majority party. The ideal would be to have all committee chairmen working competently as a team to put together a coherent and comprehensive legislative program.

Once again, this is never-never-land talk. The seniority rule is certainly "unfair" and antithetical to the spirit and practice of "popular government." It especially rewards senators and congressmen whose backwater constituencies suffer from voter stagnation or domination by powerful machines and remain undisturbed by the turmoil of current events and controversies. But the alternatives to the seniority rule all presuppose decision-making and enforcing capabilities far beyond those actually possessed by the parties and their leaderships in the houses of Congress. As befits headless bodies, the basic rule there is bargain, barter, compromise, and deal, all on an individual, one-for-one basis. In that context, putting up for grabs plums as personally valuable as committee chairmanships would be to invite continuing turmoil. The great virtue of the seniority rule is that it settles the question of who shall be rewarded with committee chairmanships swiftly and just about automatically. In the real world of Madisonian avaricious transactionism, the seniority rule is not merely an advantageous one; it is a practical necessity. All the alternatives are day dreams, even if they may get partially acted upon from time to time.

The myth of the responsible American two-party system makes our nation's electoral politics appear meaningful in the longer term. By making each election a test of responsible voter decision on the course of government action, it turns the historical succession of those elections into an epic struggle of victory and defeat, as the people march toward fulfillment of their mission to reveal their truth and secure justice for all.

"Progressive historians" have made this view of American political development popular. Especially during the early twentieth century, they worked in terms of a good guy/bad guy thesis, in terms of American history being a contest with strong class and ideological connotations.[17] Allied to these historians in spirit are a number of political scientists, scholars who were particularly prominent in the founding of the American Political Science Association at the turn of the century and are now to be numbered among the leading writers of American government textbooks. These are the decisive voices insisting upon the long-term meaningfulness of American electoral politics. And the electoral rhetoric of almost all American politicians reflects the themes and images of this scholarly community.

In summary form, these themes assert two primary propositions. The first is that the American electorate is apathetic, ignorant, and neglectful of their responsibilities. The second is that American government has been perverted, or perhaps stolen outright, by antidemocratic forces of one description or another. To these propositions, the barons at least are quick to add that the "right man" is here at hand to lead the people back into possession of their inheritance. This addendum is the subject of the next section of the present chapter. But first the mythic element of the two basic propositions must be exposed; each must be shown false and inoperative.

The first proposition is false because, compared to almost any other electorate in the modern world, the American people are well educated, broadly informed, and morally conscientious. If they are cynical about their politicians, they have good reason. If they are doubtful about their personal opportunities for meaningful political action, they have reason for that too. And if they are apathetic in the face of public problems, it may well be because their native Liberalism, to which all pay obeisance, has taught them as of old that the best solution to all problems, both public and private, is private scurrying on one's own behalf. Of course most Americans are thoroughly bemused by what happens to them in their politics, but is that their fault? More to the point, could they become unbemused? Could a

17. See the Appendix.

whole nation be lifted out of its constitutive myths by moral hectoring and a plethora of courses in "American Government"?

The proposition that citizen apathy lies at the root of the failures of American democracy is also inoperative. No argument can show positively how increasing citizen participation would alter the form or quality of American government. In the long record of increasing citizen participation that resulted from the broadening of the franchise there is very little evidence of what effect these advances had beyond leaving the electorate somewhat larger. There is also considerable experience with such citizen-involving devices as the initiative, referendum, and recall and primary elections. The results have been either inconsequential, disappointing, or, especially in the case of the primary, destructive of the very objectives hoped for. But the issue can also be put analytically. Democratic activism is only possible at the base of the American political system. Madisonian fragmentation long ago precluded its going higher.

The proposition that sinister forces have somehow made off with American democracy to pervert it to their own ends can also be shown to be false. The identities of these sinister forces are almost as numerous as the persons making the charges. Puritan theocrats, colonial commercial interests, Federalists and Hamiltonians, foes of Andrew Jackson, robber barons, the proprietors of Wilson's "invisible empire," the vested interests that fought Roosevelt's New Deal, Truman's tycoons of Wall Street, and nowadays "the military-industrial complex" and "the power elite" have all been named as oppressors of American democracy. The problem is to find these "bad guys" in any coherent form or to locate the seats of power from which they are said to operate.

There is no question that American government works disproportionately in the interests of large and powerful institutions and individuals. From its beginning American government has been biased in favor of one sector of the society at the expense of the rest. But to make that point is a long way from proving that any one organized group has been, is now, or could be in a position to control the American political system. American elites are numerous but noncongruent. They do not build to a single pinnacle of power, either overt or hidden.[18] Too many factors of dispersion and fragmentation keep them endlessly jockeying amongst themselves. In the political sphere, Madisonian fragmentation sees to that.

The mythic element in all this stands out when the issue is reduced to operative terms. Operationally, it is never clear when the sinister groups took over American government. It is even more unclear how they can be ousted. Citizen participation will not do it, however often that trumpet is sounded. The alternative, if hope and meaning are still to be read in the history of American electoral politics, is to put "the right man" into presidential office, a myth to which we now turn our attention.

PRESIDENTIAL GREATNESS

Any potential hero in America's electoral drama will also have to be a baron for there to be reasonable hope of getting him into office. Consequently, there is about all the heroes of American political life a paradoxical, two-faced quality. The biographer of America's most complete politician and ideal paradigm for all the rest titled his book *Roosevelt: The Lion and the Fox*. The phrase is Machiavelli's. It fits the American hero politician so snugly because, like Machiavelli's prince, the American baron as hero is compelled to play a double game. He must be both tribune of the people and ruthlessly skillful avaricious transactionist. There is no point in winning the people and losing the game.

An observation of this sort is not cheap cynicism. The charge is not that American politicians are dishonest hypocrites, a worthless breed of trumpeters beneath contempt. The argument is rather that America's more prominent politicians, the worst as well as the best, are the ultimate empirical projection of the Protestant-Bourgeois syndrome. They are all self-tortured men divided against themselves, and in rather simple terms.

The most prominent of American hero-barons is, of course, the president. That office is the single most concentrated focus of myth formation in American government, so much so that at

18. On this much befogged point, see Andrew Hacker, "What Rules America?" *New York Review of Books*, May 1, 1975, pp. 9–13.

times the White House appears to be a qualitatively different kind of place from any other in the political system. The American presidency is unique, and there is no denying its primary significance for American government. But it is important to realize that the presidency is not qualitatively different from the sundry offices occupied by America's lesser heroes.

One way to see this is to seek the prototype of the hero baron in a fictionalized account of him. Art can sometimes portray life better than factual accounts. *The Last Hurrah* is the fictionalized biography of a Boston politician, Mayor James Curley, by Edwin O'Connor,[19] an experienced journalist who knew his subject thoroughly. The book is nothing more than an impressionistic narrative of the mayor's last disastrous run for office. Whatever its artistic faults, it sketches out in broad relief the major characteristics of the hero-baron's life in American electoral politics.

A compelling point O'Connor makes is the crucial importance in American elections of the contrasting personalities of the candidates. His account of the campaign shows the perfunctory discussion of policy issues to be patently insincere. Most of the rhetoric is concerned with charges of "inexperience" by those experienced enough to know much of dishonesty and charges of "dishonesty" by those so inexperienced that they have had few opportunities to be dishonest. Even the talk of ethnic slurs and aspirations is blurred, because both candidates have the same background. There is virtually no evidence of formal party identifications and organizations. On the other hand, it is clear that the challenger is backed by a tight if quarrelsome group of powerful individuals —bankers, publishers, and the like — who have coalesced solely for the purpose of ousting the mayor. The mayor, in turn, is backed by his personal organization, the traditional "machine" bound to him by near-feudal ties.

The pivotal personalities of the candidates play off youth, family values, religion, and empty-headed (but photogenic) earnestness against age, humor, and practical judgment. In this context, the mayor's personality is clearly the more interesting and the book deals with it extensively. It is a split personality almost to the point of schizophrenia. To his supporters, es-

19. Bantam, New York, 1957.

pecially his personal entourage, the mayor appears and is warm, generous to a fault, outgoing, loyal, courageous, and deeply wise. To them all he is a chosen leader, larger than life, whom they have come to know and love over the years with fawning devotion. But to his enemies this same man has for decades been a ruthless, calculating, political maneuverer without scruple or shame, probably a rogue and certainly a thief, even if largely in the behalf of others.

The Last Hurrah is fictional documentation by an informed observer of major themes advanced in the present book. But O'Connor's novel goes on to put a kind of summary stamp on American electoral politics which is directly pertinent to the coming discussion of the presidency.

O'Connor's mayor loses disastrously without forewarning and almost without explanation. The mayor has fought his campaign with discipline, the incumbent's resources, and all the skills of a half century's experience. Yet he is ambushed and crushed by events. There is some talk that this may have happened because the mayor is the last of the big-city bosses and has outlived his time, but he is depicted as too wily for that explanation to be convincing. What O'Connor seems to be saying is that the mayor's downfall is simply unfortunate, a conclusion buttressed by the author's continued stress on two points.

First, besides being an empty-headed weakling, the mayor's victorious opponent is supported by his principal backers only because of their confidence that they will be able to control his every move in office and that he is as marketable to the electorate as soap. In other words, the Mayor is seen as having been quite unjustly brought down by a conspiracy in which the average voter played a wholly unadmirable role. The voter in fact appears to be as foolish and fickle as the winning candidate himself.

Second, O'Connor lugubriously stretches out a mournful account of the mayor's death, from a heart attack, immediately following the election. But in all that long account there is almost nothing said of the mayor's accomplishments. Why not? Because there is very little to be said, a slum clearance program here, some monuments, hospitals, and schools elsewhere. There is not the slightest suggestion that the mayor's many years in office had ushered in any kind of renaissance for any aspect of the city's life beyond perhaps bringing a little pride to a formerly despised ethnic group, the Irish. O'Connor's summary judgment on American electoral politics seems to be Macbeth's conclusion about life itself: full of sound and fury, signifying very little.

It is easy to accept that kind of judgment on the career of a fictional big-city mayor. It is almost as easy to subscribe to the further judgment that *The Last Hurrah* typifies large chunks of American political life and that its hero, for all his being a boss of the old school, stands as a prototype of the American political baron today. Somehow the book's literary shortcomings, its endless clichés and stereotypes, and its lapses into sentimentality and shallow characterization verify its authenticity as a political document. The book reads as realistically and breezily as a newspaper. But to go from these judgments on the barons to comparable ones on the American presidency will not be easy.

That American presidents must be barons was argued at length in the preceding chapter. But have not these men, at least the half dozen or so "great" ones, also been real heroes, bringing leadership, meaning, courage, and comfort to the whole people in times of national crisis? Is this not why their monuments abound, their heads are carved into mountains, their words, their hopes, their challenges, their visions reverberate through the nation's classrooms? And for every Grant, Harding, and Nixon, has there not been a Washington, Lincoln, Wilson, or Roosevelt? Has the nation not come to look to the presidency when times are troubled? Is it reasonable to write a last hurrah to that?

As if in response to such questions, it is fashionable in some circles to say that in the post-Watergate era we must demythologize the presidency. The American people must learn to reduce their reliance on the White House. But it is not fashionable in any circles to take that charge with full, analytic seriousness, to go beyond "cutting the office down to life-size," to insist in fact that the American presidency's actual powers are and have been from the beginning radically incongruous with the hopes even moderates place in the office or that critics fear in it. Moreover, it can be argued that the talk of Washington, Lincoln, Wilson, and Roosevelt and the monuments and sculptures in mountains are not so much measures of heroic achievement as enduring expressions of the nation's underlying anxiety, of a will to believe myth in the face of the facts.

As mythic heroes, the "great" presidents have welded the nation into the unity of its dreams. That is a political function of considerable significance, sometimes admirable, sometimes dangerous. But operationally, in terms of practical achievement, even the greatest of the great presidents were continually hamstrung by the structural logic of the political system they sought to dominate. In their times of desperation and crisis, and through their soaring words and acts, myth mightily challenged ideology, but myth inevitably lost. This is not the fault of the great presidents or of their advisors. Even under the most inspired leadership, myth in America cannot command and organize resources for the victory it craves. Consequently the great presidents were, without exception, tragic figures. They were dragged back from the fulfillment of their inspirations not by personal failure but by the tides of history, by patterns of events they had no hand in creating.

To make these points in analytic detail, we should begin by confronting and defining the myth of presidential power, the notion that the presidential office is a grand place filled best by great men, saviors of the people. This myth in the American political mind gives rise to all the symbolism, rhetoric, and legend crowded around the nation's memory of the great presidents. In the works of certain scholars, this broad, vague evidence takes on surprising precision.

These scholars divide into critics of presidential power and admirers of it. Both groups are prominently represented in the corpus of scholarship on the presidential office that has developed since Edward S. Corwin published *The President: Office and Powers* in 1940. This book has been enormously influential. Through innumerable reprintings and a number of revisions, it virtually defined the field of contemporary presidential studies. Corwin was a critic, and his book carried on its title page a statement by Secretary of State Seward.

We elect a king for four years, and give him absolute power within certain limits, which after all he can interpret for himself.[20]

20. New York University Press, New York, 3rd ed., 1948, p. iii.

Corwin argued that over the years the presidency had accumulated enormous powers, and as the long administration of Franklin Roosevelt came to an end, he became greatly concerned about the degree to which Roosevelt had enveloped the office with his personality and a perpetual sense of crisis. Corwin feared that the enhanced powers of the national government generally and of the presidency in particular gravely exposed personal and private rights and violated the constitutional separation of powers.

Corwin's charge that Roosevelt had "dangerously personalized"[21] presidential power is mild compared to the swelling fury of some contemporary scholars toward particular uses of it of which they disapprove. For example, when American war planes were bombing Hanoi in December of 1972 at President Richard Nixon's command, Arthur Schlesinger, Jr., published an article which began by quoting an old letter on presidential powers by Abraham Lincoln: ". . . see if you can fix *any limit* to his power . . . ." and then went on to declare, in his own words, that Mr. Nixon, by greatly extending a long-term trend among activist presidents, had

. . . by 1973 made the American President on issues of war and peace the most absolute monarch (with the possible exception of Mao Tse-tung of China) among the great powers of the world.[22]

Lest it be thought that this is a scholar losing his objectivity to partisan heat, it may be noted that the same crisis prompted David Apter and Robert Dahl, two of the most respected names in American political science at the time, to comment in a jointly signed public letter that President Nixon's ordering out the bombers,

. . . reveals more starkly than ever before the complete breakdown of the American constitutional system in the domain of foreign policies involving the employment of military forces.

In this domain the arbitrary power of the President has over three decades swelled to a magnitude flatly inconsistent with both

21. *Ibid.,* p. 372.

22. "Presidential War," *The New York Times Magazine,* January 7, 1973, p. 12.

the intentions of the Founders and the requirements of a democratic political order.[23]

These frightened comments should be compared to positive appreciations of supposed presidential powers of vast magnitude. The major expression of this view remains the work of Clinton Rossiter. Rossiter wrote his doctoral dissertation on presidential government under Corwin's direction and gave it the title *Constitutional Dictatorship*. Later, in his most important book, *The American Presidency,* he more glorified than questioned the office and set out to present

... the American Presidency as what I honestly believe it to be: one of the few truly successful institutions created by men in their endless quest for the blessings of free government.[24]

More analytically, the first chapter of this book is a serial explanation of presidential powers listed under these headings:

Chief of State	Voice of the People
Chief Executive	Protector of the Peace
Commander in Chief	Manager of Prosperity
Chief Diplomat	World Leader (or, less
Chief Legislator	grandly, President of
Chief of the Party	the West)

Although the heading of the chapter refers to these titles as "powers," the text often refers to them as "roles" or "functions" of the presidential office, implying that actual presidents have been able to summon up the powers and other wherewithall to carry them out more or less sufficiently. This implication is strengthened by Rossiter's repeated insistence that the president is not each of these roles separately but all of them in sum, bringing to the execution of each the aura of his possession of all the rest.

No other writer, past or present, has matched the expansive terms Rossiter used to describe the capacities of the presidential office for greatness. But it is not belaboring of the point to stress his rhetoric. His approach to the office through an analysis of its supposed roles has become common in the

23. Letter to the Editor, *The New York Times,* January 4, 1973, p. 36.

24. Second rev. ed., Mentor, New York, 1962, p. 13.

academic literature and is clearly the dominant approach in the textbook field. Moreover, Rossiter's language in *The American President* and his feelings about the presidency accurately project nationally held beliefs and sentiments about the office.[25]

Significant variations from Rossiter's central theme appear among those scholars who have found, regretfully, that in actual practice the presidency does not quite come up to his expectations. Under the Madisonian Constitution, actual presidents simply cannot carry out with any semblance of success all those roles Rossiter assigned them. A vivid anecdote in Richard Neustadt's study, *Presidential Power,* illustrates the disillusionment that attends realization of this fact.

In the early summer of 1952, before the heat of the campaign, President Truman used to contemplate the problems of the General-become-President should Eisenhower win the forthcoming election. "He'll sit here," Truman would remark (tapping his desk for emphasis), "and he'll say, 'Do this! Do that!' *And nothing will happen.* Poor Ike—it won't be a bit like the Army. He'll find it very frustrating."[26]

Once this lesson has been learned, many scholars go on to analyze the situation the best they can and to suggest means for improving it. It has been argued that the federal bureaucracy has considerable latent capacity to absorb, disperse, and/or deflect even the most pointed of presidential initiatives, and there is a sizable literature arguing that White House administrative control and coordination should be increased. There is also extensive literature on how intelligence gathering and policy formulation in the White House could be improved, and how relations between the president and Congress and between him and his party could be reorganized and strengthened. The implicit hope in all this, that the presidency is not but should be what Rossiter said it is, is rarely articulated openly, and as a result, the ultimate causes of the president's difficulties in these various areas are rarely plumbed.

25. "The President, in short, is the one-man distillation of the American people. . . ." (p. 16) "The final greatness of the Presidency lies in the truth that it is not just an office of incredible power but a breeding ground of indestructible myth." (p. 103) "It is a priceless symbol of our continuity and destiny as a people. Few nations have solved so simply and yet so grandly the problem of finding and maintaining an office of state that embodies their majesty and reflects their character." (p. 250).

26. *Op. cit.,* p. 9.

A signal exception to this rule is James MacGregor Burns. In a recent book aptly titled *Uncommon Sense,* Burns, another of America's most distinguished political scientists, has faced squarely the question of whether, under present constitutional and political arrangements, the presidency can rise to the responsibilities which the crises of our time impose upon the office. He answers that question with an emphatic negative. But Burns, pausing only to observe for the benefit of the young that in the American context revolution is not a practical alternative, nevertheless goes on to proclaim:

> We need a president who will change the institutional structure around him because he will see that he cannot achieve his goals within it, and who will understand what changing this structure means. It means organizing a new popular movement of people . . . to create a genuine national party. . . . It means ruling in partnership with Congress if national goals can thus be met, but acting without Congress if the national legislature is unable to come to grips with the job ahead. . . . It means the transformation of state and local government to the extent necessary to work with the national government to achieve national priorities.[27]

In this passage the myth of possible presidential greatness is carried to its ultimate limit. On its face, the references to mobilizing a "popular movement of the people" to support the president, to governing *with* Congress if it will, and *without* it if it will not, may strike some as verging on a call for a quasi-fascistic dictatorship. But in Burns' own view he is only arguing that these extraordinary things must be done if we are to have a president who could truly be ". . . chief legislator, chief executive, chief propagandist, and all the rest."

It remains to show that the myth of presidential greatness is both false and inoperative. The myth is false primarily because it presupposes the presidency capable of generating a kind of political power it does not and could not possess and, beyond that, a kind of political power alien to the operative American political system generally. Talk of a national government led by the president to the achievement of national priorities, talk of the president as tribune of the people, talk of the president taking the nation, by a new deal or across a new frontier to a rendezvous with destiny and the great society, is talk envision-

27. Harper and Row, New York, 1972, pp. 172–173.

ing a political figure of the dimensions of Napoleon, Lenin, or Castro. It is not unreasonable to suppose such figures seeking to mass, organize, release, and totally control the energies of an entire society in the systematic pursuit of major community objectives. Such figures might bind up a nation's divisions, reconcile its failures, and lead it forward into patterns of broad social renewal. Of they might fail at such tasks. But it would not be absurd to think of them trying to do such things. It is absurd to talk except rhetorically of actual American presidents attempting this kind of work.

Operationally, the American president is a baron; he is bigger, more visible, and certainly louder than most, but in terms of broad social power, he is no stronger than any because he is as individualized as any. The constitutional basis for presidential power is narrow indeed; it does little more than make him a participant ex *officio* in the political process along with other designated elements of the government. Most of the president's actual and supposed powers are political in origin, that is, they devolve upon him from precedent, statute, and above all, daily practice. Hence presidential powers, contrary to the myth and even when swollen by mythic misrepresentation, are no more than what that daily practice can generate. That means that the president's powers, like those of barons generally, are mostly personal, episodic, and negative.

The president has very considerable personal power. It comes to him immediately because of the highly personalized character of presidential elections, and the White House is a fine vantage point from which to exercise it. With a far broader reach than any other baron, the president can get himself involved in an extraordinary number and variety of political activities. There are few areas of public life immune to presidential intervention. But these interventions are invariably of a personal sort. Given the dispersed character of the political system generally, no president can build up and extend his authority into objective patterns of sustained control. In consequence, it is seriously misleading to suggest that he is "chief" of anything, except for the purely ceremonial role of "Chief of State." He is a principal figure in the legislative process, but he is certainly not in charge of it and rarely sets its general pace. He is the most prominent member of his party, but often enough, especially when running for re-election, he has to be reminded of its existence. As for the federal bureaucracy, the first thing to be remembered is that it does not constitute some massive monolith which could support a chief at its pinnacle. It is a vast, dispersed melange, and the president is best pictured as scrambling somewhere in the middle to control this or that aspect of it.

This is obvious commentary but it may seem to fail to support the general argument in two prime areas. First, it may seem that the president is truly by constitutional warrant, "Commander in Chief" of the nation's military might. This point, however, is easily refuted. The president can order out the bombers. Nixon did so against the judgment of most of his advisors, although there were other occasions when the bombers went without being ordered. But giving commands of this sort is a long way from "running the Pentagon." Pentagon politics is a book in itself, not always a pretty one, and many of its pages are notable for the total absence of the president or his influence.

Second, it is often asserted that the firmest base of the president's general prestige is his virtually exclusive authority in foreign affairs. But this observation more underlines the personal character of presidential power than the opposite. On the world stage the president can walk with an extraordinary individual eminence, to his great personal political benefit. But that is a very different thing from managing, in an ongoing comprehensive pattern, the nation's foreign relations. To the contrary, the persistent presence in presidential entourages of special advisors and envoys of the order of Colonel House, Harry Hopkins, and Henry Kissinger, are testimony to the difficulties presidents have had in this area.

Largely because of the personal nature of presidential power, his use of it is bound to be episodic. He can veto a bill here, browbeat a congressman there, fight a senatorial committee chairman, in a dramatic confrontation, to a standstill, or bully some segment of the bureaucracy into doing his will on a particular issue. Above all, or at least most noticeably, he can from time to time, in a clarion call to his public at large, chart a new course for the nation. The initiation of debates on national issues is perhaps the president's outstanding power. But to plan, program, and systematically allocate resources in a sustained pattern of national priorities is another matter. The president can suggest. He can, with national, self-serving fanfare, undertake bold new initiatives, announce that we have nothing to fear save fear itself, declare unconditional war on organized crime, go to China, or the like. But in the American political system, to follow through on such initiatives requires the cooperation of a host of other political actors, some of whom may be distant and openly recalcitrant. Even in foreign affairs, a president must take care not to extend his commitments to leaders overseas too far. No matter how great his personal world stature, his capacity to deliver on his given word to foreign statesmen will be often dependent in large part upon shifting patterns of support and interest at home.

Finally, much of the president's actual power is negative. Positively, the president can in the main only propose and seek to persuade. In trying to get things done the president is greatly dependent on others whose wills he cannot command. But negatively, with much greater relative independence, he can veto bills, refuse to support others, impound funds, block appointments, and so forth. In this the president is no different from other barons. To refuse to use the powers they have is usually the barons' trump card. Perhaps surprisingly, once appropriate allowances are made for differences in scale, compared to other barons the president has rather less elbow room for use of his negative powers. Because of the enormous prominence of his office, the president is under constant pressure to give the appearance of movement. It is dangerous for him to block, stop, and refuse. Almost always, it will be better for him to give in and then, on some other issue announce a bold new initiative, however empty.

In sum, presidents have very considerable powers and, as Neustadt suggested, they can make those powers work to their own advantage, sometimes to the benefit of the nation, often at its great cost. But inflating those personal, episodic, and negative powers into transcendent capacities for leading the people forward in programs of national renewal simply cannot be done — except in myth.

Even if it could be done, the American people are of no mind to see it attempted in actual fact. The mood of the general electorate across the nation, in the words of those who are expert in these matters, is conservatism laced with fear for personal property and safety. It is difficult to dispute the contentions of Richard Scammon and Ben Wattenberg that the "Middle Voter," representing seven out of ten actual voters, is "middle-aged, middle-income, middle-educated, Protestant," and more likely "a forty-seven-year-old housewife from the outskirts of Dayton Ohio whose husband is a machinist" than "a twenty-four-year-old instructor of political science at Yale."[28] Out of such stuff, dreams of social transformations are not made.

In the same vein, it is most unlikely that occupants of the White House, for all their talk, would ever realistically set out on social crusades. The record shows that only Americans get to be presidents of the United States, and Americans, being fundamentally Liberals, are not cut out to be great national leaders, even if they had the institutional opportunities. This is a broad but technical point.

It is a technical but important fact that most of what we suppose to be presidential power is political and conventional in origin. This means that presidential power must be mustered up and sustained in ongoing confrontations between the president and his various constituencies. This is what Woodrow Wilson meant when he said ". . . the office will be as big and as influential as the man who occupies it."[29] But how big are the men who go to the White House? This is the second side of the question, for the White House occupant will be as big as his conception of himself allows and no bigger. The limits as well as the motives for action are set by the occupant's ideological equipment. This is a matter of basic political socialization, and as American Liberals, those who go to the White House cannot think of themselves as leaders in any operational terms grander than those appropriate to Hobbes' sovereign, whose essential function was merely to keep men "in awe." The thought patterns, general conceptions, and specific propositions of Plato, Aquinas, Rousseau, Hegel, Marx, and Lenin for social leadership, organization, and betterment are simply not available, as operative ideas, to American presidents. In fact, anyone of a mind along the lines of those mild intellectuals who defined British Socialism before World War I is not likely to get far on the road to the real world of Washington politics.

28. *The Real Majority*, Coward-McCann, New York, 1970, pp. 70–71.

29. Quoted by Rossiter, *op. cit.*, p. 81.

Thus the myth of presidential greatness both radically exaggerates the possibilities of the actual office and presupposes a political imagination essentially absent or inoperative in the American political mind. Why, then, is this myth so broadly, so persistently, so fervently believed in America?

The myth is believed in the first place because the American people are fully equipped to believe it, even while they are wholly unequipped to act upon it. By their biblical heritage, they possess the full vocabulary of charismatic leadership. Instinctively, and with characteristic biblical prejudice, they believe that the people's savior will be a man, not a woman. They believe, too, that he will be in many ways an ordinary man of humble origins but nevertheless one who, in vaguely supernatural ways, has been granted special strengths. He is called to greatness in service, often tragic, to his people. Americans have firmly in their minds the image of Moses telling the people who were in great fear, "Fear not, stand firm, and see the salvation of the LORD, which he will work for you today." (Exodus 14:13, R.S.V.) They have the image of Samuel who, as a lad in service to the temple, was called by God in the night and "the LORD was with him and let none of his words fall to the ground." (1 Samuel 3:19, R.S.V.) They have the image of David, founder of the kingdom of Israel, receiving the pledge of loyalty from Ittai the Gittite, "As the LORD lives, and as my lord the king lives, wherever my lord the king shall be, whether for death or for life, there also will your servant be." (2 Samuel 15:21, R.S.V.) They have the image of the Messiah himself, teacher and suffering servant, a mantle they have draped especially around Lincoln as they hear him in memory:

Fondly do we hope, fervently do we pray, that this mighty scourge of war may speedily pass away. Yet, if God wills that it continue until all the wealth piled by the bondsman's two hundred and fifty years of unrequited toil shall be sunk, and until every drop of blood drawn with the lash shall be paid by another drawn by the sword, as was said three thousand years ago, so still it must be said "the judgments of the Lord are true and righteous altogether."

With malice toward none, with charity for all, with firmness in the right as God gives us to see the right, let us strive on to finish the work we are in. . . .

In the second place, the presidential myth in the form of the charismatic hero is easily placed in the American political context. Institutionally the president is but one figure occupying the political system's one significant national office, and to it the people can repair as a single congregation. Moreover the White House, as that one man's office and home, is peculiarly vulnerable to legend-gathering and fantasy. These facts create an opportunity for charismatic identifications which ambitious individuals, party managers, and the mass media cannot be expected to do other than exploit to the full. Furthermore the charismatic image suffers, philosophically, from almost no disadvantages. The messiah does not work through any systematically argued plan for organizing social resources or patterns of disciplined common action. Such means smack of socialism and bureaucracy and will always be offensive to the American Liberal mind. The messiah works through signs, promises, and hopes, through calls to glory, distant horizons, and faith. He inspires each and every one of us, but with a wonderful lack of specificity, and through our hearts, not our heads.

But above all else, the myth of presidential greatness is believed because it meets great needs and satisfies deep yearnings to believe in the American political mind. The actual presidential office, for all its capacity for getting and commanding attention, is a weak office in terms of social power and the generation of community achievement. The myth of presidential greatness masks that and makes us feel that in the White House "the people" have a noble defender. More important, the myth of presidential greatness masks our own weakness and national political incapacity. In the face of actual, systematic, and comprehensive egoism and irresponsibility built into the very foundations of the national political life, presidential greatness promises that we can transcend ourselves, that in the train of great leaders we have, can, and will strive to make our beloved land a progressive, humane democracy with justice and dignity for all. In *fact*, lacking the institutions and ideology for anything even approaching that kind of accomplishment, we will do no such thing. But it is comforting to conscience and self-understanding in the deepest existential sense to believe that we have, that we can, and that tomorrow we will again.[30]

30. "There is a Presidency in our future . . ." Rossiter, p. 229.

THE IDEOLOGY/
MYTH CYCLE

THE CYCLE
TENSION AND OUTRAGE
CRISIS AND RECOVERY

THE CYCLE

The argument so far has presented the mythic and ideological formations in the American political mind in static terms with one lying in front of and shielding the other. This is their basic relationship and it is of fundamental importance. However, it was suggested earlier that in times of crisis the relationships between myth and ideology in America can undergo dramatic shifts.

This suggestion was put in the form of the hypothesis that as a crisis unfolds, the normal, largely covert relationship between myth and ideology will burst into open contradiction, precipitating some form or another of political breakdown, but finally resolving into a recovery stage that restores the normal relationship. America's crises are of special interest because each of them has carried the promise that through it the American political system will be pulled out of its usual despond and that issues will be resolved and progress achieved. The proposed hypothesis argues against these promises and maintains that America's moments of crisis have proved largely sterile. Their primary accomplishments have been no more than to restore the status quo and what was termed its "neutral" equilibrium.

It is now possible to begin fitting into this hypothesized pattern of crisis interaction the myths of American democracy as described in the last chapter and the ideological elements of the operative government sketched in the preceding ones. Doing so will reveal certain general features of the actual process by which myth and ideology interact during crises in America.

The first general characteristic is that the crisis interaction can take place on a variety of planes. In most cases, only individuals are involved and the general public pays little attention to them or to what they do. An unemployed and bitter black man became enraged with his common-law wife one night in his Detroit tenement flat and threw her children, aged six and eighteen months, out of a seventh story window. He was arrested by the police without a struggle, pleaded guilty, and was jailed. This essentially private tragedy has important public dimensions that in racial and economic terms go well beyond the crime that was committed and the presence of officers of the law. And the myth/ideology cycle now being discussed parallels what happened here to a considerable degree. The strain in the subject between his expectations and his actual circumstances is triggered by some untoward event into an exhibition of senseless violence disproportionate to any possible immediate provocation, but afterwards, the preceding order and strain are reimposed. On the other hand, for all the frequency of events like this, and for all the significance which crimes such as murder and rape have as indices of intersubjective, communal breakdown, events of this order are not central to the focus of the present book.

Our prime concern is with those public incidents, events, or conditions in which political actors move through the crisis cycle, commanding our attention or even drawing some of us into the action with them as participants. In such public crises the shifting relationships between myth and ideology have meaning for us all. They can be as singular and sudden as the assassination of President Kennedy. They can be as drawn out and nationally involving as the Civil War. Mostly they range well between these extremes.

Before analyzing any of these events in detail, we must define certain further conceptual problems more closely. These arise at the three points where the cycle moves from one stage to the next. Only the first two need attention. The third is simply the moment of absolution, which usually signals the beginning of the recovery stage; it needs little comment besides notice that it occurs often.

Stage one is a state of *normal strain*. Some triggering event causes it to erupt into the *outraged concerns* of stage two, but the event itself is comparatively insignificant. Who can remember how, why, or precisely when a family quarrel began? Was it Lincoln's election, the firing on Fort Sumter, or some more distant incident leading up to that firing, that actually kicked off the Civil War? Is it not more reasonable to see those incidents as the opening of hostilities and then to put the real start of the war, in the sense of the beginning of confrontation, much earlier — in the hardening of attitudes following publication of the flood of abolitionist tracts, or more specifically, the Dred Scott decision? In fact the war was the culmination of broad and decades-old contradiction, fear, mutual distrust, and guilt. Therefore the war and its array of "causes" can only be understood in proportionately broad terms. What triggered the nearer approach to it and the shooting itself hardly matters in that perspective.

Determining the events that mark the transition into the cycle's third stage is a matter of great importance and some difficulty. This stage is one of *political breakdown* frequently scarred by overt violence. But what is violence, especially in political contexts, when we speak in conceptual terms that will bear considerable analytic weight? If the term means open and sudden physical force, then even the most controlled, efficient, and socially constructive hammering will have to be included. It would seem better to find a definition which connotes moral breakdown and loss of political control. This can be achieved by focusing not on the appearances of violence but on its sources and on what collapses in violent situations. In this light, situations of political violence are those in which actors lose control over their actions in the sense that they either have no idea what to do next (their activity becomes mindless) or they feel driven to use inappropriate and/or illegitimate ideas to govern their acts (their activity moves outside established constitutional and political channels.) Whether a situation is truly one of violence then becomes a question of detecting in it the breakdown of political order and not just a business of measuring noise and blood.

This characterization of violence aligns it with a wide variety of other forms of political behavior that strike at (do violence to) the formal bases of political life. It equally suggests that when a breakdown of the political order occurs, the expressions of the breakdown can vary widely. Thus a man can "break," and start shooting with a gun wildly, or with cold fury and great skill, or after careful planning and conspiracy with fellows. Or he can engage in some form of protest and demonstration which, however overtly "peaceful," is patently extra-constitutional and even treasonable. Or if he has no idea how to proceed, he can lapse into hopeless apathy, just give up, in effect commit political suicide. But no matter which of these courses he follows, violence has been done, in concept more importantly than in physical fact, to the possibilities of political life as an intersubjective effort to live and act intelligently and purposively with others within the confines of established norms. The smashing of that fragile possibility of controlled social life is the core characteristic of the third stage of the myth/ideology cycle.

As we review each stage of the crisis cycle, it will be important to include references to actual events and to notice which of the great myths is principally involved. But our primary concern must be to show how each stage bears the seeds of its own dissolution into the next one, until the final return to "normalcy." This is the inevitability that establishes the perpetual sterility of the American political mind.

TENSION AND OUTRAGE

When the schematic outline of the myth/ideology cycle was introduced in Chapter 1, the first stage, normality, was described as already a condition of considerable strain. This is important because it underlines the persistent contradictions between Protestant conscience and Bourgeois practice in American political life. As the American political process moves along, it is punctuated more or less continuously by random expressions of surprise, outrage, and condemnation by academics, journalists, and others who have taken on the role of keepers of the national conscience. Gross inequalities caused by racial, sexual, religious, economic, and age discrimination are regularly exposed. So too are breakdowns in the governmental process — its corruption, its meaningless and irrelevant elections, and its misleading rhetoric. The "inside dopester" is a perennial feature of American public life. And there are always scholars here and there burrowing away on the reputations of American political heroes, present as well as past, showing that their achievements were far less than myth supposes.

But the persistence of Protestant mythic pressure on Bourgeois practical politics is also important because it means that where and when that pressure will break into the open are virtually unpredictable. Normally the critics of American democracy are easily put down as utopians, trouble-makers, or sentimentalists, people whom practical, realistic men of affairs do not need to heed carefully. But given the degree to which all Americans are vulnerable to appeals to conscience, there is simply no telling when some event will thrust the critics before very large audiences indeed. The critics always have a case. All that is required to get the rest of us to give them a hearing is a sufficiently dramatic incident to remind us all of our persistent guilt.

Sooner or later, the flood of guilt will flow again and again. And the incapacity of Bourgeois practice to deal substantively with the charges is as persistent as Protestant conscience. Witness the ways in which Bourgeois practice systematically violates Protestant conscience's first great myth, the ultimate source of most of America's political discomfitures. When confronted with clear evidence of serious instances of discrimination, the barons of American politics will attempt to respond, either because they themselves have been stung to the quick by the charges or find it advisable to still the hullabaloo. But how can they respond? They can pass laws to include the discriminated groups more generally in the processes of "popular government," but these moves achieve little beyond allowing the victimized groups to participate more fully in the national myths. The barons can also work to ensure that the discriminated groups get to have barons of their own. But what will that accomplish? More fairness in the distribution of what is going, perhaps. Unfortunately such cosmetic measures cannot touch underlying sociological problems, will not much alleviate poverty, unemployment, racial bias, or, in the case of blacks, the dreadful accumulated penalties of four hundred years of social oppression. Even the feeblest efforts to attack these real problems, such as affirmative action and busing-for-integration programs, sooner or later collide with that characteristically Liberal legal blindness which can claim that all patterns of discrimination, even those specifically created to atone for those of the past, are illegitimate.

Consequently, Protestant conscience and Bourgeois practice work to an impasse guaranteed to generate increasing critical pressures, frustrations, and every kind of opportunity for the kinds of dramatic incidents which trigger American politics into crisis. John Brown leads a raid on Harpers Ferry, and the confrontation leading to the Civil War is in the open. Or a century later the Supreme Court hands down the coincidentally titled decision, *Brown* versus *Board of Education,* and ushers in another very different kind of crisis period orbiting the same problem. Or burglars are apprehended in the offices of the Democratic National Committee in the Watergate building. Or prisoners at Attica begin a rebellion, a terrorist group abducts the daughter of the wealthy Hearst family, a strike begins to protest the treatment of migrant farm workers by California fruit and vegetable growers. Or news reports force into the open events which suggest widespread corruption in the police department and the mayor of the city is compelled to appoint a wide-ranging investigative commission. Each of these incidents is related to a broad, unattended social problem of long standing. And all of them grasp and hold the attention of the general public, and thus they spark general concern and debate.

Sometimes the dramatic incident involved in shocking the nation out of normal acceptance of its internal contradictions is itself so serious and sudden that the crisis is over before national awareness fully develops. In these instances the debate stage is conducted retroactively. This was the case with the asassination of President Kennedy and, in somewhat more extended ways, the urban riots of 1967. Both of these events shook the nation with their horrors. Both were also seen as related to social problems of long standing. But these connections were made in the wake of the actual events, in endless articles in the press about "the gun culture," adolescent alienation, and so forth, and in the widely read and discussed Kerner Report on the causes and significance of the urban riots.

Once under way, the primary characteristic of the second stage is outraged condemnation of social evils laced with promises of corrective action. If the majority of incidents triggering the second stage originate in the nation's first great myth being somehow pushed away from the facts, this stage soon also pulls up the other two myths for testing. Clarion calls resound, leaders must respond to the challenges of the time, the people must be organized for action. These calls are usually initiated by the barons themselves. Professing at every turn their faith in the Constitution and the promises of American democracy, they flagellate themselves into ever-loftier promises. Perhaps they sincerely hope the promises will be redeemed. But as experienced operatives in the American political system, they must also know that they will probably never be called to account, that they will have all kinds of opportunities to blame mistakes and failures on sundry enemies, real or invented. So the promises are tendered. Our house will not remain divided against itself; government will be restored to the people; the trusts will be broken; the world will be made safe for democracy; the workers will gain their rights; one third of the nation will be clothed, fed, housed, and employed like the rest of us; the world will be made one; the tides of barbarism will be rolled back; there will be prosperity for all; the black movement will overcome; international aggression will be punished, democracy defended, peace achieved, and national honor restored; corruption will be rooted out; and truth, openness, and lawful processes will once again reign in government. The American dream will come true.

It is doubtful if any nation in history has so regularly and exquisitely teased itself with hopes fantastically beyond its capabilities for realization. But fueled by deep guilts, American hopes burn higher and higher. They reward the barons' rhetoric with applause, devotion, and votes, but suspecting that the barons may not persevere enough, they may form organizations of their own to sustain the pressure and keep hopes alive. These volunteer armies of the moment are scattered throughout America's political history in a wide diversity of forms. There have been narrow bands of fanatic publicists, sudden mass movements, good-government groups of all sorts, political splinter parties, and underground groups. It is sometimes supposed that this last type, especially in the form of terrorist organizations, are a recent feature of American political life, but history shows that secret societies of more or less violent bent, from the Ku Klux Klan back to the Know-Nothings, the Order of Cincinnatus, and even the original organization of Phi Beta Kappa, have existed in this country from colonial days. They are not to be confused with organized criminal elements. They are more akin to the relatively harmless fraternal organizations which also abound in America. But their objectives are political, their methods often dangerous. They are a tribute to what has aptly been called "the paranoid style" in American politics. As such they have general significance as the extreme type of citizen response to the mythic promises of the American tradition.

The barons are alarmed by all these groups, and with good reason. Impatience and uncompromising demands are a threat to any operative political system, none more so than the

American. Even in times of genuine and broadly perceived crisis, its capacities for moving beyond its inherent avaricious transactionism are minimal. So the barons, without abandoning their overflowing promises, begin to talk darkly about extremists and to urge one and all to put their trust in established procedures and traditional norms. Once this kind of talk begins, the stage is set for confrontation and breakdown.

CRISIS AND RECOVERY

There is no need to press to absolute limits our hypothetical pattern for the ways in which myth and ideology interact through America's periodic crises. Political breakdown has occurred so often in American history that there is no need to maintain the extreme position that every national debate on a pressing public issue dissolves in the end into some kind of chaos. Nevertheless, it can be persuasively argued that whenever a long-neglected social problem has been brought to public view in a sustained and dramatic way, exposure will have generated so much anger, frustration, guilt, recrimination, distrust, and fear that some kind of explosion, breakdown, or massive withdrawal sooner or later is all but inevitable. The protesting groups must realize that normal channels hold little prospect. On the other hand, those who believe themselves responsible for maintaining the public peace have every reason for increasing nervousness. They know they are not responding to the substantive challenges. They know (without the benefit of a single book of political theory) how precarious in a Liberal society are their claims to respect. Again and again as these crises develop, authority figures compress their understanding of what is at stake into the single, profoundly Hobbesian imperative that they must maintain order and show who is in charge. The need to defend and assert the authority and power of the state is rawly exposed in pure form.

Predictably, the result is often enough a Hobbesian shootout, open, visible violence between officers of the law and some group of citizens. The classic and most catastrophic American shootout was the Civil War. Lincoln made it plain again and again that his prime concern was to preserve the Union. As a good Hobbesian on his Bourgeois side, he elected to do this by force, claiming that the insurgent South, being Hobbesians also and making the same election for their cause, left him no choice. The result was monumental tragedy. Exactly mirroring Grant's claim in that war that he would hold "this line if it takes all summer" were the attitudes of the authorities involved at the Haymarket riots, the Veterans' March on Washington, Kent State, the Attica uprising, and the Los Angeles shootout with the tiny remnants of the Symbionese Liberation Army. In every one of these cases, like hundreds of others, the authorities moved up a massive display of force. The opposition was futilely armed but borne up by visions that in death they could testify to the possibilities of mythic fulfillment, that oppressed people everywhere would be lifted up and become truly equal. And in every one of these cases and many, many others, order in America was restored, Bourgeois order on the ashes of Protestant conscience.

The shootout is the ultimate example of breakdown in American political life, violence at its most visible. At the other extreme is the invisible violence of withdrawal, alienation, and apathy. Stage two of the myth/ideology crisis cycle splutters to a conclusion and the third stage is simply a retreat into political silence. Alternatively, stage two can conclude with visible violence appalling enough to shock numbers of otherwise concerned persons into silence and withdrawal. Alienation and apathy do violence to core values of democratic politics. If anything, this kind of breakdown is more threatening to the political order than violence of the visible sort.

It is impossible to estimate the extent or the practical significance of actual political alienation in America. Some evidence of its extent crops up in election statistics. In the 1972 presidential election, which Richard Nixon took by a landslide, a third of the electorate did not vote. That is an extraordinarily high percentage for one of the world's most educated and organized democracies, and the percentages of non-participants in other, less dramatic elections are even higher. But why individuals stay away from the polls is almost impossible to put into quantifiable terms.

There is, however, impressionistic evidence of political alienation in America. It can be seen in people's faces, heard in their muttered comments, read in their occasional declarations. But the alienated are by definition unorganized, and how representative what is seen and heard may be is impossible to say. Finally, a high proportion of deviant behavior in America is at least related to political alienation. Epidemic alchoholism and other sorts of drug addiction are expressions of it. Many of the violent, mindless crimes committed in America are displaced expressions of bitter political frustration. But all efforts to total these instances are guesswork. Political alienation is an extensive and serious feature of American political life. It is also a dark, frightening, uncharted area. The most we can say about it analytically is that its massive extent can probably only be explained by reference to guilts and disappointments on mythic scales.

There remain two further forms of the breakdown that characterizes the third stage of the myth/ideology crisis cycle in America. One is the organized resort to extra-constitutional political behavior which, while overtly "peaceful," often invites violence, whether by authorities or others, and is itself illegal and/or deliberately contrary to established norms. This kind of behavior was central to the activities of the Civil Rights and Peace Movements of the 1960s and it has occurred frequently throughout American history. The techniques used range from civil disobedience to massive demonstrations by hordes of aroused citizens designed to urge a desired political response by their sheer bulk. The barons resent this kind of behavior, though on occasion they find it advisable to tolerate it and even to support it in special situations. But what was said about the extreme examples of overt violence in America is true also of these milder forms: they arise out of mythic frustration with the operative features of American politics, and they are almost uniformly futile. The Peace Movement did not stop the war in Vietnam, even if it did help tip Lyndon Johnson into the decision not to run for re-election. For all the changes in laws and registration patterns it may have won, the Civil Rights movement did not materially alter the social and economic status of the mass of black people in America. Like hundreds of other of America's protest movements, they are now historical relics.

Much more interesting is the breakdown in political life which the barons themselves can bring about in the face of crises they cannot handle. While giving every appearance of acting within the norms of the system, they can reduce its workings to the level of public farce. Farce — the absurd filling up of form with meaningless or inappropriate content — is a standard feature of American politics, especially of its periodic election campaigns. But it is in times of crisis that the barons show consummate skill at paralyzing farce.

The pattern has been repeated many times. When a crisis develops, especially one involving the exposure of corruption or other crimes within the baronial fraternity, the machinery of government freezes; rhetoric, piety, and investigatory zeal are applied in abundance; one or more of the barons are dramatically cashiered; and underlying problems are hardly noticed, much less attended to. But it took the effort to impeach President Nixon to play out this kind of farce and its attendent destructiveness of possibilities for meaningful government on a truly grand scale.

The farcical elements involved in the effort to impeach President Nixon include his own absurd posturing before the public, his blundering arguments to those investigating and passing judgment upon his conduct, and his repeated egregious errors of political judgment. On the other hand, it is difficult to label as farce either the acts or the motives with which he was charged. His character flaws of greed, vanity, paranoia, and arrogance are usual throughout the American political mind, even if they appeared in somewhat unusual combination in Nixon. And his acts were simply those of an avaricious transactionist who lost his balance as many others have, though rarely in so exalted an office. Nixon went much too far and got caught. It is especially important to stress that his decision to "fight like hell," use any argument, delay, announce that he was not "a crook," and give every appearance that the presidential office adhered in him as a personal possession was the standard response of any baron cornered in his bailiwick. In other words, focus on Nixon reveals in his impeachment mostly ordinary factors.

The grand elements of farce in Nixon's impeachment are only revealed when the whole process is set out. Its first farcical element was its elephantine pace. More than two years elapsed from the time it became public knowledge that the Watergate affair raised serious questions about White House involvement to the final denouement of the impeachment effort. During this time hardly a week went by without its quota of headlines, and fascinating details emerged month by month. By coincidence, during this same period other important nations of the world also faced unexpected crises over their executive heads, most notably Australia, Britain, Canada, France, Israel, and West Germany. Every one of these nations, including Israel where the problems went to the very bone of its national existence, faced its crisis and resolved it with decorum and dispatch, often in a matter of weeks. Even more significantly, these nations acted in the belief that continuity in the executive branch must be maintained with the least possible interruption. As if openly mocking all these examples, the American impeachment process ground on inch by inch, sterilizing the capacity of the national government for executive leadership.

The second farcical element in Nixon's impeachment was its grandiose scale. Only one question was at issue: the fitness for office of Nixon himself. For the governance of the country, the guilt and complicity of his associates were secondary matters. But a half dozen or more of the nation's major political institutions became involved, and through them literally hundreds of senators, congressmen, judges, their regular staffs, and a great assortment of specially recruited lawyers, investigators, and other experts, to say nothing of the clerical help required for all of them. And these official actors were only half the story. For months on end, the press and public could think of nothing else to discuss. In the end, all national attention was focused on the impeachment issue alone. But while all this went on and on, a large proportion of the nation's general population had long since come to believe that the answer to the central question at issue had been obvious from the beginning.

A more ominously farcical element of the impeachment process lay in its imprecision and blunderbuss quality. It was a relatively safe bet from early on in the proceedings that "they," to use Nixon's propagandistic terminology, would "get" him in the end. But even after it was all over, it was not clear who "they" were. In retrospect it seems that the House Judiciary Committee, by formulating the specific charges to be brought against Nixon, played a critical role. It did, but no more so than others. The House Judiciary Committee undertook its task reluctantly and worked almost exclusively with materials provided by other agencies earlier and more energetically in the field: the Senate Watergate Committee, the Special Prosecutor's Office, the original Department of Justice investigators, and the press. From time to time these agencies cooperated, but hardly more than that. The general picture, from start to finish, was the standard American political situation in which a host of actors stumble forward in complex and irregular patterns that defy the assessment of responsibility that democratic theory and popular imagination require.

These factors also made it uncertain almost to the last why Nixon needed to be "got." Gradually the charges were formulated and pressed. Along the way, very important ones were dropped. Some argued that the dropped charges, such as Nixon's tax problems, the embellishment of his homes at government expense, and the secrecy with which he conducted certain bombing operations in Cambodia, were more serious than the charges that were leveled. Others argued that the most serious charges of all, such as Nixon's conduct of the closing phases of the Vietnam war, were never even raised during the impeachment process. One matter that came up again and again and was almost universally lamented was never cast in formal charges by even the President's most severe critics. In presidential addresses to the American people, Nixon lied repeatedly and systematically, in speech after speech, and thereby debased the most fragile and precious feature of the nation's democracy, its political dialogue. But lying on television to the people is not an impeachable offense.

The final important farcical element in the impeachment process was probably the source of much of the widespread unease when Nixon was brought to book. Those directing the effort against him strove at every turn to make the entire process "judicial" in form and spirit, believing that only in this manner could its conclusions be and appear fair and legitimate. Their effort was largely successful. But that success flew in the face of the fact that any impeachment process is fundamentally a political one. Nixon understood that from the outset and he and all his men fought accordingly. For them, "impeachment politics" was the name of the game. Almost every one else talked laboriously about weighing the evidence, preserving the law, and consulting reason and personal conscience. Yet it was obvious from the beginning that the outcome of the process depended on the decisions and votes of professional, full-time politicians, all expert in the arts of political survival, all weighing necessarily personal political interests against whatever else they chose to put into the balance.

If they had had the chance, the American people would have undone Nixon's 1972 election and voted him out of office. In other words, they would have made a political choice and acted upon it. But they were forbidden that route by their Constitution. The matter was forced into a judicial charade instead. As social and economic problems accumulated and Nixon's executive utility evaporated, the argument about how to remove him while observing every legal and moral nicety went on and on. Desperately the barons in charge strove not so much to get Nixon out as to save the system, their system as much as his, from a wave of political revulsion. So they dressed it out in judicial robes, banished politics from every corner, reduced the government to grand farce, turned the whole process into a long, long joke so mythically solemn no one dared laugh. That constituted neither violence nor even breakdown in the usual meanings of the words, but it certainly brought the political process to as full a stop as any open rebellion could have.

As the breakdown stage of the myth/ideology crisis cycle concludes, the recovery stage may begin with a moment of absolution. Taking a number of examples of these together will expose the logic of the whole recovery stage.

At the Appomattox Court House Grant told Lee that once his army had been disarmed of all save side arms, "each officer and man will be allowed to return to their homes, not be disturbed by United States authority so long as they observe their parole and the laws in force where they may reside." These terms are now interpreted as exceptionally generous. It is also thought they expressed Grant's intelligent recognition that the war had been a civil one, that the Southern soldiers were not ordinary enemies but fellow Americans, and that the imperative of the moment was the restoration of common life. On both these counts, Grant's behavior contrasts sharply with that of many other Northerners of the time.

On the other hand, Grant asked for and received an unconditional surrender. Hobbesian sovereigns will accept no less. Secondly, in demanding only the disarmament of Lee's men, Grant was effectively telling Lee and the world at large

that in the Civil War rebellion was the only issue. He was saying that once the violence ended, everyone could go home and
forget. Grant refused to pass judgment on the Southern cause.
Perhaps to do so would have exceeded his authority as a military commander. But he also promised that no other authority
would pass such judgment. In so doing, he was expressing more
than the policy of the Lincoln administration. He was upholding
the underlying Liberal tenet that even on racial questions each
group and each man is the best judge of their own interest
within the law. In giving Lee a blanket all-is-forgiven absolution, Grant was declaring with the finality of the force of arms
that in the Civil War no substantive problems of public policy
were involved.

He was very probably right on this issue too, although he
is given little appreciation for it. The war came on because the
contradiction between mythic egalitarian aspirations and the
South's "peculiar institution" imposed upon the nation's operative political institutions and ideology an intolerable strain.
When the war was over slavery was abolished, but not the
black's effective social and economic subcitizen if not sub-
human status. And within thirty years, with the Supreme Court's
Plessy versus *Ferguson* decision, the South had regained the
right to regulate the relationship between the races. In the same
period, the North had fully solidified its own hypocrisies. The
collapse of the nation's political institutions was hardly noticed
at the time and its implications have rarely been discussed
since. Grant's judgment on Lee sealed up that question as
effectively as it did questions about the morality of the Southern cause. Regardless of the facts, the war was declared meaningless, and the way was open for a rapid restoration of the
nation's myths and its operative ideology to the status quo
ante bellum.

Much the same social function was performed for the
myth/ideology crisis cycle by the Warren Commission Report
in the wake of the Kennedy assassination, but with a twist.
That assassination and the subsequent murder of the assassin
himself on national television shocked the American public as
few single events in their history have. But the debate it in-
flamed was largely diluted by the Warren Commission's comforting reassurance of what all desperately craved to hear, that
Lee Harvey Oswald had acted alone. This judgment was com-

forting because it seemed to rule out any disturbing ideological significance and relieved us of the burden of making a response. Objectively, the presence of a rationally organized conspiracy pursuing intelligently formulated goals would seem less alarming to the general public than the scary notion that the streets are haunted by half-demented quasi-children capable at random times of blowing out the brains of even presidents of the United States. But Americans understand personal problems better than societal problems. Moreover, shrink a great crisis into terms which have a solitary figure break, shoot, and run, and the American cultural soul will empathize with every fiber. And if the man so unjustly shot is a glittering mythic hero of epic dimensions, a glorious president thought seated in Camelot even in his own time, then the stage is set for American tragedy in its purest form. But what finally made this imagery so acceptable was that it rendered the event meaningless — as meaningless as Grant made the Civil War. By saying that the assassination was the work of a single madman, the Warren Commission absolved the rest of us of all blame and of all responsibility to act. Shocked to the core by what we had seen and read and seen again and read again, we craved reassurance that we could retreat unchanged and unchallenged to our myths.

The resolution of crises into the work of one aberrant man or narrowly identified group is a standard American technique. In fact it is a variation of its obverse: that the solution of crisis is putting "the right man" into office. But a final variation on this technique declares that no one is to blame, not even the principals.

The best example of this approach came as the American involvement in Vietnam ground to an end. By then, it was almost universally agreed that the war had been a national disaster, a view that came to be held even by those who had been most active in getting it started. Arthur Schlesinger, Jr. was one of these. He had been a member of President Kennedy's White House staff and had actively supported the decisions by which Kennedy precipitated large-scale American involvement. When Schlesinger came to see the error of these policies, he looked back and tried to explain how it all had come about. But he could not find any one point in time, any one person or group, any one conscious and deliberate decision on which to hang the blame. He concluded that the American involvement in Vietnam had come about because of what he called "the politics of inadvertence." Political scientists were quick to point out that for all its apologetic tone, Schlesinger's analysis was probably not far off the mark. All American policymaking, even when war and peace are at issue, is a patchwork process in which one minor decision here leads "incrementally" to another there and another again, each satisfying particular interests and none capable of addressing or assessing the general drift. But this seemingly comforting analysis has terrifying implications. If America slid inadvertently into the Vietnam involvement, how were we to get out? History soon unfolded the answer: much the same way we got in, by a gradual, stumbling, often inadvertent process. And the implications for America's future are unnerving.

Schlesinger's analysis was widely accepted for reasons having little to do with its political acuity. His conclusion was an absolution not only of the Kennedy and Johnson administrations but of all of us as well. Despite the characteristically American, barbaric use of violence to confront social and political movements, the public was told the war was a mistake, an accident, one of those things that happens. Who can be blamed for things like that? Regardless of what we did, we are our aspirations, and these, noble, humane, and transcendently promising, we do not need to change.

And so it was with Nixon's impeachment. Eventually it ended, suddenly and almost inadvertently. Forced to reveal evidence he had concealed to the end even from his own lawyers, Nixon effectively convicted himself and resigned his office. Immediately the moment of absolution began to develop. In his resignation speech, Nixon took the first step by wholly obscuring the central issues. He admitted only to errors of judgment and argued that he was resigning only because he had lost his base of support in the Congress. He gave no explanation of why he had lost it or why he had needed it.

The next morning there were tears all around and the successor Gerald Ford in strong voice told the nation that its "nightmare" was over. Our Constitution works. Our great republic is a government of laws not men. Here, "the people rule." This theme, with the refrain that the day of shame was actually a day of triumph, already echoed from every side as commentators outdid themselves to remark on the simplicity, swiftness, and sureness of the transfer of power. Few noted that those were characteristics only of the final moments of the process. Before then, all had been enormously complicated, agonizingly slow, and wholly unpredictable. Nevertheless, editors could declare:

> Out of the despair of Watergate has come an inspiring new demonstration of the uniqueness and strength of the American democracy. A mammoth task of self-cleansing has been carried out under the principles and procedures established by the Founding Fathers almost two centuries ago.
>
> The checks and balances of a tripartite system, strained by the abuses of an aberrant Chief Executive, have proven adequate to restore faith in the integrity and responsibility of that system.[1]

With that kind of absolution, who needs to learn? No wonder that within months President Ford gave Richard Nixon an unconditional pardon.

Thus proceeds the recovery stage. The mistakes, horrors, and guilts are put aside. They are not connected to the preachments of myth. These are independently reaffirmed. The veil between self-image and action is drawn again. Three final points remain to be made about the myth/ideology crisis cycle. Each is in the form of a reminder.

First, if it seems that undue emphasis has been placed on violence, the defense is not simply to point to the plethora of violence in American political history. Remember also that in the American Liberal ideology, as much as in Hobbes' original philosophy, violence is the "natural" condition. The achievement of society requires continuous effort. The urge to violence is so pent up in each of us that we greet a break-and-run situation with ideological relief. H. Rap Brown was pointing in this direction when he said, "Violence is as American as cherry pie."

Second, like most social theory, the myth/ideology cycle outlined here is primarily useful for the way it can order our understanding of events. American political life is a kaleidoscope of incidents. If these assume crisis proportions, they may become susceptible to analysis in terms of the four-stage cycle presented in this chapter. Sometimes such incidents pass through the cycle's stages relatively quickly, as did Watergate.

1. The New York Times, August 9, 1974, p. 32.

In contrast, the Civil War crisis originated in the Declaration of Independence and extended through the Missouri Compromise, the war itself, and on to *Plessy* versus *Ferguson,* a span of 120 years. Sometimes these incidents in American life are easily distinguished from the rest. Other times they feed into and grow out of each other in apparently random ways. This was especially true of the assassinations, riots, overseas disasters, and other moments of high drama that cluttered the 1960s and early 1970s. The myth/ideology cycle is a heuristic device, an analytic frame by which to bring these incidents into revealing and consistent focus. Its aim is to bring out meaning that might otherwise be smothered by vividness of details and the emotions which these incidents so powerfully engender.

Third, the illustrations and analyses presented in this chapter buttress the general conclusion that over and over again the cycle has repeated itself, stage following stage with every appearance of inevitability. The historical and analytic evidence supports the judgment that the American political system and the mind it articulates exist in a condition of "neutral" equilibrium. Yet some may still ask, why, even after the most horrendous events have exposed the myths as hollow and the operative political system as crass and socially self-demeaning, do we so swiftly and uncritically return to them again? After all the other answers are put down, one stands as overriding: we have nowhere else to go. That vast, inherited national mythic and ideological preformation of consciousness in which our history has mired us gives us no alternatives.

THE PUBLIC INTEREST

7

THE RATIONAL/
PROFESSIONAL MIND
LEGAL ORDER
PUBLIC SERVICE

THE RATIONAL/PROFESSIONAL MIND

The third of the great tasks of American government is to get the work assigned to it done with some regard to the public interest. Over the years, the work assigned American government has grown enormously in scale, complexity, and cost. It ranges from the primal needs of preserving the public peace and defending the community from invasion through the more modern concern of regulating economic activity to such contemporary imperatives as supplying a host of services to specific groups or on behalf of the public generally. Any reader can draw up a detailed list of examples of this colossal work assignment. And most can recall the specific government agencies expected to participate in their performance, such as law enforcement agencies at all levels of the government, monetary authorities at the federal level, and educational bodies which are mainly local. This chapter analyzes the ideal mental type which can undertake to do all this work well. We have chosen to designate this ideal mental type the *rational/professional mind,* a mind at once reasonable in itself and highly skilled by training.

The present chapter will also show that, while the rational/professional has been brought in to serve the political system and its needs by irrepressible demand, it nevertheless radically contradicts fundamental features of the system's dominant Protestant-Bourgeois ethos. Because of these contradictions, the rational/professional mind in the American context, while it strives nobly and competently to go about its work, finds its motives as often frustrated as encouraged and its efforts harassed as often as harnessed.

The resulting confusions and strains are in excess of those already observed within the dominant Protestant-Bourgeois ethos itself and they split that ethos into its mythic and operative ideological elements. Hence, it may sometimes appear that the rational/professional, teased and demeaned beyond patience, may be in a position to take off on his own, rather as if the genie had been let out of the lamp by too small a boy. There have been very important occasions when the rational/professional mentality, in its legal guise and speaking especially through the Supreme Court, has seemed to be not only settling controversies appropriately within the limits of the law, but also defining and extending the limits of public policy. And in its bureaucratic guise, especially in the great Washington headquarters, the rational/professional mentality seems under more or less continuous temptation to take on a life of its own and go its own way. Nevertheless, as we have seen, the American political system has powerful capacities for maintaining its overall stability and sterility. To date, it gives every appearance of being able to disperse, suppress, and generally contain the outstretching tendencies of its judicial and bureaucratic elements within the same limits it has set for the endless war between its mythic and operative elements.

The discussion must begin with the usual reminder that here, as elsewhere, we do not review an actual group of people — judges, civil servants, the military, and others in public employment. The rational/professional mentality is a particular preformation of political consciousness, a special way of viewing political life for the purpose of participating in it. It is used especially by judges and other public servants, but it also shows up in the work of regular politicians from time to time, sometimes very prominently. Equally important is the fact that in America actual judges and civil servants regularly become infected with both Protestant and Bourgeois enthusiasms characteristic of the system's dominant ethos. This sometimes happens simply because they are Americans like everybody else and get caught up in the general mood of the political culture. More interestingly, it happens in particular cases where an individual rational/professional person is compelled to put on the colors of outraged conscience or, alternatively, to go cunningly the avaricious transactional route in order to preserve cherished programs or just keep his or her footing in the bureaucratic hierarchy. In any event, the rational/professional mentality should be regarded as the third mode of political consciousness available to American political operatives. It is more readily available to some political actors than others, but as much as the other two it is an important part of the total political system.

As such, rational/professionalism's contrasts with the Protestant and Bourgeois elements are of decisive importance. The most immediately noticeable difference is that the rational/professional mentality is not linked to its partners in the system. Those partners are linked to each other, albeit unhappily, by their common history and their fundamental attachment to individualism. But the rational/professional mentality is wholly different and apart from both of them, and it must meet and contradict the Protestant-Bourgeois syndrome externally.

Secondly, unlike the Protestant-Bourgeois syndrome, the rational/professional mentality suffers few if any schizophrenic tendencies. Internally it is a unified way of understanding and acting in the political world. This is not to say that actual judges and other public servants cannot find themselves confused. In America such persons regularly get caught between competing modes of political consciousness, and the consequences for them personally can be traumatic. The point here is simply that as public servants their vision is clear, and their self-assurance, while limited in ways we must notice, is calm and uncomplicated. In their assigned roles they know what to do, how to do it, and why they must. As professionals, they do not experience or empathize with the ambitions, doubts, and guilts which wrack Protestant-Bourgeois politicians, the barons who are their nominal masters, or the ordinary Americans whom in theory they serve.

The reason for their assurance lies in the unified complete-ness of the rational/professional's outlook, a quality which stems from its general rationality. This is not meant to suggest that the Protestant-Bourgeois outlook is inherently irrational, although in their paroxysms of self-hatred, Protestant-Bourgeois individuals and communities plunge deeply into irrationality with some regularity. But for the Protestant-Bourgeois, rationality is only an instrumental factor, a capacity for dealing with prob-lems as they may arise. It is not a definitional element of the Protestant-Bourgeois ego, nor is it a decisive Protestant-Bour-geois society. The central element in the Protestant-Bourgeois sense of personal identity is will, life-energy, and its restless search for achievement, power, and security. Correspondingly, the Protestant-Bourgeois social sense is defined as either a sentimental transaction in humanity or an avaricious transaction in self-satisfaction. In contrast to this, rationality for the rational/professional is the essence of both self and society.

The rational/professional achieves a sense of selfhood through no assertion of ego. It comes instead through de-monstrable and acknowledged professional competence. This means two things. First, the competence must be recognized.

Typically this is achieved through training, examination, and admission into an orthodox professional group of an appropriate and socially recognized specialty, as in the legal, medical, and other professions with similar histories of extended, formal organization. On the other hand, the required sense of recognized admission can often be gained simply by holding an appropriate job. In American government, especially in the federal service, the whole process is elaborately structured and codified, in terms of both admission and advancement and tenure. But in whatever detail the matter is handled, the end result is that the rational/professional's self-understanding is objective, not subjective. It comes not through some inner experience, but through the recognition of others.

Secondly, the rational/professional is recognized as simply the possessor of a certain skill, learning, or other competence. Who am I? For the rational/professional, the answer is not the existential "me," the unique self that I have become in my time. It is certainly not, in the nominating language of the American political baronage, "The man who . . ." The answer is rather, a tax lawyer, an oceanic hydrographer, a judge, a soldier, one of a class of persons who can perform to a set standard of competence — rationally, impersonally, by reference merely to the prescribed techniques and canons of one's professional fraternity.

Even at this level of analysis it is plain that as an ideal mental type, the rational/professional will think, talk, and act through a vocabulary of political self-consciousness very different from that employed by the Protestant-Bourgeois. We only begin to get at these differences by contrasting the "communitarianism" of the former with the "individualism" of the latter. The differences become sharper when we think first of the Protestant-Bourgeois, strong in will and brave in faith (or weak and whimpering), setting forth as one soul to pursue a self-defined interest: nirvana, fame, power, wealth, whatever. Then think of a uniformed police officer, trained, disciplined, starchly correct, arresting a law-breaker. What prompts the arrest is the logical congruence between wearing the uniform and upholding the law. Action here is solely in response to the imperatives of the profession. How shocking is the thought, in rational/professional terms, that the police officer might not act unless self-interest were first satisfied, unless some kind of deal were made with the criminal. It would be as if a sailor, skilled in the ways of the sea, deliberately set his craft upon the rocks in order to destroy his vessel and commit suicide. It would be an irrational act, a kind of professional insanity.

During the long story of the unraveling of the Watergate affair, leading ultimately to the resignation of President Nixon, a particular crisis along the way was Nixon's firing of Special Prosecutor Archibald Cox. Cox, the very model of the rational/ professional mind, believed that to do his job he had to pursue certain lines of investigation. President Nixon, the quintessential Protestant-Bourgeois baron, resisted, knowing only too well what was only later revealed to the public, that to allow Cox to go on would be disastrously contrary to Nixon's interest. Just hours before the crisis in this contest broke with Nixon's ordering Cox discharged, Cox held a news conference in a room jammed with excited reporters. The atmosphere was one of extreme tension, yet Cox conducted the conference calmly, with traces of dry wit, firmly, but with unfeigned self-effacement. In particular, he began the conference by noting a headline in one of the morning newspapers, "Cox Defiant." Cox insisted that he was not defiant and that he was not engaged in defying anybody. He had, he said, the greatest respect for the Attorney General, his immediate superior, and for the presidency. As a loyal American, he understood the need to be obedient to constituted authority. But, he said, he was trying to do a job in the best way he knew how. If that was unsatisfactory, he would be happy to retire and go back to teaching law. Which, of course, is exactly what happened.

These attitudes and understandings of the self carry over into the rational/professionals' understanding of their social situation. As professionally competent, especially if in government work, they see themselves summoned to serve neither this person nor that one, and certainly not themselves, but society generally. Of course they get their pay and think of possible promotion, but that all fits into the pattern of career potential. Of course they are subject to superiors and discharge their functions under orders. But all of this only becomes meaningful and defensible as the whole professional situation is set in the context of the public interest. For in the final analysis, it is the public interest — and it alone — that they must serve, loyally and to the end.

The public interest is an abstraction. Because of that, many students of politics, especially those political scientists most attuned to the speech and behavior of American barons, believe the notion of the public interest to be either operationally meaningless or only emotively significant. In terms of their field of reference, they are right. Ideologically the barons are driven to serve individual interests, either their own personally, or, in pursuit of that, the interests of their clients and fellow barons. All of these interests are identifiable immediately in experience by simply asking the relevant persons what they want.

To rise to any higher perspective, the barons know only two routes. Individual interests can be added, identified as shared, or otherwise conjoined. As a practical possibility, this process has finite limits that stop well short of anything so ethereal as "the good of all," or "the greatest good of the greatest number." In fact, given the minoritarian nature of the operative American political system, totaling of individual interests cannot go even so far as "the good of the majority." The most the barons can achieve in this regard is the empirically given in each situation, the good of those who combined to promote their interests in the first place.

On the other hand, in conscience the barons of the American political system have available a more generalized notion of the public interest, one they can derive from the system's humane Protestant feelings for the community. Appeals to the good of this collective will be emotively powerful, certainly for the general electorate and perhaps even for the barons themselves. Nevertheless, given the operational weakness of the whole Protestant side of American politics, these appeals are mostly to mere sentiment and vague feelings of social responsibility. The clarion calls to ask not what the nation can do for each of us but ask rather what each of us can do for the nation are grounded in and can only be worked out through the political system's myths. For all the force with which they may be put and felt, mythic appeals to the public interest compare poorly to the hard empirically felt definitions of personal interest which are the lifeblood of the system's daily work. Repeatedly they are sent nobly aloft; as regularly, they are soon deflated as unrealistic, impractical, utopian, the soft-headed enthusiasms of the pious.

None of this deters or even distracts the rational/professional. If the concept of the public interest he must serve is abstract, so also and equally is the concept he has of himself, a mere impersonal, desubjectified skill. Moreover, for him, the concepts of self and of society are reciprocally related in mutual presupposition. Neither can be given practical definition except in the context of the other. As thus mutually defining, the thought linking them becomes the ground for an ongoing experience in which the rational/professional's sense of himself and his skill becomes concrete only along with his growing awareness of his actual social situation and of the particular ways in which he can contribute through his skills to the general welfare. The ultimate expression of this complex but comprehensively coherent process is to be found in Hegel's description of perfect social freedom, an ideal situation in which the individual finds fulfillment in service to the universal interests of the state without loss of particularity.

The state is the actuality of concrete freedom. But concrete freedom consists in this, that personal individuality and its particular interests not only achieve their complete development and gain explicit recognition for their right ... but, for one thing, they also pass over of their own accord into the interest of the universal, and, for another thing, they know and will the universal; they even recognize it as their own substantive mind; they take it as their end and aim and are active in its pursuit. The result is that the universal does not prevail or achieve completion except along with particular interests and through the co-operation of particular knowing and willing; and individuals likewise do not live as private persons for their own ends alone, but in the very act of willing these they will the universal in the light of the universal, and their activity is consciously aimed at none but the universal end.[1]

That Hegel wrote metaphysical implications of cosmic proportions into this process should not put us off. He is describing the ideal thought process by which the modern civil or military servant develops the particularities of his personal talents, training, and ambitions and relates them to the needs of the community and public authorities he serves. For such a servant to the public interest, not only are the concepts of his service and the public interest reasonable, and in fact, necessary, but

1. *Hegel's Philosophy of Right*, tr. T. M. Knox, Oxford, London, 1942, pp. 160–161.

they are also unthinkable except as mutually related in and through his personal concrete experience. It is in these terms that letter carriers, soldiers, judges, bureau chiefs, administrative assistants, field agents, and all the rest walk through their days of loyal service in the public interest.

But there are limits to the definition of the skillful self in the context of an understood public interest. That it goes on as far as it does is important, and within it individual public servants can sharpen their skills and perfect their employment of them with very considerable precision. Yet in time they will inevitably face questions they cannot answer. The letter carrier is to deliver the mail, swiftly, surely, at minimum cost, and to all citizens without favor. But what about pornography, subversive materials, or assassins' bombs? The soldier can develop weapons and train himself in their use. But whom is he to fight, within what limits, and for the achievement of what purpose? What is to guide the judge through conflicting laws or controversies on which the law is silent?

These questions arise from the rational/professional's fundamentally instrumental character. A servant requires a master in thought as much as experience. Although the line separating servant and master, administration and policy, is never as clear as the argument might suggest, all governments face this division and all strive to handle it by giving the public servant what may be loosely called political leadership.

The American effort to give political leadership to its public servants is fraught with more than the usual difficulties. It will be useful to list the most important of these together before analyzing their particular ramifications for courts and judges on the one hand, and the public bureaucracy and civil service on the other.

At the institutional level, the prime difficulty American public servants experience when they look beyond themselves for guidance in their work is the extreme fragmentation and dispersion of political leadership in America. From the point of view of those who want to get on with their job, authority structures in America are horrendously scattered and pitifully weak. In situation after situation, American public servants are given only faltering, incomplete, ambiguous leadership. As often, competing masters make conflicting demands upon their talents and energies. And sometimes they get no direction at all and are left to their own devices. This last situation is an important feature of much of America's bureaucratic life, but it is also an especially important problem for the Supreme Court.

Secondly, when public servants are given a lead, the clash between the mental processes by which the typical Protestant-Bourgeois politician formulates his conception of the public interest and those understood in the mind of the public servants can sometimes be so serious as to cause paralysis. Theoretical in origin as this clash is, it can bring on quite painful complications for the public servant.

Thirdly, when public servants are given an insufficient or ambiguous lead or left to work things out alone, they are likely to stumble simply because they are not well prepared, by training and temperament, to set about defining ends. They are like illustrators. Given a text, they can do well, but they lack the artistic sense to paint their own pictures. However popular, generals and bureaucrats make notoriously ineffective politicians. They are too much given to vacuous generalizations learned by rote from school books or singular concerns regardless of competing needs.

Finally, there is the most serious difficulty of all. When faced with failures of actual political leadership, American public servants will turn instinctively to the general value structure of the overall political culture. There they confront the weaknesses and insufficiencies of the nation's dominant Liberalism. Of course these plague all Americans, but they torture public servants. Public servants have a clear concept of the public interest, and their problem is to give it content in particular circumstances. But it is precisely in the area of public concerns that American Liberal political theory is most deficient. As we have seen, even the concept of public authority was hamstrung in Liberalism's origins, and subsequently it has been able to develop only the most inexact vocabulary of social organization and social justice. Over and over, American public servants are told to do something constructive about poverty, racism, crime, and a host of other problems which agonize the nation's Protestant conscience. But these problems are broadly and deeply social in both quality and extent. As public servants, American rational/professionals can put these problems firmly into the context of that concept of the public interest which they inherently possess. But in the American environment they experience grave difficulties in going from this theoretical grasp of the issues to practical programs for their solution. Typically, like any other American Liberal, they wind up merely talking about people's "rights," as if one could organize and manipulate sociological perspectives by such radically individualized means.

LEGAL ORDER

The unity of the American political system lies in its being a constitutional construct, a legal "cage." The prime service to the public interest performed by American courts and their judges is their unique capacity to perceive, preserve, and maintain that cage as a single totality containing a nation of self-motivating, quarrelsome egos.

Implicit as much in Liberalism's Hobbesian presuppositions as in Madisonian constitutionalism is the assumption that an individualistic, competitive society will be wracked by controversies between interests of every sort. The vast proportion of these controversies are minor and are resolved by the parties to them. This also happens sometimes with controversies of serious proportions. And many more controversies occur within institutional settings which provide specialized machinery for resolving them without formal appeals to the law. But there remain disputes which threaten the stability of our self-imposed legal encagement. These must be dealt with firmly, because they attack the only barrier in our Liberal society standing between us and what we regard in self-fulfilling prophecy as our anarchic nature.

To settle such disputes we turn to the courts, whether in civil or criminal actions. From a philosophical perspective, it is both significant and characteristic that the Americans have sustained the ancient English procedure which brings these actions before courts as adversary proceedings. This pattern is followed even in criminal cases: the courts treat criminal actions as disputes between public authorities and alleged law-breakers in which the accused are presumed innocent. But of even greater interest are the assumptions made in all these actions about the judges of the courts, the nature of their work, and the motives for their actions.

These assumptions can be put simply by saying that judges are different. They are different because they are not, or at least are not supposed to be, in any way parties to the disputes that come before them for settlement. Locke put the traditional view well when he argued that no man should be a judge in his own case, and as traditions go, this one has been well observed. But there is also a larger sense in which, in the Anglo-American tradition, judges are supposed to be different from other political actors. In the Liberal view, ordinary men are invariably self-serving, interested parties in all they do. That is why they get into disputes and why the disputes are so often dangerous and difficult to resolve. But judges called upon to settle these disputes are supposed to be "disinterested" persons by character, training, situation, demeanor, and function.

Judges are expected to be merely judicious, clearly members of the group we have labeled rational/professionals. Symbolically, our expectations are revealed in the ways we clothe judges in priestly robes, put them in chambers that look like churches, and often house them in exact replicas of Greek temples. Along with the honorific rituals that permeate their formal conduct, these trappings emphasize the distance that is supposed to separate judges from the likes of the rest of us. And at the more important level of substance, the wholly disinterested judicial mind is supposed to appear in two central characteristics.

First, the good judge is expected to be firm and skillful in conducting the proceedings that go on in his or her court. The good judge is expected to be able to discipline the parties before the bench and to expedite resolution of their dispute. The good judge is expected also to be adept at applying the general rules of the law to particular situations. In other words, like any rational/professional, the judge should know the job and perform it competently, without favor or thought of personal advancement.

More important, as servant to the public the good judge is expected to know the law and preserve it through all disputes. The good judge is servant, not master, of the law. The law is decreed in solemn compact, and in the promulgations of sovereign legislative authorities. With the aid of counsel, the good judge obediently studies the decrees of the legislative authorities and applies their particular rules to the disputes that arrive in court. Through all this, the good judge is pure rational/professional, disinterestedly doing an assigned job as well as possible.

In other words, the judge does not find out what the law is by magisterially inventing it, or by consulting some superior wisdom of justice and truth. Equally, in Anglo-American Liberal theory ordinary citizens do not go to judges to obtain, except in vague, distant hope, justice. Citizens go to court, or are brought there, because they are parties to dangerous disputes. And what they get from the courts are resolutions of those disputes within the law. In this way, we ordinary folk are all kept within the limits of our legal cage by the judges, rational/professionals whose first obligation is not to themselves, to us, or to any one else — but to disinterestedly keeping the cage intact as king of us all.

The role of the judges as uniquely qualified keepers of the legal cage that Liberal theory erects to entrap all ordinary people was recognized from the beginning of the Anglo-American tradition. The early kings, as lawmakers of their realms, delegated to the judges the task of preserving the public peace. The same theory was implicit in Hobbes' basic formulations of both the law's nature and its prime utility to people generally. And it has been central to the claims of American judges from John Marshall on for the respect they believed the rest of us owe them and their courts. Even Madison, in the all-important Federalist Paper No. 51, allowed that judges had to be recruited differently from other political actors.

In the constitution of the judiciary department in particular, it might be inexpedient to insist rigorously on the principle [of election, direct or indirect], first, because peculiar qualifications being essential in the members, the primary consideration ought to be to select that mode of choice, which best secures these qualifications; secondly, because the permanent tenure by which the appointments are held in that department, must soon destroy all sense of dependence on the authority conferring them.

That judges must be supposed to possess these "peculiar qualifications" underlay Marshall's argument throughout *Marbury* versus *Madison,* above all the central assertion that

It is emphatically, the province and duty of the judicial department to say what the law is. Those who apply the rule to particular cases must of necessity expound and interpret that rule. If two laws conflict with each other, the courts must decide on the operation of each.

Marshall's argument in that case was directed to supporting the right of the court to review acts of Congress for constitutionality, and it is primarily in this sense that the power of judicial review is known through the textbooks. But the special stature of judges as keepers of the legal order is better revealed in those cases in which the power of judicial review was extended to bridle the pretensions of executives, especially the president. In these cases the Liberal imagination can be immediately excited, for in them the judges take on, stare down, and put back within the law individual usurpers of power. Thus, in the post-Civil War case *ex parte Milligan,* the court found itself confronting the proposition

. . . that in a time of war the commander of an armed force (if in his opinion the exigencies of the country demand it, and of which he is to judge) has the power within the lines of his military district, to suspend all civil rights and their remedies and subject citizens as well as soldiers to the rule of *his will;* and in the exercise of his lawful authority cannot be restrained, except by his superior officer or the President of the United States.

As interesting as the words in this proposition which the court chose to italicize is the choice of argument the court made to put against it.

This nation, as experience has proved, cannot always remain at peace and has no right to expect that it will always have wise and humane rulers, sincerely attached to the principles of the Constitution. Wicked men, ambitious of power, with hatred of liberty and contempt of law, may fill the place once occupied by Washington and Lincoln; and if this right [recited above] is conceded, and the calamities of war again befall us, the dangers to human liberty are frightful to contemplate.

Observers with broader perspective on the possibilities of politics than Americans might wonder whether the dangers the court conjured up with these words were real. Would the American people be likely to put such tigers into office, and if they did would they have no method of their own for ousting them before real hurt to human liberty had been done? But that kind of thinking radically underestimates the limitations of the American political system. Again and again the American people have had to beseech the judiciary for relief from executive usurpations and corruptions at all levels of their government. And again and again relief has come by that route, sometimes spectacularly as when President Truman's seizure of the steel mills during the Korean War was disallowed by the Supreme Court. But it took the case of *United States* versus *Richard Nixon* to expose the full implications of these issues.

The case was brought by the Special Prosecutor investigating the Watergate affair. He claimed before the court that he needed materials held by President Nixon to press charges against a number of Nixon's assistants in a case in which Nixon himself was named but not indicted. The President had steadfastly refused to surrender such materials on the grounds that to do so would undermine the "executive privilege" that adhered to his office and assured its occupant unrestricted discretion in revealing private conversations. In its ruling, the court allowed that presidents had a privilege of confidentiality but held that it was rooted in practical requirements and not in law. It further held that this privilege was not absolute. In particular it argued that

The impediment that an absolute, unqualified privilege would place in the way of the primary constitutional duty of the judicial branch to do justice in criminal prosecutions would plainly conflict with the function of the courts. . . .

and that

. . . the allowance of the privilege to withhold evidence that is demonstrably relevant in a criminal trial would cut deeply into the guarantee of due process of law and gravely impair the basic function of the courts.

The court then faced the central question, marshaled the precedents, and concluded that they "cannot be read to mean in any sense that a President is above the law."

In retrospect, three further points about this case need to be emphasized. The first is that after initial hesitations President Nixon was squeezed into announcing the obvious, that he would obey the court's order to release the materials. He thereby admitted to posterity the rightness of the court's central claim, that all persons, even presidents, are subject to the law. He also effectively conceded the court's implied role to sustain that claim.

Secondly, the release of the materials not only led directly to Nixon's resignation but also aborted the cumbersome congressional impeachment process which had been underway quite independently for many months. In consequence, the honors, if not in any firm poltical sense the responsibility for administering the coup de grace to presidential lawlessness went, once again, to the courts and their "impassive," "unemotional," wholly disinterested judges.

The third point is that of the eight judges participating in the court's unanimous action, three had been appointed by Nixon himself. One of these, the chief justice, had actually written the court's opinion. Nixon had personally selected these men for appointment to the court. More particularly, he had lauded each of them at the time of their appointments not only for their personal qualities but also for their supposed judicial philosophies and their agreement with his own. But when the issue was of legal and judicial supremacy, old loyalties and gratitudes counted for nothing. In Madison's words, the judges' sense of duty destroyed "all sense of dependence on the authority conferring them" in office. They depended exclusively upon those concepts of duty and public interest symbolized by their robes.

The day after the decision was announced, *The New York Times* editorialized the conclusions of informed opinion generally.

> In a unanimous and firmly-worded opinion, the Supreme Court has reaffirmed the supremacy of law over Presidential pretensions and restated its own authority as the ultimate arbiter of the law. . . .
>
> If this nation was to remain the Republic established by the authors of the Constitution, the Court could only have ruled as it did yesterday. A decision in Mr. Nixon's favor would have meant that he or any future President could operate outside the law. . . .[2]

There is irony in this horror of presidents outside the law, for it is lost on almost all observers that this is precisely the position the judges occupy in their role as keepers of the legal cage. Because of the weight of tradition enveloping their functions and also because of the inconstant pace at which they

2. July 23, 1974, p. 32.

work, taking disputes only when and if they come, the judges are not as frightening to the American Liberal imagination as are all shades of executive authority descending from George III. Moreover, as rational/professionals defining themselves in terms merely of the concrete application of their traditional skills to non-controversial social needs, the judges do not often display the unusual character of their status in the political system. Nevertheless, this status is the source of real difficulties.

Some of these difficulties are administrative in character. The ideal judge is a pure rational/professional. Actual American judges, especially at the local level and the lower levels of the State systems, often fall well short of that ideal. Judicial appointments and, where judges are elected, many judicial nominations are a form of patronage bestowed through arrangements made by barons working elsewhere in the political system or in the legal profession generally. For example, after a not-otherwise-memorable State legislative tussle over State aid to metropolitan areas, a baron on the losing side complained openly to a reporter that the winners had gained much of their strength from being able to hand around judgeships "like cookies." In this kind of atmosphere many judges, despite the monumental weight of professional tradition, are corrupted in sundry devious ways, sometimes systematically. There is ample evidence to support this supposition "from the street" and from occasional press reports of trials and convictions of judges. Corruption in the judiciary may be almost as prevalent as it is in other branches of the American political system. But because of the special position judges occupy in that system, their corruption is a more than usually serious matter.

For the barons generally, as we have seen, corruption is virtually politics by another name. But in a political system based on Liberal understandings of the nature and functions of the law, judicial corruption cannot be regarded as a norm. If judges are keepers of the legal cage for the rest of us, corrupting them not only demoralizes them personally; it also directly threatens the security that legal encagement gives us all. Judicial corruption in America is probably a critical link in the chain of factors accounting for the sustained success of syndicated crime across the nation. But because of the special position of judges in the political system, judicial corruption is doubly difficult to detect and prosecute successfully.

These difficulties also lie behind more routine kinds of administrative irregularities among American judges. Judicial independence, to be practically meaningful, must allow relative independence of the judiciary from other branches of the government and relative independence for each judge in the courtroom. But granting that kind of independence entails wide variations in the application of the law, especially in regard to criminal sentencing and damage reward standards, and causes grave problems for those attempting to level out such variations. Much more serious, at least in the field of direct law enforcement, is the problem of getting judges to play systematic and cooperative roles vis-à-vis other government agencies with responsibilities in the area. Whatever extraordinary theoretical and practical significance may be assigned their work, the judges play only one part in the administration of justice. Often enough, from the perspectives of other participants they do not do their part well. Yet because of the necessity, rooted in Liberal doctrine and practice, of never submerging judicial independence, judges are relatively immune from efforts by police, prison personnel, and correction officials to force systematic and integrated patterns of cooperation upon them.

These are all sticky problems. Some of them, at least, could be moderated by changes in laws and administrative practices. The same cannot be said of the major substantive difficulties arising from the special position the judges have in the American political system. These are occasioned by those disputes which the judges find they can only settle by "making," not just applying, law, and they can be seen most vividly in the work of the Supreme Court.

The Supreme Court finds the opportunity to "make" law in ambiguities, imprecisions, and silences in existing law, especially in the Constitution itself and the Bill of Rights. There is no way in which a phrase like "equal protection of the laws" can be given precise meaning in the context of a heated social or political problem except by coining such a meaning more or less arbitrarily on the spot. Over the years, the Supreme Court has consistently shown a coy reluctance to hand down such meanings, some would say to the point of irresponsibility. On the other hand, the opportunity to do so has been transformed often enough into unavoidable demand by the failure of other branches of the government to meet problems ade-

quately and by the eagerness of the American people to let
judges confront and declare upon issues of even the broadest
sort.

All the "great" cases settled by the Supreme Court, from
Marbury versus *Madison* on, have had a law-making dimension.
But for all their legal trappings, some of the most outstanding
of these have involved public policy problems pure and simple.
Any important Supreme Court decision will reaffirm the underlying policy preferences of the law itself and of most judges
and lawyers as well, but the cases now being cited go far
beyond that. Thus, perhaps the most notorious of the court's
"political" cases, the Dred Scott decision of 1857, could be
interpreted as plain application of the bias built into the roots
of American law in favor of property rights over human rights.
But interpretation that stopped there would have to ignore all
the where, when, and why of the case and all the contextual
questions which made the court's decision momentous. In that
context, the action of the court can be seen as a powerful move
on behalf of slave-holding interests and as a major blow against
the Republicans seeking to limit those interests. Moreover, this
same contextual light also shows that the court's action hardened attitudes all along the line and pushed the nation on
through the stage of increasing frustration toward the inevitable
stage of violence. It is at least arguable that a legislative
decision to the same effect would not have so dangerously
aggravated the situation. Legislative decisions are clearly re-
versible. But the Supreme Court, at least in appearance, speaks
with the implacably final voice of the law of the land. To oppose its rule requires an ultimate defiance.

But too much blame can be heaped on the members of
the Supreme Court when from time to time they employ its
voice on major policy questions confronting the nation. They
are largely compelled to do so by the failure of the other
branches of government to give clear political leadership. The
general fumbling of the slavery question from the Missouri
Compromise of 1820 on meant that one day, sooner or later,
the issue would get to the courts. In *Dred Scott* it did and the
Supreme Court took its stand. Disaster followed. But for all
history knows, a different decision in that case might have precipitated the Civil War even more quickly. *Dred Scott* is largely
known as a "bad" decision because the interests the court

favored by it went on to lose the war. Later, in *Plessy* versus *Ferguson,* the Court was given a chance to reaffirm its initial policy preference on the race question, which it did. The nation hardly blinked. Half a century later the nation was in a very different mood, and the court, in *Brown* versus *Board of Education,* went the other way.

In all these cases and in many others raising comparable questions in different areas of national concern, the Supreme Court has played a clear policy role with little "political" guidance from the other elements of the government, and there is every probability that from time to time it will be called upon to play this role in the future. How important is this role? What are the consequences for the political system generally? The answer, perhaps surprisingly, is that the Supreme Court's significance in this area is small, despite the enormous attention given it in the press and the schools.

The first reason for this judgment arises directly from the nature of the Supreme Court as a court. A court is not an administrative body, and only with the greatest difficulty can it display the kind of ongoing force which the administration of a policy requires. Consequently, while it may pronounce a policy, administration must be left to others who may be quite variously sympathetic to its objectives. This fundamental weakness is supplemented by another. When the court lays down a policy, it does so in the course of its work in settling specific disputes. The policy may incorporate broad value preferences, but the decision of the court is directed only to particular issues raised by the dispute before it. The practical effect of the court's policy decision is often much narrower than is generally supposed. Thus, in *Brown* versus *Board of Education,* the Supreme Court obviously spoke in behalf of the general advancement of black people in American society. Its decision, however, was directed only to the integration of schools, and it said little about and influenced even less the host of other factors, economic, social, and political, in which the status of blacks in America is rooted. Inevitably, a broad policy so narrowly focused will be of little general consequence.

The inconstancy and narrowness of the Supreme Court's policy-making role are compounded by unavoidable clumsiness in the way it goes about its work in this area. We can illustrate this by looking at a quite different range of cases, those leading up to and on from the *Baker* versus *Carr* decision dealing with malapportionment of electoral districts. Problems of apportionment had long been held to be questions for legislatures to decide, but their discharge of this responsibility was so glaringly inadequate over the years that the pressure on the Supreme Court to undertake to review it was eventually irresistible. In *Baker* versus *Carr* the court claimed jurisdiction by arguing that malapportionment was a violation of the "equal protection" guaranteed by the laws to each citizen, a strange way, to say the least, of interpreting the opportunity to vote. It then argued, in *Gray* versus *Sanders,* that

The conception of political equality from the Declaration of Independence, to Lincoln's Gettysburg Address, to the Fifteenth, Seventeenth, and Nineteenth Amendments can mean only one thing — one person, one vote.

Whatever (if anything) the Gettysburg Address may mean in specific political terms, has it ever been suggested that it had the force of law? Clearly the court was pressuring itself into a Solonic role of interpreting broad ranges of general political tradition. But judges are not philosophers; they strive for rules of applicable and enforceable precision, not general understandings of the political process. So for them, the Gettysburg Address and all the rest meant no more or less than "one person, one vote."

In *Wells* versus *Rockefeller* they held that congressional districts must be so drawn within a State that their respective populations are as nearly equal as the modern technology of head counting and map making will allow. Effectively, they were saying, good constituency design is just a clerical problem. Gerrymandering was only a distant concern. For them, the central issue was purely a question of individual rights: did my right to vote count or weigh as much as yours? At no point did they raise questions about how constituencies should be designed as viable political communities or about what requirements should be met to promote political dialogue and meaningful confrontation. In consequence, the court's malapportionment decisions, for all their being policy ("political") decisions, heralded no revolutions in political representation in America. Legally, they were too narrowly conceived for anything of that order. They signified at most a shifting around of numbers. Questions about fundamental changes in the quality of American electoral politics were not so much postponed indefinitely as never raised at all.

The courts in the American political system do play an indispensable role in maintaining the system's legal frame. Currently, the performance of this role is dangerously marred by corruption and poor administration, but the courts appear capable of sustaining themselves. On the other hand, there appears to be no warrant for the notion that the judges might lead us, through their policy-making role, to a redefinition of the constitutional limits and style of our political life. Neither in theory nor in practice have they demonstrated any transcendent capacity in this regard To return to the metaphor used at the beginning of this chapter, the boy rubbing the lamp may well be small, the limits of the dominant political system being what they are, but so far as the judges are concerned, the genie coming out of the lamp is only that: a mythic wonder propounding landmark decisions and milestones in the law, but actually transforming American politics very slowly, if at all.

PUBLIC SERVICE

The vast army of public servants civil, military, and paramilitary employed by American governments federal, State, and local, has some very important problems. Most of these problems, however, are internal to the public service itself and are of little direct interest to the themes of this book. Typical of such generally interesting administrative problems are questions about improving management capabilities and patterns, information gathering, storage, and retrieval, resource allocations, personnel recruitment, job definition, training and promotion techniques, discipline, and, above all, communications.

The problems posed by the public service which have a direct bearing on the themes of this book concern the ways in which the public service is related to and affected by the other elements of the political system and its dominant Protestant-Bourgeois ethos. Most of these problems have been touched upon at various points in the preceding discussion. To pull them together for a final summary treatment, they will be discussed under three heads: the general pattern of the relationship of the public service to its Protestant-Bourgeois masters, specific questions arising from the clash between the ethos of the public service and that of the dominant political system, and the question raised centrally throughout this chapter about the capacities of rational/professionals for self-direction in the wake of failures of political leadership. Is the public service or some element of it any more able than the judiciary to lead the political system into a measure of self-transcendence and regeneration?

The basis for the general relationship between the American public service and its employers is the extreme fragmentation and dispersion of political authority in this country. An immediate consequence is that the public service, ideally a single monolith dedicated to the national public interest, is itself fragmented into 90,000 or more separate governmental units and beyond that, effectively, into a separate service for each baron in the system. This situation creates a problem, sometimes open, but never wholly escapable, for every person in the public service. To whom should he or she be loyal, the baron above or the more distant concept of the public interest which, for all its abstractness, gives the public servant identity and ethical justification?

Since every baron's job is to make the powers of his office work for him, the conflict between him and his servant's sense of public duty is inevitable. For masses of public servants, this conflict is hidden by distance in hierarchical relationships and the bland requirements of routine job performance. But at the higher reaches of bureaucratic structures where policy decisions are made with visible consequences for both the baron and the public, the conflict of loyalties for public servants can be severe. Typically they straddle the issue and only cut off one or the other of the sources of tension in extreme situations. But often enough, as will be noted more fully later in this discussion, public servants take on the coloration of the barons themselves to protect their own rising personal interests.

Before looking at that kind of development, we must note another aspect of the general relationship between barons and the public service, a point that will go a long way toward explaining the general tenor of American political discourse on public policy issues. Because the barons are fundamentally uninterested in problems of public policy, and because public

servants fundamentally are, the initiation of public policy proposals in American government regularly occurs at the bureaucratic, not the political, level. That is one reason why so many
of the policy proposals that show up in American political discourse are so occasional and specific. Public servants, as
rational/professionals, define themselves as the possessors of
specific skills. Seeking ways to contribute those skills to the
public good, they work out proposals and programs in which
their skills are more or less prominently featured. Most public
servants developing policy proposals of this sort, whether for
building a new military aircraft, controlling inflation, or improving job training programs, will do so from within a particular bureaucratic structure with which they have had a long
personal involvement. It is only natural, therefore, that such
proposals should be not only specific in their content but
narrow in their perspective.

This analysis also explains why barons' statements on
public policy questions, such as the president's annual State of
the Union Address, are usually grab-bag affairs not united by
any consistent political philosophy. The preparation of these
statements is the responsibility of the baron's staff. They collect
and winnow proposals they have dredged up from a wide
variety of bureaucratic depths. Any such occasion is an opportunity for a public servant with a proposal for public policy
to shop it forward, but he must sell his proposal to both levels
of the baron's personality. He must show how his proposal will
serve the baron's own interests or those of the baron's client
groups and principal allies. And he must also show how his
proposal can be made to appeal to the Protestant conscience
of the general electorate. If his luck fails on either of these
counts, the public servant can still hope, given the dispersed,
flattened character of American political hierarchies, to sell his
proposal elsewhere to other barons with whom he has or can
develop appropriate contacts. And through all this, he must
strive to maintain, however faintly, his own understanding of
his proposal's advancement of the public interest.

When a proposal has been sold to one or more barons,
their style of politics takes over. This does not mean that the
public servant drops out. He or she must continue to lobby
and push for the proposal all along the line, supply arguments
and information as requested, and be prepared to modify the

original design as the political process requires. This can be a grueling business. Nevertheless, in some cases it will not be unreasonable to push forward in the hope that some semblance of the original suggestion will be returned for administration. Because of coincidence with the rhetoric of Protestant conscience, the final product may even contain much of the public servant's original concern, however specialized and narrow, with the public good.

After enactment, however, the return of a policy proposal to a bureaucracy for administration may not turn out to be a happy day for the public servant who originated it. It may be a payoff point of great personal satisfaction, but it will also be the beginning of a series of payoff points for the barons. They will not be content to sit back and collect plaudits for enacting great legislation. Baronial interest in the administrative process is always intense, for that process supplies the fodder of their daily political lives. Indeed, seeing to it that all relevant barons are well fed may be the public servant's first obligation for personal survival. Again and again, he or she may have to suffer seeing programs conceived in the public interest used to satisfy selfish baronial needs. This gobbling process can affect staffing, budgeting, and contract allocating as well as more general decisions about program beneficiaries. At municipal and State levels as well as federal levels, it regularly results in such swollen emphasis on what are called "input" factors that "output" factors are stripped of operational significance.

This happens readily in such programs as weapon procurement, highway construction, development of community mental health facilities, and the like, where implementation lends itself to the kinds of particularization of disposable benefits required in baronial negotiations. It also happens on momentous questions of war and peace. Thus, as the Johnson administration came to a close, a group of the President's advisers and assistants, and others more widely placed in the executive branch, became convinced that the President's policy of increasing involvement in the Vietnam war was a mistake and had to be reversed. They consulted among themselves and agreed, in an undeniable public spirit and at considerable risk to their personal careers, to initiate debate within the administration to see to it that the policy of intervention was reversed. In the end, this group achieved their immediate objectives, but the debate by which they did it went on for over a month and later merited this description:

> One dramatic record of its progress appeared in the 12 versions of a Presidential speech that evolved during the month — the last draft pointing in the opposite direction from the first.
>
> The entire episode also provided a remarkable demonstration of how foreign policy is battled out, inch by inch, by negotiation rather than decision. The turnabout emerged through sharp confrontations and subtle, even conspiratorial, maneuvering — with compromises struck for bureaucratic purposes and with opponents in agreement for contrary reasons.[3]

What this description omits is that the decision it refers to was taken in 1968, and direct large-scale American involvement in Vietnam did not end until four disastrous years later. On the other hand it does suggest that a major reason for the extended American involvement in Vietnam was that "input" considerations were regularly allowed to obscure, at times nearly totally, "output" yields.

In this context we can look more closely at the clash between the duty ethos of public service and the interest ethos of the dominant system of baronial politics. At its most poignant, the contest between these conflicting modes of political consciousness appears within the personality of the public servant, and as such it is vividly familiar, for example, to those Americans who watch television police dramas. However melodramatic such fare may be, its very exaggerations point at such real problems as the prevalence of corruption in actual police departments. A former police commissioner of one of the country's largest forces, a man who came up through the ranks, put it in a private interview in approximately these words:

> The guys are out on the street all day. They do pretty much what we trained them to do, and they do it pretty well. But all around them they see people on the take. Not just crooks but all the ordinary business people too, everybody grabbing what he can. So it's pretty hard for the guys not to think that there's not much harm in their taking a little too when it comes their way.[4]

---

3. *The New York Times*, March 6, 1969, p. 14.

4. By the rules of this Kenyon College conference on violence, the commissioner's remarks were not for direct attribution or quotation.

When the commissioner, a man of unquestioned integrity and devout Catholicism, was asked if he was referring to an insoluble conflict between "professionalism" and "capitalism," he answered unhesitatingly in the affirmative and then repeated his thought with the bitter phrase, "The whole country is on the take."

These reflections were confirmed by the findings of the Knapp Commission, which investigated corruption among the New York City police in 1969–1972. They reported that corruption was serious and widespread in the department. But they also reported that the men themselves distinguished between what they termed "meat-eaters" and what they termed "grass-eaters." "Meat-eaters" are officers who take corruption seriously and who spend many on-duty hours aggressively seeking out situations they can exploit for personal financial gain. The commission estimated that they represent only a small percentage of the force but that their graft incomes amount to many thousands of dollars per year. Socially and politically, the "grass-eaters" are a more interesting group. These are the numerous officers whose graft is small-scale, almost casual, but regular. They are relatively efficient and brave, but they accept gratuities (personal gifts in the form of television sets, suits, furs, jewelry, theater tickets, liquor, and even automobiles) and solicit five- and ten- and twenty-dollar payments from contractors, tow truck operators, gamblers, prostitutes, and the like. About such men, the commission further wrote:

One strong impetus encouraging grass-eaters to continue to accept relatively petty graft is, ironically, their feeling of loyalty to their fellow officers. Accepting payoff money is one way for an officer to prove that he is one of the boys and that he can be trusted. In the climate which existed in the Department during the Commission's investigation, at least at the precinct level, these numerous but relatively small payoffs were a fact of life, and those officers who made a point of refusing them were not accepted closely into the fellowship of policemen. Corruption among grass-eaters obviously cannot be met by attempting to arrest them all. . . .[5]

The conclusion in that last sentence was reinforced when the commission remarked later in its report that the situation they

5. Michael Armstrong, Margo Barrett, et al., The Knapp Commission Report on Police Corruption, George Braziller, New York, 1972, p. 65.

found was hardly different from that uncovered by many previous commissions of the same sort.

Compared to many other forms of public service, police work is especially vulnerable to corruption. Moreover, corruption of the police is much more painful, contradictory, and socially dangerous than corruption of the political barons for whom, in campaign financing for example, the difference between the acceptable and the unacceptable is simply a question of what is legally allowed. On the other hand, the prevalence and persistence of corruption in American police departments exemplifies the prevalence and persistence of frustration within the lives of American public servants generally.

These frustrations are expressed in many different ways besides corruption. Among America's public servants cynicism, depression, and resignation are so plentiful as to be the norm. But other developments can arise too, particularly as the public service becomes involved in one or another of the nation's periodic passages through the myth/ideology cycle. To return to the example of police work, as the American community struggled forward through an increasingly agonized stage two over its involvement in Vietnam, police departments across the country generally displayed commendable restraint in the face of provocation by peace demonstrators. But sometimes the discipline broke. It broke in 1968 in Chicago during the Democratic Convention when the police rioted the better to beat up the demonstrators in the street. It broke again during the Columbia University strike when the police took to knocking around Barnard and Columbia College undergraduates. And some of the same tensions and frustrations were at work when discipline collapsed in the shootout at the climax of the Attica rebellion. What was happening in these extraordinary examples of lawlessness by the forces of the law? The answer in its shortest compass would appear to be that the police, although (when in uniform) technically not parts of the Protestant-Bourgeois syndrome, nevertheless got caught up in it and came to feel doubly threatened. They came to believe that the students, supposedly subservient blacks, and effete professors were threatening not only basic American values of masculinity and patriotism, but also that particular sense of order for which they stood as police. In the end random paranoia drove them over the edge.

This discussion leads naturally to our last question. What do public servants in America do, tortured and teased as they so often are by the encompassing Protestant-Bourgeois political environment in which they work, when they are faced with a lack of leadership from their nominal superiors in the political system? The answer is that when they can, they become barons.

Consider two examples. The following is taken in its entirety from a front-page news report in 1974.[6]

'MODEL' POVERTY PROGRAM FALTERS
By Michael Knight
(Special to The New York Times)

NEW HAVEN, Nov. 17 — The country's first anti-poverty program, which pioneered many of the Great Society programs of the early nineteen-sixties here and was the model for hundreds of similar projects in cities across the country, is in deep trouble, according to both its friends and its foes.

The program, Community Progress, Inc., a bold experiment in social reform, was begun in 1962 with the help of the Ford Foundation. It invented Project Head Start, the Neighborhood Youth Corps, the legal-service program, the comprehensive manpower-training program and dozens of other projects later adopted nationwide.

Now, however, according to state and Federal officials who have been investigating the program for months, it has deteriorated into fiscal and administrative chaos and has become little more than a political pork barrel dominated by the city's powerful Democratic party machine.

. . . . the [Connecticut] Department of Community Affairs is calling it a "sick shambles" and is planning to replace it as the local conduit for $1.5 million a year in state anti-poverty funds.

"We've never taken action this drastic before," said Susan Hobbie Bennett, commissioner of the department. "But the irregularities and incompetence are amazing and they've given us every indication that they have no intention of improving."

"The sad part," she said, "is that they have lost the long view they had years ago, got tied up on politics and the pork barrel and City Hall politics. And they forgot what was on the end of the line, which was helping poor people."

Commissioner Bennett's implication that the degeneration of New Haven's Community Progress, Inc. and its loss of focus

6. From " 'Model' Poverty Program Falters," by Michael Knight, *The New York Times* (November 18, 1974), p. 1. © 1974 by the New York Times Company. Reprinted by permission.

on its original goals was unusual is misleading. On the contrary, such dangers plague programs of this sort all across the country. On the other hand, her suggestion that the downfall of this organization was a consequence of its becoming involved in what she termed "City Hall politics" is more than just conventional wisdom. Given the nature of the American brand of "City Hall politics," involvement in it forces even the most idealistic of rational/professionals to lose focus.

This point can also be illustrated by the career of New York's Robert Moses. Moses was a singular man, and his career was extraordinary. But both were archetypal of those situations in American politics when the public service and its rational/ professional idealism and ambition are unleashed, genie-like, from the body of the political system.

Moses' career spanned more than 50 years. During that time he never once held elective office. The one time he ran for such an office he lost ignominiously. But beginning with a close relationship to "Al" Smith, soon to become Governor of the State of New York, Moses rose in the 1920s to a position of considerable influence in that State's politics. From this position he designed and then accepted appointment in the commissions created for the development of the State park system on Long Island, notably Jones Beach, and the parkways connecting them. The extraordinary speed with which he completed these jobs, together with the ebullience, imagination, and energy with which he accomplished them, propelled his career upwards.

Without in any way diminishing his ever-growing involvement in State construction programs, he simultaneously undertook major responsibilities in the government of the City of New York. At the zenith of his career, in the post-World War II era, he held nine major administrative positions, some in the State government, some in the city government, and some as chairman of certain public authorities, the most important of which was the Triborough Bridge and Tunnel Authority. Some of these positions, such as Commissioner of Parks for the City of New York, were regular, established offices. Others were not only created expressly for him but also, like his first position, in legislation actually drafted in minutest detail by Moses personally.

During his long career, governors of the State, including

Smith, Roosevelt, Lehman, Dewey, and Rockefeller, came and went. So also did such mayors of New York City as LaGuardia, Wagner, and Lindsay. None of these men had the power or resources to guide or restrain him. Moses' power and influence were such that he never had to treat them as anything more than equals. During one critical three-year period he had the Mayor of New York, one Vincent R. Impellitteri, virtually in his pocket. His most exhaustive biographer has written that he developed his various offices and personal power

into a fourth branch of government, known as "Triborough," which was so powerful that he was, in effect, free from control by the officials who had appointed him. Through Triborough, he mobilized banks, labor unions, contractors, bond-underwriting syndicates, real-estate manipulators — a dozen key economic interests — into a unified, irresistible force, and with that force he warped the city off its democratic bias. During his decades of power, the public-works decisions that determined the city's shape were made on the basis not of democratic but of economic considerations. During most of his reign — including, despite legend, most of the LaGuardia portion of it — the city's people had no real voice in determining the city's future. He and he alone — not the city's people, not the government officials the people elected to represent them, not the power brokers who dominated some of these officials — decided what public works would be built, when they would be built, and to what design they would be built. He was the supreme power broker.[7]

Moses was personally responsible for the development, planning, engineering, financing, and construction of an incredible number of parks, parkways, arterial highways, bridges, cultural centers, dams, and apartment buildings, mostly in New York City but also along the St. Lawrence and Niagara Rivers. The total cost of these has been estimated, in 1968 dollars, as in excess of twenty-seven billion dollars, making Moses "unquestionably America's most prolific physical creator. He was America's — perhaps the world's — greatest builder."[8] But our interest here is not the size of this achievement but the political methods by which it was done. Beyond that we have a direct interest in assessing the quality of that achievement. Moses acquired a reputation as a man who got things done, often

7. Robert A. Caro, "The Power Broker," *The New Yorker*, July 22, 1974, p. 36. See also the issues of July 29, Aug. 12, and Aug. 19.

8. *Ibid.*, p. 35.

against incredible political odds. But what did his doing them represent in terms of the values of the political system and the possibilities of transcending those values?

Moses came from a moderately upper-class background. He was educated at Yale, Oxford, and Columbia Universities, from the last of which he obtained a Ph.D. in political science. His first forays into politics were as an idealistic proponent of civil service reform at the municipal level and of administrative reorganization throughout the executive branch of the State government. In the first of these efforts he failed utterly. In the second, because of his friendship with Governor Smith and under the astute supervision of the Governor's advisors, he was more successful. He began to learn the basic lesson of American baronial politics, that achievement comes only with power, a term Moses' biographers and the man himself assumed needed no definition. Nevertheless, Moses became adept at all those techniques by which power is won and used in the American political system. He could marshall public opinion to his side by proclaiming his independence from "bosses" and declaring himself a champion of parks for the people. With skill that became legendary in his own time, he mastered the more arcane arts of personal manipulation, conspiritorial planning, and ingenious bill drafting.

Two techniques Moses used with unsurpassed skill over the years. The first of these was dreaming up situations that would be lavishly profitable to those from whom he sought cooperation. He could also contrive to maneuver such people into painful developments, costly to them both materially and in reputation. But he relied largely on tempting bankers, union leaders, contractors, and politicians of every sort into his grandiose schemes. He cultivated the reputation of being "a practical guy, a guy you can talk to." The corruption involved never tainted Moses himself, and much of it was so skillfully arranged that it was not overtly illegal. But it is certain that Moses made many men wealthy far beyond the most generous estimates of their social worth. Moses' other principal technique was that in all he did, he made the powers of his office work for him. Moses' power was huge, and it was his own.

Moses, then, became a baron par excellence. He had to. But he was more than that. Even at the height of his baronial power, Moses retained something of his objective role of public servant extraordinary. However hard he rode on this aspect of his career for public relations purposes, it was not mere rhetorical flourishing. Moses came into public life with a dream, a vision in concrete and steel of the public interest, and he lived his professional life in pursuit of it. It is by reference to that dream, so clearly beyond the imaginative powers of the ordinary baron, that the qualitative assessment of Moses' accomplishment must begin.

Moses' achievements have been sharply criticized in recent years by those who believe his multiplication of facilities for the automobile and corresponding neglect of mass (especially rail) transit have compounded the city's transportation problems. Critics have further charged Moses with systematic and disastrous bias in favor of the automobile owner and his white, middle-class, suburban lifestyle. The chief symbol of this bias is none other than the Triborough Bridge itself: from all three ramps one views some of the most notorious slums in the world. The critics see this bias even in Moses' earliest achievements. Urban dwellers could go to Jones Beach only by driving out on superbly landscaped parkways where only private cars were allowed. But it is also evident in the harsh, unsympathetic design of Moses' public housing projects.

These criticisms are of great theoretical importance. They point to that unavoidable, incurable limitation in the mind of the rational/professional that dooms his attempts to dream beyond himself. Though not an engineer, Moses had the mentality of one. He did not understand either the social values assumed in his public works or their effects in the social context. He was blind to the whole social world which his physical creations shattered or transformed even to the point of having almost no regard for the problems of their maintenance and occasional renovation.

Finally there is the ultimate limitation imposed by the very nature of the American political system upon all those who hold power within it. The power they hold is nothing but the kind of power the system can generate. However large the power Moses held, it retained the basic characteristics of the system in which it was to be used. This meant that it was always particular power, the power to do this, get that, compel this man, buy another. His power was incremental; so were his projects. They were large, but they were neither inclusive nor comprehensive. Moses could build. But he could not fight crime in the streets. He could not fight the corruption he himself engendered. And he could not educate children, aid the needy, combat racism, or do any of the other things necessary to regeneration in American social life. Great as his power was, it was inadequate in kind and in extent. Grandiose as his dreams, they were inadequate to relieve the pains of our common life. Moses was an American, as politically helpless as any of us before the overwhelming realities of the nation's crumbling social fabric.

CONCLUSION: THE RECORD AND THE PROSPECT

THE RECORD

If the themes of this book are even approximately correct, much rethinking about the American political record will have to be done. The usual approach to that record by political scientists and historians starts with the notion that the political system that compiled it is basically sound, even more capable than most of preserving human dignities and forwarding human purposes. The primary intent of this book has been to challenge that premise and to force a reassessment of America's political capabilities.

Such a general reassessment should begin with particular reassessments of the major crises of the American political record. Some of these have been touched upon at many points in the preceding argument, but they can be summarized here as follows.

• The Revolution was fought in the name of liberty. In fact, it freed almost no one not already then free. Its more signal accomplishment was to lock the American people into a massive mythic, ideological framework of political consciousness which at once endlessly tortured their aspirations and denied them the capacities of achieving them.

• The pushing back of the Western frontier and the opening up of the continent was a triumph over nature. To many it was colorful, demanding, and personally rewarding. It was also rapacious, unbridled, and disorganized. It was conspicuously cruel to the original inhabitants. Above all, because so ungoverned, it was wasteful to the point of being a national disgrace.

• The Civil War was a tragedy. Worse, it was a constitutional catastrophe. It demonstrated two things. First, it showed that the political system was incapable of confronting and resolving moral divisions of its own devising. Extreme violence was the price of that failure. Second, the war showed that the system could survive almost anything, even its own failures and vast civil war.

• The Spanish-American War was the first important example of American extra-continental imperialism. It was also the first important instance of America plunging onto the world stage in rampant pursuit of mythic ideals but armed with operative conceptions of politics and violence so naive they verged on the barbaric. In the suppression of the rebellion in the Philippines that followed the war, American conduct was worse than barbaric and on an appalling scale, but if anything, even more in the name of the highest sounding, mythic ideals.

• World War I and World War II were further examples of this phenomenon. However, the facts that these wars were conducted far overseas, were concluded with military victory earned in concert with other powers, and were followed by rapid disengagement of the bulk of the American forces largely concealed their imperial incompetence, especially from the Americans themselves.

• The New Deal is generally credited as a creative response by American government to domestic economic and political crises. It is also credited with having overturned old power structures and setting the political system firmly on the track of new conceptions of governmental capability and responsibility. In retrospect, it can be seen that the fundamental Madisonian limitations of the political system precluded anything of that dimension. Like Woodrow Wilson's first administration and other reform periods, the New Deal was primarily successful in its rhetoric, largely presidential. It went into the history books as a *new* deal. In fact, it possessed no new philosophical commitments and was an administrative patchwork operation using programs of traditional design to smooth over social problems. The major political and economic disparities in American society were largely untouched, as were their concomitant social problems: poor distribution of resources and labor, urban blight, crime, racial tensions, and so forth. Nor was the New Deal the beginning of subsequent attacks on these problems. Qualitatively they are today much as they were then, if not measurably worse.

• The Korean War and the Vietnam involvement are the prime examples of post-World War II "Pax Americana" enthusiasms at their most mythic extreme and their most operationally incompetent. In both there were fundamental difficulties in defining political objectives and controlling military behavior, factors clearly stemming from defects in the American political mind. Also in both, military defeat was sustained and painful, if not conclusive. In the Korean conflict the very fact of defeat was largely ignored, along with the lessons that might have been learned. In the Vietnam situation, the absurdity, cruelty, and deceit of the process of intervention was matched by much the same qualities in the same proportions during the withdrawal. And because all of this became an extended public spectacle, a "never again" attitude seems firmly entrenched in the American political mood. But it remains to be seen whether anything else has been learned or whether anything has been done to prevent recurrences of the conditions which led to this disaster.

• "Watergate" is the most vivid of the American political system's overt moments of public corruption. But far from being a splendid example of the system's health and vigor and its capacity to seek out, apprehend, and bring to justice lawbreakers even in the highest places, its resolution is evidence of the system's capacity to sustain every kind of damage without significant change. The secrecy and "cover-up" mentality of the barons who conducted the original affair was exactly paralleled by the anxiety of the barons who succeeded them to "close the book." The notion that all aspects of the affair, singly and in sum represented nothing more than an extreme of the norm appears to be beyond the limit of anything but the most private of analyses.

The crises of America's political past are the notch points through which must be strung any general interpretation of the meaning of our common experience as a political community. Most of them are separated only by decades of more ordinary experience. A full explanation of American politics would also have to pay attention to those intervening years and note their ongoing qualities. These too are much less admirable than is often supposed.

The argument being advanced here about the American political record challenges American political scientists and historians to review their materials and traditional interpretations in the light of these two charges:

1. American political history is replete with examples of failures and disasters as well as sustained demonstra-

tions of inadequacy at more ordinary levels of political performance. The record is objectively accessible despite the extraordinary capacity of the system to conceal and disguise it with mythic misrepresentation.

2. The record is not of a series of unfortunate accidents, but is in large part the consequence of demonstrable defects in the nation's political institutions and, even more grievously and fundamentally, in its institutional underlay of ideological and mythic commitments.

These charges are mounted from a perspective that is well within the generality of the American political consciousness. The American political system is a failure in its own terms. We are not what we want ourselves to be.

THE PROSPECT

The future repeats the past. This is the grim lesson of almost all recorded history, despite the fascination of culture-bound enthusiasts with technological changes that suggest qualitative advances in the human condition. In America, this lesson is reinforced by the absence from our political vocabulary of those concepts by which even the prospect of radical change could be opened up. These missing concepts have essentially to do with social structure and social movement. Their lack in the American political vocabulary means that the prospects are virtually nonexistent in this country for a genuine revolution that might usher in an American nation possessed of greater capacities for self-management and forward motion.

There are several reasons for this conclusion. First, the Americans have no understanding of what a revolution of the sort that has transformed other nations of the world amounts to. As Hobbesian Liberals of an exceptionally narrow sort, their political theory is set in terms of a sovereign over and against a merely aggregated population, with the relationship between them grounded on the necessity to restrain violence. Therefore, for the Americans, revolution can only be thought of as a more or less violent coup d'etat, what has been called sustaining the legitimate by illegitimate means. They lack the political imagination to conceive of revolution in full and creative terms, as a dynamic "leap in being" by which a whole communal structure is wrenched forward into a new social, political, and economic structure.

This fundamental ideological lack is followed by two more practical ones. The Americans lack any tradition of political leadership or organization by which a Lenin-like leader could forge and master a sufficient revolutionary instrument to smash and rebuild the present establishment. Moreover, there is no revolutionary mass on the American political scene out of which such a leader and party could arise. The notion that American homosexuals, liberated women, blacks, aged, Indians, and poor could be welded into the hammer of a revolution is radically incongruous with the realities of American political life.

But if the prospects for revolution in America are nil, so are the prospects for any sustained radical political action within the present political system that might lead to its gradual transformation and regeneration. All the arguments just cited against the prospects for revolution apply here as well, especially the lack in the American political vocabulary of concepts essential to meaningful revolution. Because we lack concepts of social structure and social change, we cannot create in our political imaginations any revolutionary vision, even one to be achieved peacefully. When the cry goes up that something must be done, the suggestions that follow, if they ever get farther than the standard Liberal whimpers about giving everyone their "rights," hardly amount to more than arguments for tinkerings. Given the thinness of the American political culture, it is virtually impossible to generate within it debate with genuinely radical implications.

This argument is reinforced by noting again the extraordinary powers the established American political system has for sustaining itself through every kind of crisis and challenge. In practical terms these powers mean that when and if a radical movement arises, the Madisonian capacities of the constitutional system will be exquisitely proficient in dispersing it, distracting or buying off its leadership, and defusing its idealism with smothering rhetoric drawn from the bottomless wells of American mythic belief.

What can be done by those who believe that substantial change is urgently required in the American political system, in the American political *mind?* One answer is that a sobering period of deep reflection by all radicals on the realities of the American political situation would have immediate rewards. One of the most painful spectacles of recent decades has been the sight of self-styled American radicals dissipating their energies in politically frivolous enthusiasms and pointless actions, however energetic. Indeed, American radicals would do well to urge a period of sober reflection on friend and foe alike. Perhaps America's most pressing need as a political community is to abandon pretense and admit general political incompetence. Until that happens, the American political system will remain a dangerous actor on the world stage and a woefully self-deluding one at home, with unpredictable consequences in both areas. In this light, a period of sober reflection on the realities of American politics would have not only general spiritual and intellectual merit, but practical benefits as well. It might lead us into drawing back from at least some of our more extreme tendencies toward self-destructive behavior.

Beyond this, in the nature of the argument presented in this book, not much else can be said. This may be a depressing thought but it should not be, in the direct sense, an amazing one.

America's condition is not unique. Recorded history shows numerous examples of societies suffering from the same political immobilism in the face of major problems that afflict this country. We must beware of illusions of freedom. We have no more liberty to make over our future than our history allows us. The past is a prison. If there is to be escape from it, the keys must be found within. Keys of the right size and strength may not exist for us. If so, our predicament may be that described by Hegel in the preface to his *Philosophy of Right:*

When philosophy paints its grey in grey, then has a shape of life grown old. By philosophy's grey in grey it cannot be rejuvenated but only understood. The owl of Minerva spreads its wings only with the falling of dusk.[1]

1. Tr. T. M. Knox, Oxford, London, 1945, p. 13.

APPENDIX:
THE STUDY OF
AMERICA

No book stands alone. This one takes off from a debate that developed a clear form in the academic field of American Studies in the 1950s but then tapered off sharply. It may seem strange to revive so old a controversy, but there are powerful contemporary reasons for doing so.

With America's victory in World War II still close and her responsibilities to "the free world" in the cold war riding bearably, the 1950s were suffused with national self-assurance. There were negative factors, of course. The meaning of the Korean War, as it battered inconclusively to an end, was ambiguous. And the Hiss trial, the execution of the Rosenbergs, and above all the whole complex phenomenon called McCarthyism, spread multifaceted doubt and anxiety among moderates and critics. But these negative factors could not undercut the overall élan. If anything, they stimulated the search for more positive factors. American Studies, founded single-handedly by Perry Miller at Harvard in the 1930s, flourished; and few in the field doubted that the task of interpreting America's uniqueness — of understanding ourselves in terms of ourselves — was worthy of any scholar's best efforts.

Suddenly, in the 1960s, such endeavors appeared an excess of patriotism, an almost unbearable affectation. It seemed more important to promote civil rights for blacks and to stop the war in Vietnam. When both these efforts encountered tragedy and frustration, the result was rage and withdrawal. The American Studies movement waned perceptibly. Its outstanding practitioners took to specialized studies, and many of them gave up the interdisciplinary effort and returned to their traditionally defined departments. The effort to explain America was put more and more in universalistic terms. The United States was simply the most advanced of the industrialized, over-technologicalized nations, an imperialist power on the Leninist model, and so forth.

Yet as the 1970s move on, a return of interest in the particularity of the American experience seems increasingly likely. One reason is the way the Vietnam war dragged on, horror piled on horror, combined with the utter futility and meaningless of American violence. It passed from a military defeat to a crisis of conscience and on to the very edge of a death of concern, of national heart. Then there was Watergate, a matter of small practical moment compared to Vietnam but of great symbolic significance in the context of history. In fact, Vietnam and Watergate together, coming after the assassinations of the 1960s, the frustrations of the civil rights movements and the war protests, the urban riots, and the events at Kent State, Jackson State, and Attica, were failures laced with terrible meaning. They cannot be made to go away in a universalistic interpretation. Whether or how other nations suffered such events is not to the point. These were *our* events and *our* failures, and if we are to understand them we must explain them to ourselves. The problem of America's uniqueness has returned, though in a new form.

The debate of the 1950s left matters suspended. There were at least four sides to that debate, of which three had origins going back to the turn of the century or earlier. First, there was a revival of interest in the work of Frederick Jackson Turner. Turner had achieved wide recognition in the 1890s in the long wake of Civil War divisions, and the thrust of his "frontier thesis" had been essentially nationalistic and unifying. America, he argued, was not so much divided by a line between North and South as it was bound together by the sustained experience of westward expansion. What had brought the original colonies together and what still made the nation one community was the constant presence, in both memory and anticipation, of the potential for development across the line of furthest settlement into the empty beyond. Out there, enduring characteristics for the whole nation had been formed.

From the conditions of frontier life came *intellectual traits* of profound importance. . . . That coarseness and strength combined with acuteness and inquisitiveness; that practical, inventive turn of mind, quick to find expedients; that masterful grasp of material things, lacking in the artistic but powerful to effect great ends; that restless, nervous energy; that dominant individualism, working for good and for evil, and withal that buoyancy and exuberance which comes with freedom. . . .[1]

There is truth in these remarks, but in the 1950s they had a special meaning for some. Sixty years after Turner first proposed his thesis, Daniel Boorstin called it "the most influential, if not the only significant, general interpretation of our history. . . ." More specifically, Boorstin used Turner's insights to explain what Boorstin regarded as The Genius of American Politics,[2] the nation's apparent unconcern for political theory and especially ideological dispute of the European sort. As much as Turner, Boorstin traced to our frontier experience the distinctively American democratic spirit. But Boorstin insisted more emphatically than Turner that Americans owe their vigorous pragmatism to the frontier. In his eyes, what most put America ahead of all other nations was her people's cheerful willingness, born of having to make do on the very edge of civilization, to solve problems and conflicts only as they arose and on their merits alone. Ideology could not divide us, because we had none. Our greatness was our seamless unity.

For all the force of the Turner-Boorstin thesis, it does not explain major aspects of the American experience. In its light America's famed diversity of religious, sectional, and ethnic groups must be given considerably less emphasis than usual. Even from the perspective of the 1970s, there really is a powerful sense in which we have been and are *all* Americans, and this sense seems to be rooted in our shared experience in the continental environment. But granting that in no way asserts that Americans are untroubled by deep divisions. That kind of talk, at least in Boorstin, seems to stem solely from his all-too-transparent and fervid patriotism. Boorstin glided past divisions struck through the American experience much too glibly. Witness these sentences on the Civil War:

Not the least remarkable feature of the Civil War — apart from the fact that it occurred at all — is that it was so unproductive of political theory. This, the bloodiest single civil war of the nineteenth century, was also perhaps the least theoretical.[3]

1. "The Significance of the Frontier in American History" (1893) in *The Frontier in American History*, Holt, New York, 1920, p. 37.

2. *The Genius of American Politics*, University of Chicago Press, Chicago, 1953, p. 25.

3. *Ibid.*, p. 131.

Even while allowing his main point, one longs to catch Boorstin by the sleeve, take him back to that yawning apostrophe in his first sentence, and ask him point blank how the war happened. How could a nation so generally agreed fall into such a catastrophe, especially a nation having a "genius" for politics? It does no good for Boorstin to add, a page later,

The mere fact that the nation had survived the ordeal of civil war seemed itself to prove the strength of the thread which bound the present to the past and to confirm the common destiny of the nation.

That explains how the division was healed. It does not explain how the division arose, between whom, or why. And it says nothing at all to the question of how the division could have gotten so dreadfully out of hand. In the 1970s it is that last question which presses hardest for an answer.

Other scholars, not only in the 1950s but long before as well, had paid more attention to our national divisions. So-called "progressive" historians from J. Allen Smith to Arthur Schlesinger, Jr. made them their starting point, and the same concerns were reflected after World War II, on the left in the work of C. Wright Mills and his followers, and on the right in the work of Willmoore Kendall and his associates.

The common theme of all these writers constitutes the second major approach to the problems of American history. This theme might be labeled "the good guy/bad guy thesis." It held that American history has been marked from the beginning by severe and meaningful struggle between sharply opposed, clearly identifiable contestants. How far this thesis departed from the "frontier thesis" is revealed in its contention that the divisions between the contestants in America's internal war were not only founded in social and economic factors (classes) but also expressed from the outset in profound and broad ideological terms. Vernon L. Parrington's vision of the first phase of this strife can stand as a model for all the rest. Writing in the Introduction to his massive work, *Main Currents in American Thought* in the 1920s, Parrington declared:

The line of liberalism in colonial America runs through Roger Williams, Benjamin Franklin, and Thomas Jefferson. . . . Over against these protagonists of liberalism must be set the complementary figures of John Cotton, Jonathan Edwards, and Alexander Hamilton, men whose grandiose dreams envisaged different ends for America and who followed different paths.[4]

The conservative version of this thesis simply reverses the "good guy/bad guy" roles assigned principally to Jefferson and Hamilton.

The advantages of this interpretation of American history are wider than its focus on the obvious divisive events in the nation's past. The thesis also touches sympathetically upon a broad national feeling that our rending struggles amongst ourselves over the years have not been meaningless quibbles, but significant and productive steps toward progressive solutions. The way has been hard but progress has been made. The New Deal, in this view, really did overcome entrenched interests and moved the nation toward social justice.

However few the doubters of such interpretations may be even today, the difficulties with the general theory on which they are based are as serious as those with the frontier thesis. The problem is to distinguish between the ideological positions of the contestants. Hamilton, as the long-time opponent of Jefferson, clearly had what would now be called an ideological position. He was an eighteenth century, English-style commercial liberal schooled in the works of Adam Smith and the rest, with a remarkable grasp of the practical needs of America's infant, capitalist economy. The difficulty is that Jefferson occupied much the same general ground philosophically, and the problem of distinguishing between his position and Hamilton's becomes one of shading and emphasis — difficult business when dealing with so chameleon-like a creature as Jefferson.

Difficulties of this order arise not only with the supposed progenitors of America's civil strife. When Arthur Schlesinger, Jr. tried in the 1940s to apply the thesis to Jacksonian democracy as an intellectual movement, he began boldly enough.

The Jacksonians believed that there was a deep-rooted conflict in society between the "producing" and "non-producing" classes — the farmers and laborers, on the one hand, and the business community on the other. . . .

The specific problem was to control the power of the capitalistic groups, mainly Eastern, for the benefit of the non-capitalist groups, farmers and laboring men, East, West and South.

4. Harcourt, Brace, New York, 1927, Vol. I, p. vi.

But by the end of the paragraph he had given the game away.

Jacksonian democracy was rather a second phase of that enduring struggle between the business community and the rest of society *which is the guarantee of freedom in a liberal capitalist state.*[5]

Freedom for whom? Presumably anyone and everyone, without regard to "class." Freedom to do what? Presumably to become a liberal capitalist. But what has become of the distinction between "producing" and "non-producing" classes? What, in fact, has become of the good guy/bad guy thesis? One must suspect that it was never more than a mask for a much simpler thesis, a this guy/that guy thesis, or, at most, a big guy/little guy thesis.

The suspicion that the good guy/bad guy thesis simply concealed the rampant competitiveness characteristic of any thorough-going liberal capitalist society is powerfully reinforced by a third view of American political experience, the so-called "pluralist" school of American political scientists. This school was founded at the turn of the century by A. E. Bentley, but it did not become prominent until after World War II in the writings of David Truman and Robert Dahl. Eschewing formal institutional and ideological analysis, the pluralists concentrated their attention on the behavior of political, social, and economic groups, on their formation and interaction, on their tendencies towards not only competition but also ad hoc coalition, negotiation, and compromise. The pluralists especially noted the skill with which groups individually and collectively sought out "access points" in the political system, through which they could make their influence felt in the gradual process by which government policy and administration "incrementally" evolved.

The pluralists taught many Americans, almost for the first time, the realities of how the political system worked. But their insistence on being merely descriptive got them into trouble with facts and critics. They described what they saw, the politically visible activity of powerful interest groups. They neglected all else and were unprepared for times when the politically weak in America burst into flaring visibility, as did ghetto

5. *The Age of Jackson,* abr. D. P. Geddes, New American Library, New York, 1949, pp. 118–119 (emphasis added).

blacks in the urban riots of 1967. Critics argued that these errors were caused by tendencies to view politics only from the top, from the perspective of the offices of chief executives, mayors, governors, and the like. These tendencies were tracked back to deep-seated pluralist biases towards conservatism and, more importantly, elitism. At least in part, the criticism was misplaced. The elitism was more in what they studied than in the pluralists themselves.

A more serious criticism was that the pluralists could not account for the extraordinary uniformity of behavior across that part of the political spectrum that their approach illuminated. Bentley had crudely equated activity to interest and interest to activity and left it at that. But this kind of psychology raises more questions than it answers. What, substantively, is this interest which the groups so actively pursue, and why do they with an almost animal ferocity pursue it? What halted the post-World War II pluralists from exploring these questions any more than Bentley did was their unwillingness to take ideological questions seriously. In his study of the governmental process, Truman admitted that the competitive struggle between the groups goes on within a presupposed and sustaining value context, but with characteristic (unconscious) denigration he labels it "the democratic mold" or "the rules of the game."[6] And he defines it as a generalized, unorganized interest which more specialized and tightly knit groups must take care not to violate.

But the problem cannot be solved so tangentially. The values or norms of a political society are not a mere "habit background" against which real political activity goes on, nor do they contain and moderate it by mere occasional imposition. The norms of political life are creative. They define into existence the situations in which political actors appear, and they define the actors themselves, their roles, their goals, and their means. What is needed is a methodology which will unite ideology and behavior as jointly constituting the world of politics. By throwing the emphasis in studying American politics decisively back toward ideological considerations, this book attempts to make possible such an advance in the development of political studies.

6. *The Governmental Process*, Knopf, New York, 1960, p. 129 and elsewhere.

The need for a bridge between behavioral, pluralistic studies of American politics and ideological problems was not appreciated until after the 1950s. Nevertheless Norman Jacobson in an article titled "Political Science and Political Education," published in 1963, did see that need and where it had to be met.[7] His thesis was that the reason why the pluralist explanation of American politics worked so well was that the pluralists' methodology exactly mirrored the underlying ideology of the American political system. The connecting link between the two was provided by the work of no less than the founding fathers. Prefiguring in their own political science all major aspects of the political science of Bentley and his disciples, they also created out of their political science the American political system. The American people adopted that system as their operative political ideology and worked it well, becoming in the process at once good citizens and good specimens. Putting it another way, Jacobson declared that the American polity is "a gigantic self-fulfilling prophecy."

Uncovering the broad ideological consensus, which Jacobson saw undergirding the American polity, was a task which had been under way in the United States for some decades, although the pluralists paid no heed to it. R. H. Gabriel, Richard Hofstadter, and Clinton Rossiter, to say nothing of a host of others, were exploring the nation's ideological consensus throughout the 1940s and 1950s. Moreover, all members of this group worked on the basis of what might be called "faith of our fathers" assumptions and thereby constituted a fourth, distinctive approach to American experience. They perceived what the earlier progressive historians had not, even though it had been staring them in the face all along — that behind all the conflicts Americans were united in broad ideological agreement about the merits and meaningfulness of liberal capitalism. Moreover, these new historians made clear that the commitment to the general ideology of liberal capitalism, with its attendant doctrines of personal freedom secured through legal rights, was present at the nation's founding and had broadened and deepened its hold in the years since. As early as 1948, Hofstadter summed up these findings.

7. *The American Political Science Review,* September 1963, p. 562.

[My] studies in the ideology of American statesmanship have convinced me of the need for a reinterpretation of our political traditions which emphasizes the common climate of American opinion. The existence of such a climate of opinion has been much obscured by the tendency to place political conflict in the foreground of history. . . . However much at odds on specific issues, the major political traditions have shared a belief in the rights of property, the philosophy of economic individualism, the value of competition; they have accepted the economic virtues of capitalist culture as necessary qualities of man. . . .

Above and beyond temporary and local conflicts there has been a common ground, a unity of cultural and political tradition, upon which American civilization has stood. That culture has been intensely nationalistic and for the most part isolationist; it has been fiercely individualistic and capitalistic.[8]

The evidence cited in support of these conclusions by Hofstadter and the others in his company is overwhelmingly persuasive. Close analysis of materials drawn from periods ranging from "the seedtime of the republic," in Rossiter's phrase, through the revolutionary interval, past the Civil War to the present consistently dissolved supposed extreme ideological divergence. A singular commonality emerged between federalist and anti-federalist, supporters of the Bank and its opponents, North and South, and such major individual figures as Theodore Roosevelt and Wilson, and Hoover and Franklin Roosevelt. All are Americans; all are Liberal, individualistic capitalists.

The consensus school was the 1950s' major contribution to the debate about America's uniqueness. But what this literature did was to return the argument to the point where Turner left it, though at an ideological rather than an environmental level: America is a simple monism. And as with Turner and Boorstin, the same question is left hanging, the problem of conflict in America. If America is ideologically uniform through both space and time, how are we to account for the divisiveness which has so marked our history, and for the range, volume, persistence, and violence of that divisiveness? In the last years of his life, more than two decades after the date of his first major publications, Hofstadter himself restated all these questions

8. *The American Political Tradition,* (1948), Vintage Books, New York, 1954, pp. vii, viii, and x.

and significantly backed away from his former consensualist position.[9] But he did not have time to develop new answers.

This is somewhat surprising because in *The Liberal Tradition in America*,[10] the most prominent of the consensualists, Louis Hartz, whose work Hofstadter had examined with care, had pointed in the direction where answers might be found. That book still stands ahead of any other in its field, largely because Hartz brought to his work an unusually broad cultural and historical perspective. More firmly than any other American intellectual historian of the period, he could place the nation's dominant Liberalism in the context of its European origins. Having done so, he advanced two central hypotheses. The first was that American Liberalism was in origin an eighteenth century English — that is Lockean — Liberalism which alone, of all the available European ideological systems, was exported to the American environment. There, deprived of nourishing cultural opposition, it became firmly implanted but also provincialized, and it ceased to develop. In these terms, Hartz accounted for our national (Liberal) consensus.

But Hartz's second thesis was that the nation's commitment to Lockean Liberalism was "bizarre," and in saying this he moved well beyond his fellow consensualists. What he meant was that Americans, being merely Liberals and knowing nothing of possible alternatives, became exceedingly nervous when their one basic commitment was questioned or in any other way subjected to pressure. In these terms Hartz was able to explain McCarthyism, a phenomenon of special concern to American intellectuals in the years Hartz wrote. When the argument is buttressed by noting both the rigidity of American provincial thought and the bellicosity inherent in Liberalism's original revolutionary role back in Europe (a bellicosity deprived of any object in America's wholly non-feudal environment), Hartz was also able to explain at least in some measure America's all-too-frequent explosions into conflict, without compromising the evidence of the nation's ideological uniformity. All those outbursts were effectively psychological breakdowns, instances of hysteria, basically meaningless conflicts.

9. See *The Progressive Historians*, (1968), Vintage Books, New York, 1970, Part V.

10. Harcourt, Brace, New York, 1955.

Insufficient attention was paid to Hartz's explanations of American divisiveness, partly because he himself did not press his highly promising suggestions very far. As a historian, he was interested in tracing American Liberalism's story. He accounted for the difficulties it experienced almost entirely in Turneresque, environmental terms. At no time did he undertake a systematic analysis of the content of America's commitment to Liberalism.

One suspects that, besides a lack of professional interest in such matters, there may be another reason why Hartz did not press his second thesis as far as it might have been taken. In saying that America's commitment to its dominant Liberalism is "bizarre," Hartz was on dangerous ground. He was pointing at the notion that there might be something fundamentally awry in the nation's ideological equipment. In the 1950s, to do even that much was strong stuff.

There is an adage that the social function of the academically tenured historian — and political scientist? — is to write or rewrite about the nation's past in such a way as to preclude our having to do anything about our future. All too obviously Boorstin meets this test. So too did Turner himself, declaring that with the passing of the geographical frontier the nation could turn to new ones, economic development for example. The pluralists, when pressed, made the judgment necessary to legitimize their work: that group politics, with its characteristic dispersion of power patterns, assured all interested participants reasonable opportunities to influence the democratic process, while achieving at the same time a relatively stable harmonization of incipient conflict. The "faith of our fathers" historians, of course, trumpeted the values of the past, even while some of them perceived threats to those values in the crises of the present and the unpredictability of the future. Even the progressive historians, for all their sense of besiegement, were assured that all would be well if only we soldiered on.

On the last pages of his book, Hartz reformulated his position with care. He stated without qualification that what would be "shattered" by America's advent as a world power was merely its "provincialism," and he then added:

For if America is the bizarre fulfillment of liberalism, do not people everywhere rely upon it for the retention of what is best in that tradition? . . . In any case, given the totalitarian nature of Russian socialism, the hope for a free world surely lies in the power for transcending itself inherent in American liberalism.[11]

Twenty years after those words were written, they seem less reassuring. In fact, from today's perspective, does it not seem that what Hartz's extraordinary book best proves is the incapacity inherent in American Liberalism to transcend itself?

Once again, the two events that most prepare us to ask questions of this order are the war in Vietnam and Watergate. Both diminished our faith in ourselves as a nation to unparalleled extremes. They were symbolic failures, the first of America's "mission," the second of America's "democracy." In the principal personae of these events, Lyndon Johnson and Richard Nixon, more and more of us see not accident, inadvertence, or personal failure, but American Liberalism's "bizarre fulfillment."

This book starts on that foot. Far more sharply than did Hartz, it focuses on the content of the nation's dominant Liberalism; it discovers divisions and agonies well beyond those at which Hartz hints. Far more sharply also than Hartz's work, it concerns itself with the relationship between crippling ideology and crippled action in the operation of the national political system. But most importantly, it sets out to investigate questions that few in professional American Studies have asked. Why has America failed itself, so often, so disastrously?

11. *Ibid.*, pp. 308–309.

INDEX

255